Understanding Precious Metal Markets

A Comprehensive Guide for Intermediate and Advanced Investors and Traders

T. Forbush

UNDERSTANDING PRECIOUS METAL MARKETS

ISBN: 979-8-9931940-0-4

Editor: W.W. Little, PhD

Published:

STEMA LLC,
6408 W Colonial Dr
Boise, Idaho 83709

Printed in the United States of America

Dedicated to:

My dad,

who first introduced me to precious metals when I was a teenager.

&

My wife and sons,

for your patience and support while completing this work.

Special thanks to:

My editor,

Bill, the endless hours, and valuable inputs are recognized and greatly appreciated. Both by me and certainly all the readers.

&

My endorsers,

None of you have received any compensation for this, many of you were valuable references, and all have given your vote of confidence. I am honored.

Table of Contents

Table of Contents

List of Tables:

List of Lists:

Preface

There are many books on precious metals, arguably too many. Enough books in fact to sufficiently deter anyone with monetary motivation from writing a new one. The problem for me however is that I don't like any of them. Unfortunately, the market is flooded with introductory material of widely varying quality. On the other side of the spectrum are highly specialized reports primarily prepared for institutions or accredited investors. There is very limited middle ground information for those intermediate level investors and traders wanting to advance their knowledge and skill set without dedicating the time to become a true specialist.

My perspective on precious metals is unique, being both broader and deeper than most "experts". I've been an investor and trader of precious metals since age 17. I hold an M.S. in Economic Geology/Geochemistry and am a Certified Professional Geologist. I have spent a large part of my career in minerals exploration and mining working for various sized companies on several deposit types through my consulting company. I've balanced my geologic consulting with a boutique financial planning practice. The latter has taught me how to manage the needs, concerns and objectives of those in the retail space. Regarding precious metals this is important because much of the introductory material for retail is predatory. While the specialized reports are usually of high quality they are almost always prepared for institutions, which by nature, have different needs, objectives, and means.

Surprisingly, many financial professionals also have a poor understanding of precious metals. This is in part due to limitations/restrictions they have in their broker/dealer contracts, complex securities and commodities regulations, and finally lack of training. For example, it was a little shocking that the 300+ page study manual for the series 65 securities exam had only two short paragraphs on gold, and nothing about silver or platinum group elements. In short, understanding metals exploration, production and development, while also being a trader and financial professional independent of a broker dealer has been a unique advantage. First, it has allowed me to see patterns not obvious to others, second, it forced me to recognize when the "common knowledge" interpretations were wrong, third, removed me from most conflicts of interest, and fourth, accelerated my ability to research, understand, and test the more accurate (but at times counterintuitive) drivers of these markets.

Very much like a research thesis, many of the ideas, interpretations, and concepts presented are not my own, but are what I have found to be most accurate through my observations and trading. Emphasizing that point, this work contains well over 200 references.

Most of the books or reports written on precious metals found today fall into one of my five categories:

1- Selling something
2- Voodoo, magic, and the supernatural
3- Conspiracy theories
4- Genuine and helpful but lacking in substance and/or scope
5- Specialized, these are usually excellent but have a narrowed focus.

Getting good advice can be difficult, there really are few unbiased professionals in this sector. Many investors will try to ask their financial advisor. The difficulty is that if the advisor is affiliated with a broker/dealer (as most will be) they will have a conflict of interest, they can only offer funds the broker/dealer sells (and can charge you for) and sadly most of these precious metals fund options perform poorly. Given their ignorance and conflicts of interest, most advisors, for good reason, avoid the subject entirely and recommend you buy something else.

After the advisor most retail investors resort to YouTube, investment blogs, and what they can find on Amazon for their "expert" advice. Because of my overall dissatisfaction with most of the "expert" advice and following the old adage "if you want something done right you got to do it yourself" I've decided to write my own book on the matter. The irony is you probably found this book on Amazon.

Preface

This work is prepared primarily for the retail investor, who unlike the institutional investor does not have access to the same resources and research. In most cases the information the retail investor receives is late or subpar at best, riddled with speculation, opinion, and marketing. While an institutional or accredited investor will likely find this book interesting as it offers a unique perspective and probably has some new information, they should, hopefully, already be well versed in many of concepts and strategies presented here.

My goal is not to teach you how to trade, recommend products, or push some socio-economic agenda. This is not a recommendation to buy or sell, and I do not provide timing information, which in this format would be near worthless anyway.

Rather, I simply do my best to teach you everything relevant, as if you were one of my own clients. The book breaks down the different subcategories of precious metal investments. I illustrate at a basic to intermediate level how each metal is formed, produced, and used, how different investments work, identify risks and opportunities, introduce some of the strategies commonly employed, and debunk several common misconceptions. Understanding these topics will improve a person's risk analysis when approaching each of the discussed instruments. I also talk about how precious metals are taxed, and how they are often employed as part of an individual's financial plan.

Doing this will save you a significant amount of time, hundreds of hours potentially, as you gain competence in this space. Truly understanding the principles herein will help you avoid costly mistakes. It will allow you to define which precious metal investments work with your strategies and risk tolerance and which do not. This saved time you will use to develop your trading skills and spend on more focused research regarding the investments and trades you plan to execute.

My intentions for writing this book were completely self-serving. Precious metals are a subject I get asked about frequently, and it takes several hours to even introduce the topic thoroughly. In short, I needed something I could hand people.

Preface

A warning, the first chapter is science heavy, if this becomes too much for you, don't get intimidated or overwhelmed, simply move on to chapter 2. That said, I think most will enjoy the science, as there are few who know it and very rarely is it explained thoroughly to those with investment interests. If you enjoy this book, please let me know and leave a positive review. In the meantime, let me show you how the precious metals markets look through my eyes.

- T. Forbush

Understanding Precious Metal Markets

Chapter 1: Genesis and Endowment

To begin, we need to start before the beginning. Before people, before dinosaurs, before our planet, even before our sun. It is always the same question just worded different ways, usually by an investor, “So where does the gold (or silver) come from?” The question is usually more than just curiosity. Every serious investor desires to understand their assets as thoroughly as reasonably possible. Unfortunately, most in the world are ignorant of where our mineral resources come from. It is not something taught in school. Sadly, even most geologists have only a vague understanding of where metals actually originate and what controls their distribution. In their defense, mineralized rocks only account for about 0.003% of the Earth’s crust (calculated from Maus et al, 2020); so even for bachelor’s level geology graduates this isn’t a topic that gets a lot of attention. Yet, all the technological advances of humanity are built upon minerals exploitation, so in that regard, we need to do better understanding the world we live in. Those who are informed compose a very small group of specialized individuals with specific graduate studies, relationships within a tight research community, lots of on-the-job training, and scientific problem-solving experience. “So, where does the gold come from?” Even with a master’s degree in geochemistry and two decades in the industry, the answer remains complex and intriguing. This chapter seeks to answer it in a way satisfactory for the average person interested in metal markets.

Fusion

On an elemental level, the metal formed in a star, a star that went supernova. That is the explanation for the silver at least. All elements are initially built by fusion reactions. It takes a lot of energy to force atoms together. The bigger the element (speaking in terms of atomic number) the bigger the star required to force the additional protons and neutrons together. For this reason, larger elements are generally less common than smaller elements. It is also worth mentioning that elements with odd atomic numbers are generally more difficult to produce than those with even numbers. Smash single atomic numbered elements (hydrogen) 1 and 1 together you get 2 (helium), 2 and 2 you get 4 (beryllium), but for 5 (boron) you need either a 2 (helium) and 3 (lithium) or a 1 (hydrogen) and 4 (beryllium), which in the realm of thermonuclear reactions is simply less probable due in part to the lower stability of unpaired protons within a nucleus (Donnelly et al., 2023). Look at the periodic table and many of the odd numbered elements you likely have never heard of; whereas you will be familiar with most of the even numbered ones as they are more common. The observation is known as Oddo-Harkin's rule, Figure 1-1 is a periodic table color coded to elemental abundance and helps illustrate this phenomenon. This plays into the relative abundance of gold and silver as both are odd numbers. They are precious metals in part because they are less common.

For example, our sun's heaviest product will likely be Oxygen (O; atomic number 8). Stars barely massive enough to go supernova will produce elements as heavy as iron (Fe; atomic number 26). Silver (Ag; atomic number 47) would require a significantly larger star, and the silver would not be part of its fusion cycle but rather a product of its spectacular supernova death, where the imploding star is subjected to unimaginable pressure. From this, we can deduce that our solar system must be made from the remnants of a star-gone supernova that had an initial mass at least 30 times that of our sun. Given the presence of gold, platinum group elements, and uranium that can only be part of the story as the creation of these elements require different astrophysical phenomena. (Kobayashi, 2020; Wall, 2023)

Even the most massive stars are not large enough to fuse the heaviest elements and produce little to none of them when they go supernova. While there is still debate by astrophysicists over the origins of the heaviest elements, gold (Au; atomic number 79), Uranium (U; atomic number 92), and others are hypothesized to originate from neutron star collisions. Neutron stars are the condensed remnants of large supernovae, see figure 1-2, where the core of the supernova is becoming a neutron star. A neutron star is typically about twice the mass of the Sun, but it is extremely dense, with all that mass compressed into 20 to 30 cubic kilometers. For example, 1 teaspoon of neutron star material can weigh as much as Mt Everest. It is probably inaccurate to think neutron stars are made of distinct elements, instead, they are more likely to consist of a dense lattice of layered neutrons (hence the name) with alternating layers of superconducting protons between them. When two neutron stars collide, they circle toward each other in an increasingly fast collapsing orbit. As they near collision, their gravitational pulls begin to rip the other apart. The masses finally collide, producing first an explosion that is followed by an implosion. These stages allow pressure to reduce to where protons combine to form nuclei neutrons, forming the heavy elements. Much of this matter is apparently ejected as the masses collapse. (Kobayashi et al, 2020; NASA, 2017) Images of the first recognized neutron star collision are provided in figure 1-3 while figure 1-4 illustrates the stages of a neutron star collision.

Attempts to reconstruct the stellar history of our solar neighborhood has caused researchers to believe our solar system's endowment of heavy elements is not explainable without inputs from neutron stars (Kobayashi et al, 2020). The possibility of this is not improbable, considering the closest known neutron star to Earth (Calvera or 1RXS J141256.0+792204) is only 250 light years away, and experts say the potential for others being nearby is high (Science 2.0, 2007). This all plays into the relative abundance of gold and platinum to silver; the former two are more difficult to fuse, so no wonder there is less of them.

In summation, how we think we got our solar system and why it has the observed relative abundances of silver and gold is:

Step 1: A collision of two neutron stars, or remnants thereof, passed through our part of the galaxy shedding heavy elements. These included a mixture from Uranium (atomic number 92) and down, including gold, platinum, silver, iron, and others. (Kobayashi et al, 2020)

Step 2: A supernova event provided the bulk of matter in our solar system. Elements probably included those as heavy as Barium (atomic number 56) and everything lighter. This material formed our solar nebula (big dust and gas cloud in space). This matter intermixed with remnant material shed from the neutron star collision that had passed through space earlier in step 1. (Kobayashi et al, 2020)

Step 3: Our solar nebula began to collapse. This could have initiated through its own internal gravity or, more likely, have been helped by gravitational waves from a neighboring supernova event.

Step 4: Once the core of the nebula had condensed sufficiently, our sun ignited. Later, our system's outer dust ring coalesced, forming proto planets. The 4.6-billion-year age often quoted for the age of the Earth comes from radiometric dating of meteorites created during this period, hence providing the age of our solar system. (Dalrymple, 1991)

This explanation as to the origin of precious metals on Earth is extremely simplified. However, those seeking further details will find (Kobayashi et al, 2020) one of the most comprehensive descriptions of star evolution and elemental fusion to date.

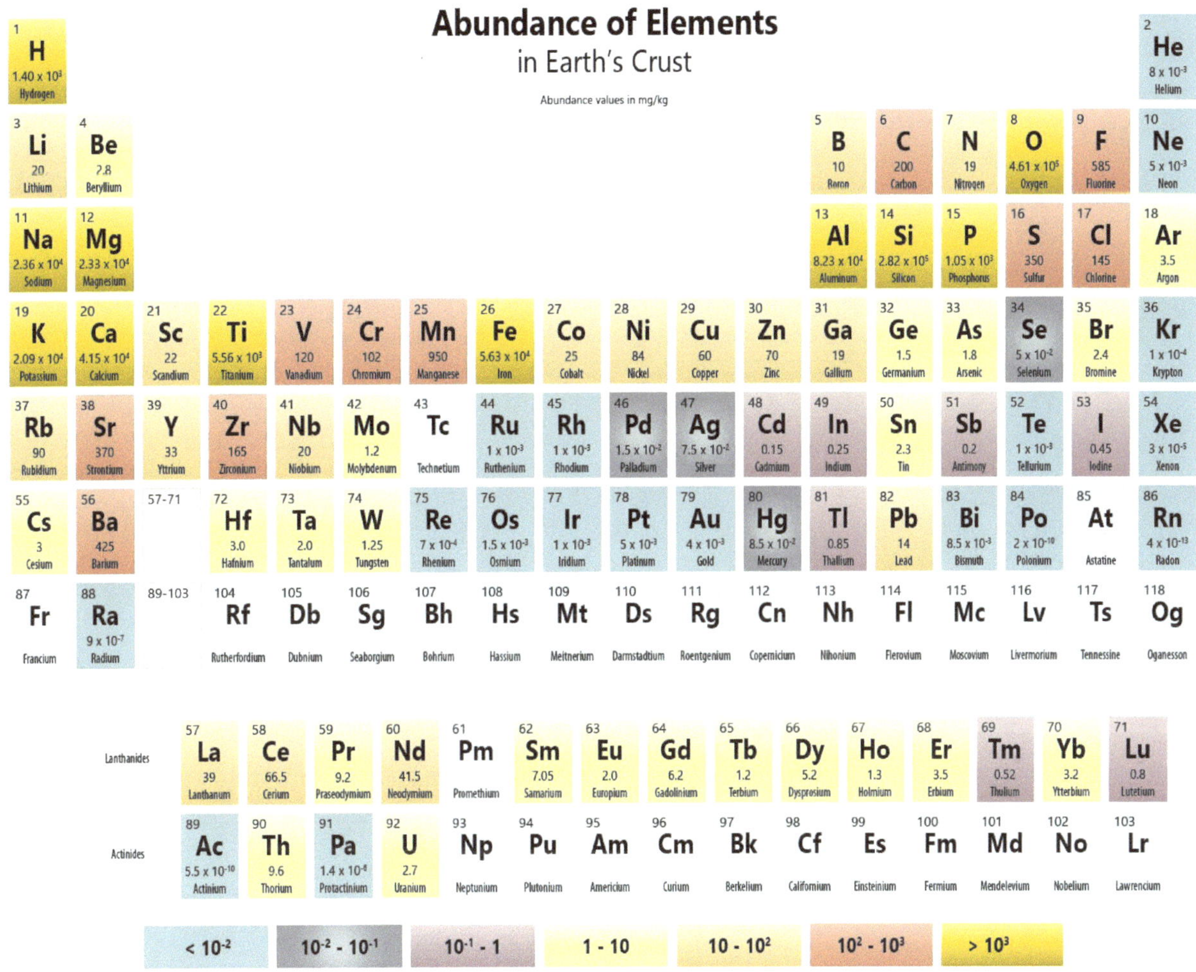

Figure 1-1: Periodic Table of Elements color coded to Earth's crustal abundance. *Notice two general trends, the first is that, in most cases, odd-numbered elements are less abundant than neighboring even-numbered elements. The second is that, elements become progressively less abundant as they increase in atomic number. Many of the more valuable metals are either odd numbered or heavy or, in the case of gold, both. (Hemenstine, 2021)*

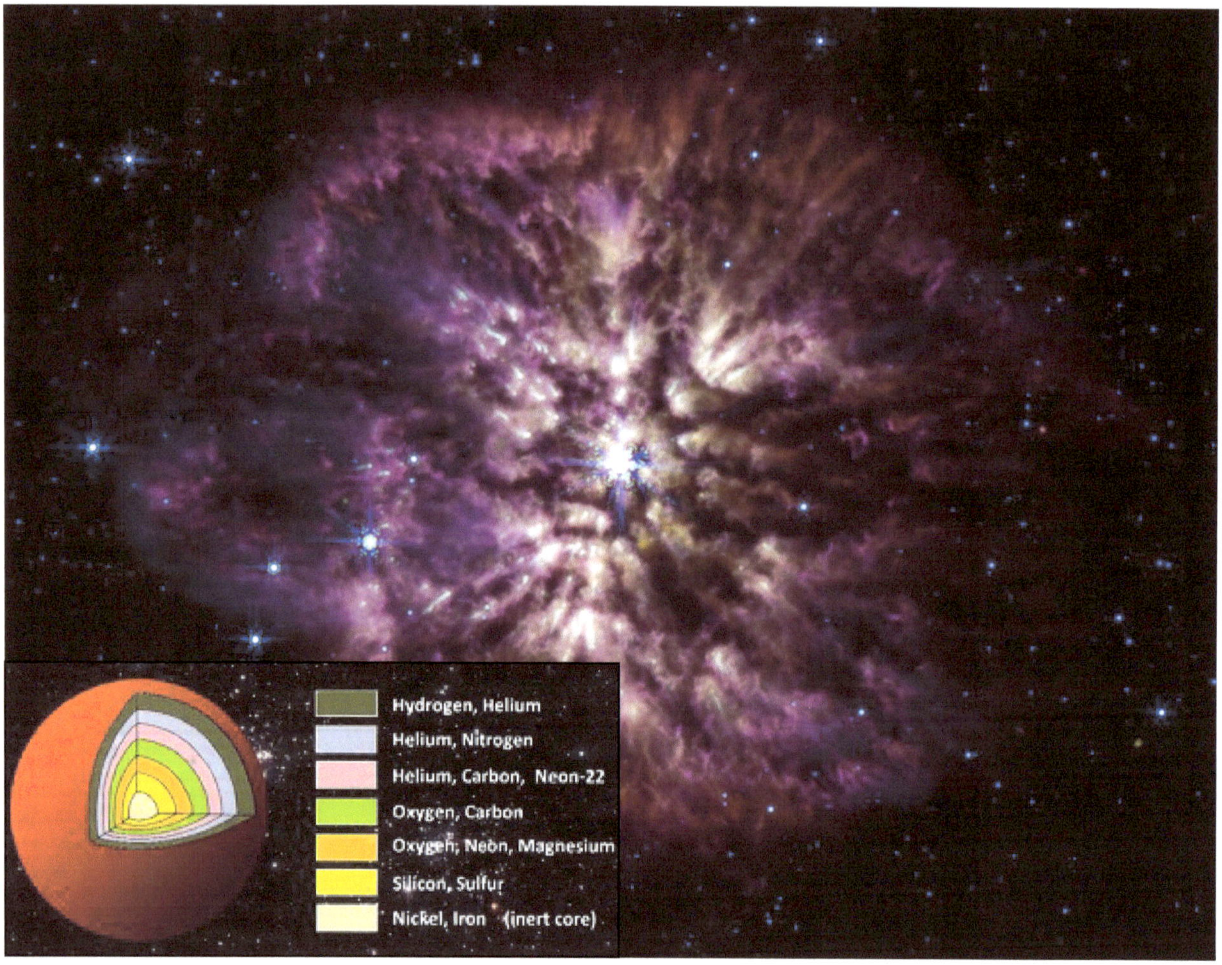

Figure 1-2: Wolf-Rayet 124 about to go supernova. *A recent infrared image courtesy of the James Webb Space telescope; shows WR-124, a star about 15,000 light years away, in its initial stages of supernova. Wolf-Rayet is a class of massive stars, about 30 times our sun's mass, in the initial stage of supernova where the star (center) sheds outer layers of dust and gas (colorful halo). These stars generally fuse elements up to atomic weights of iron (Fe). The imminent supernova will fuse and distribute elements up to atomic weights of about that of silver, leaving a neutron star in the center of a debris field. These cosmic products making up the debris field have a mass about 10 times that of the Sun and become the building blocks of new solar systems. (Wall, 2023; Kobayashi et al., 2020); Insert modified (Harvey, (2023).*

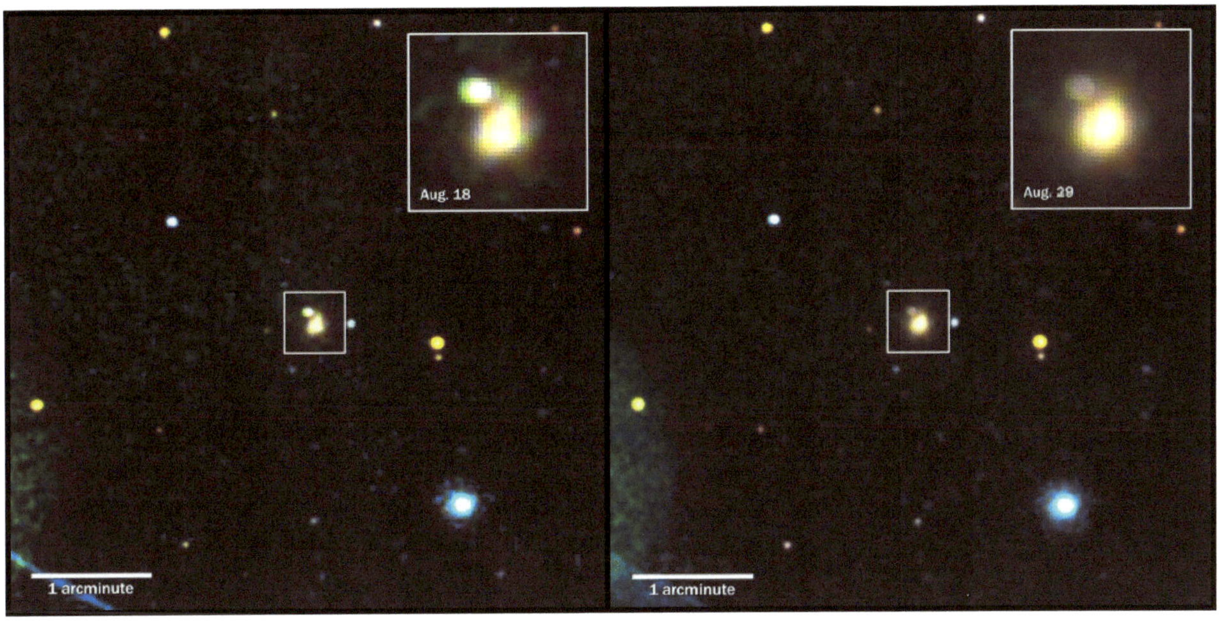

Figure 1-3: Event GW170817, *was a set of intense spectral and gravitational waves ultimately interpreted as a "kilonova" or neutron star merger, the first mankind has observed and recognized. Initially identified by the Fermi Gamma-ray Space Telescope on Aug 17, 2017, it was quickly recognized as unique, and other international space- and ground-based assets were redirected, including: the Laser Interferometer Gravitational Wave Observatory (LIGO), the European Spaces Agency's INTEGRAL satellite, NASA's Swift, Hubble, Chandra, Spitzer missions, and Pan-STARRS survey, among others. Images above show the new light source (upper) that first appeared on the 17th of August and had significantly dimmed by the 29th. Spitzer recovered the last interoperable readings of the ejecta 43 days later as the source cooled below detectable thresholds. (NASA, 2017; Villar et al., 2018)*

Figure 1-4: Stages of a "Kilonova" Neutron Star Merger, *1-Orbits collapse and increase in speed creating huge gravity waves in space-time. 2- As the neutron stars are about to merge, they rip each other apart, inner pressures ease to the point that protons can form nuclei with neutrons creating many heavy elements. The stage culminates in an explosion as masses fully collide. 3-Initial collapse of the masses, intense gamma-rays emitted from the axes. 4-Continued collapse, material, gamma, & x-rays ejected from axes, particles are moving just under the speed of light. Ejected matter radiates UV and visible light which dims as it cools. The new star quickly collapses into either a black hole or new neutron star. In the case of GW170817 the entire event transpired in less than 60 days. (NASA, 2017) (Villar et al., 2018), image (Wehner, 2020)*

Metal Mobility and Concentration

Immediately after a supernova event, as matter is cooling, atoms of different elements begin combining into minerals. It is important to note as matter coalesced to make our planet it was not necessarily in the form of native elements, but rather compounds. This understanding is from geochemical data collected from asteroids that formed during this period. Excluding hydrogen and helium gas, the solids consisted of ices (water, carbon dioxide, ammonia, methanol, and methane) and minerals including carbonates, silicates, oxides, sulfides, and iron-nickel alloys. (Taylor, 2012) Not so different from baking a cake; the ingredients, temperature, and pressure determine what the possible results are. Understanding these reactions and the minerals made under certain conditions is essentially the field of geochemistry. In most cases the metals with which the Earth was endowed were initially bound in silicate minerals like olivine and pyroxenes, oxides, and iron-nickel alloys. Through Earth's history some have and will continue to be released and then reincorporated into new minerals several times through various chemical processes, while others may remain "locked" in their original mineral for multiple billions of years. (Brownlow, 1996)

Materials that make up Earth initially formed from the solar nebula into a protoplanet through accretion; at the time the proto earth would have had a more or less homogeneous composition. The accretion process generated heat, decaying radioactive elements also added heat, and considering rocks are good insulators the internal temperature began to rise. As accretion and radioactive decay continued eventually temperatures were great enough that partial melting began to occur, gravity pulled the heaviest elements to the center while volatiles and light elements moved outward. It was hot enough that many metals like iron were liquid. There was a differentiation with the heaviest material at the center, grading upward to the lightest elements at the surface. A few cosmic events complicated things, probably the most dramatic being a hypothetical protoplanet named Theia, whose orbit brought it too close to Earth resulting in a collision that fused their cores and ejected material that became the moon. This event explains why Earth has such a proportionally large moon in such a near orbit, a true galactic rarity, and a core that is proportionally large for the diameter of the Earth. (Young, et al., 2016)

Today, Earth has several layers, scientists have two general models, one of which classifies Earth's layers in terms of rheology (flow of matter or ductility) the other based on composition. For this discussion I have combined the two models into one (figure 1-6) as it provides a more comprehensive view. Understand however, that minerology does not control rheology and that boundaries between both do not perfectly match. Also, the internal structure of Earth's common rock forming minerals have a high degree of flexibility regarding chemical composition. Figure 1-5 is an example of this, and it is important when considering compositions of the different layers of the earth as these minerals manifest chemical concentrations dominated lighter elements near the surface and progressively heavier element concentrations moving into the intermediate layers.

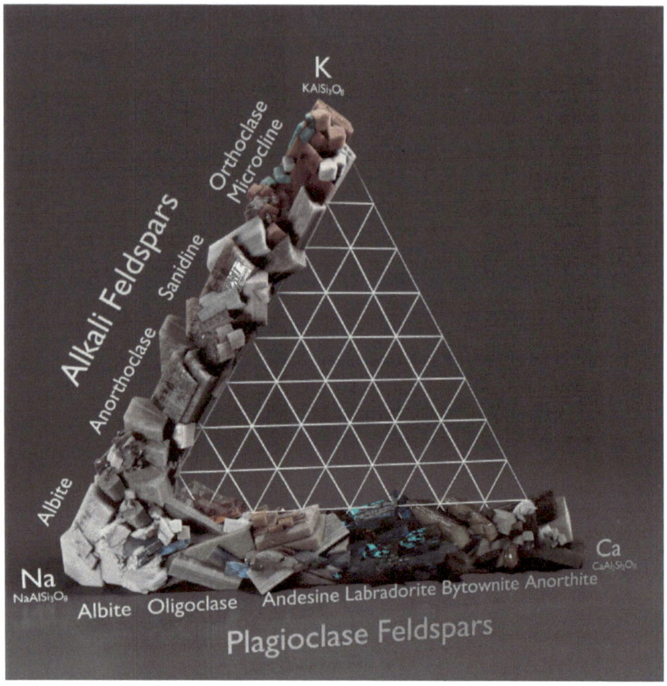

Figure 1-5: Feldspars, *are common rock-forming aluminum silicate minerals. They come in two major types, Alkali Feldspars and Plagioclase Feldspars. Their crystal structure allows them to incorporate varying concentrations of metals which, as is seen in the figure, can affect their visual and physical properties. Pyroxenes, garnets, and several other mineral groups are the same way, each group is a chemical spectrum with end members and several intermediate manifestations. This flexibility in the chemical structure is what causes these minerals to be so common, because given a significant range of physical and chemical conditions at least one variant is still likely to be stable. Instead of trying to learn all the names and specific chemistries (like us geologists do), focus on general group compositions and understand there is a spectrum between end members. Image: (Jakaitė, L., 2019)*

Moving from the outermost layer of the Earth inward (figure 1-6):

1: The crust, is a brittle, rigid solid composed mostly of silicate and other light minerals.

2: The upper mantle, is a ductile solid that flows due to internal heat. It is dominantly composed of iron silicates, 60% olivine and 25% pyroxene. Aluminum silicates like plagioclase and garnet can account for another 10%. (Langmuir & Broecker, 2012)

3: The lower mantle is made of malleable plastic-like rock, and contains a mixed concentration of metals, carbon, and silica. The two most stable minerals are believed to be perovskite $(Mg,Fe)SiO_3$ and Mannesiowüstite $(Mg,Fe)O$, (Bovolo, 2005).

4: The outer core is liquid and comprised of a Fe-Ni alloy, with up to 11% silicate and sulfur impurities (Hirose et al., 2021).

5: The inner core is solid, consisting predominantly of Fe-Ni alloy but including the bulk of other heavy metals, and less than 5% silica, sulfur, and carbon. (Chernicoff & Whitney, 2002; Hirose et al., 2021)

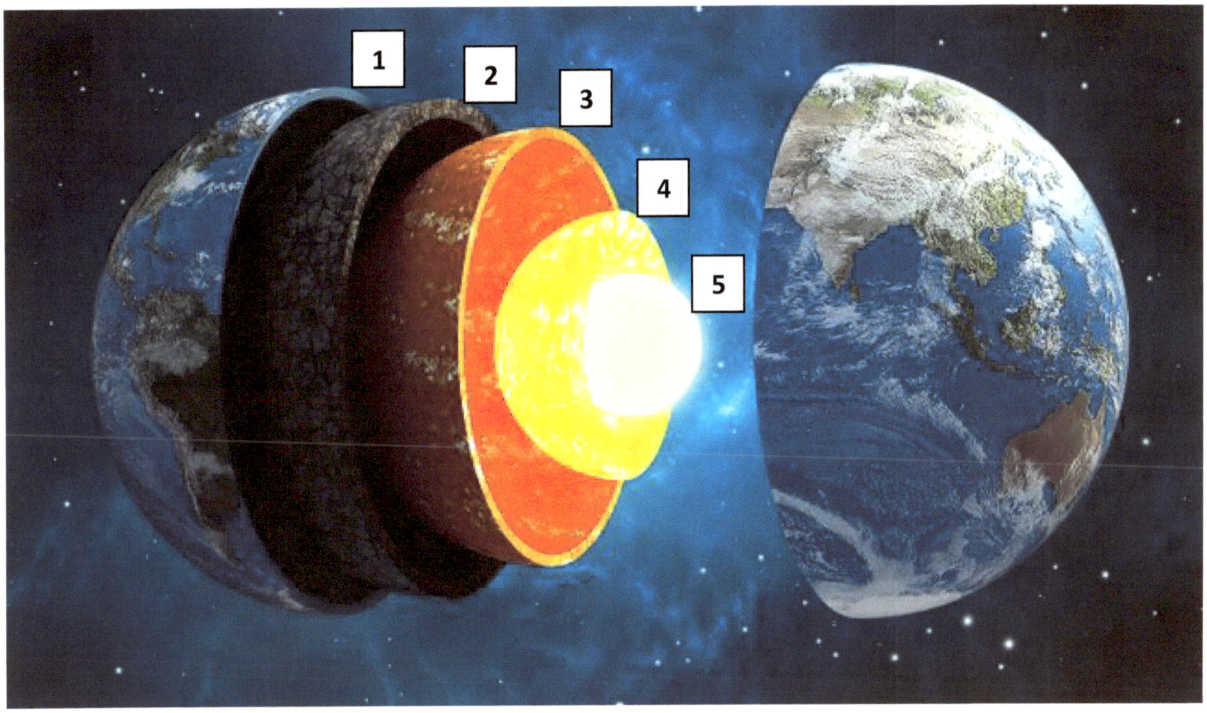

Figure 1-6: Layers of the Earth, *1-Crust: Brittle and dominated by silicate minerals and light elements. 2- Upper mantle: Solid but ductile, dominated by iron silicates. 3-Lower mantle: Malleable plastic-like rock that has a mixed concentration of metals, carbon, and silica. 4-Outer core: Liquid Fe-Ni alloy with some silicate and sulfur impurities. 5- Inner core: Predominantly solid iron-nickel alloy but includes all other stable heavy elements: zinc, copper, silver, platinum, gold, uranium, etc., and less than 5% silica, sulfur, and carbon. (Chernicoff & Whitney, 2002; Hirose et al., 2021) Image, modified from (Pappas, 2021).*

Earth is interesting in that it has natural mechanisms that allow metals to re-concentrate near the surface. Earth is technically still differentiating, while the majority of heavy metals were pulled to its center, low concentrations remain in the crust and upper mantle. This obviously creates a problem for humans wanting to exploit those metals. Thankfully, there are ways that Earth moves metal from the mantle into the crust. The first process is partial melting. As the name implies, the material only partially melts. The molten portion includes H_2O, CO_2, Alkali metals (potassium, sodium, and calcium being most common), sulfur, chlorine, fluorine (these three in the form of acids), silica, other light elements, and interestingly, several heavier metals due to low melting points and susceptibility to mobilization by acid. These melts, or magma, can generate in either the crust or mantle and migrate to the surface, where they can result in a volcanic eruption. If the magma cools and solidifies below the surface, it produces a coarse-grained igneous rock, such as granite. (Winter, 2001)

Both scenarios result in silicate rocks with varying degrees of incorporated metal. Another process is associated with the second scenario and will be discussed later. First, economically speaking, even if a rock is >20% metal but that metal is contained within silicate minerals, for example olivine, the rock is essentially worthless from an ore perspective. We currently do not have technology to economically separate metals from silicate minerals. Space junkies need to understand this to keep from making inaccurate assumptions about extraterrestrial resources. For example, Wikipedia under "lunar resources" lists aluminum (Al) and iron (Fe) in plagioclase and olivine respectively as potential resources. Both, however, are silicate minerals; if we had the ability to extract Al and Fe from silicates economically, we would have no need to go to the moon for them, as both minerals are abundant on Earth's surface. Correct, the moon does have high concentrations of metals, but don't think it as a floating ore zone, because most of that metal is locked in silicate minerals. (Faure, 1998)

Partial melting occurs in the upper mantle and lower crust; the melt or liquid portion is called magma and migrates into the upper crust. The magma is viscous fluid of mixed molecules, metal ions, and acid. If magma cools before it reaches the surface it will crystalize into solid minerals, however not all of the elements in the magma are compatible within the internal structures of the minerals forming, due to their chemistries and temperature pressure conditions. Compatible elements (e.g. silica, alkali metals, aluminum, and titanium) come together to make what are known as rock forming minerals (e.g. feldspars, pyroxenes, quartz, amphiboles, micas, and olivine). These minerals typically incorporate 5 to 20% of the total metal endowment of the melt. Everything else stays in the liquid, which now is significantly less viscous and still being hot moves upward and away from the new rock formation. This process is called fractional crystallization, a key concept all geology students are required to understand. (Winter, 2001)

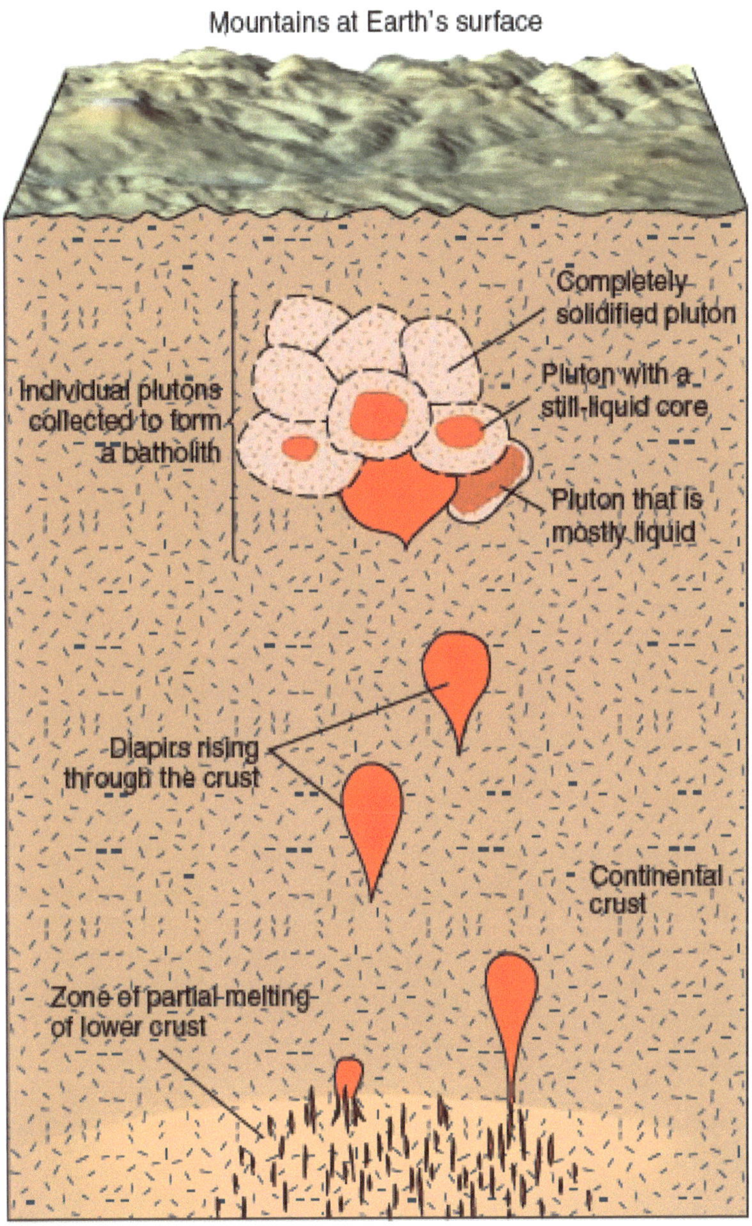

Figure 1-7: Partial Melting Model, *the lower crust or upper mantle partially melts. The melt includes aluminum-silicate magmas, is 4-9% metals (mostly iron), and about 2% water, chlorine, fluorine, and sulfur. The melt moves its way toward the surface in a diapir (inverted tear-drop shape). As they cool, they create what geologist call plutons, which are composed of crystalline igneous rocks, like granite. (Winter, 2001) (Jung, 2015)*

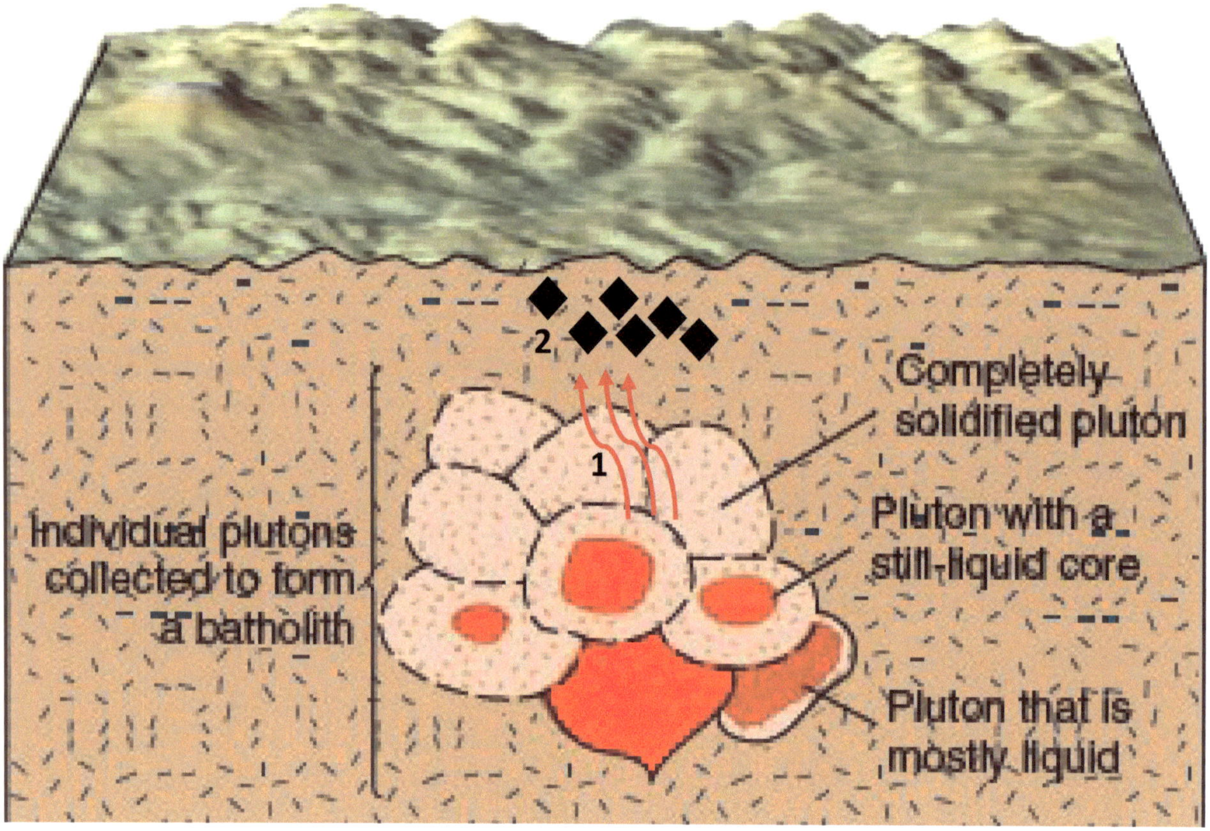

Figure 1-8: Ore Bearing Fluids, *1- As magma cools silicate minerals precipitate forming a pluton while acid and metals concentrate in the remaining fluid. This process is called fractional crystallization and is the key process in which Earth concentrates metals in the crust. These hot metal bearing fluids often move up and out of the forming pluton. 2- As these fluids interact with surrounding country rock they metasomatically alter it forming various alteration minerals, the fluids begin to cool and neutralize, precipitating their metals in the process, often in the form of sulfides. (Sillitoe, 2010) (Robb, 2020) (Winter, 2001)*

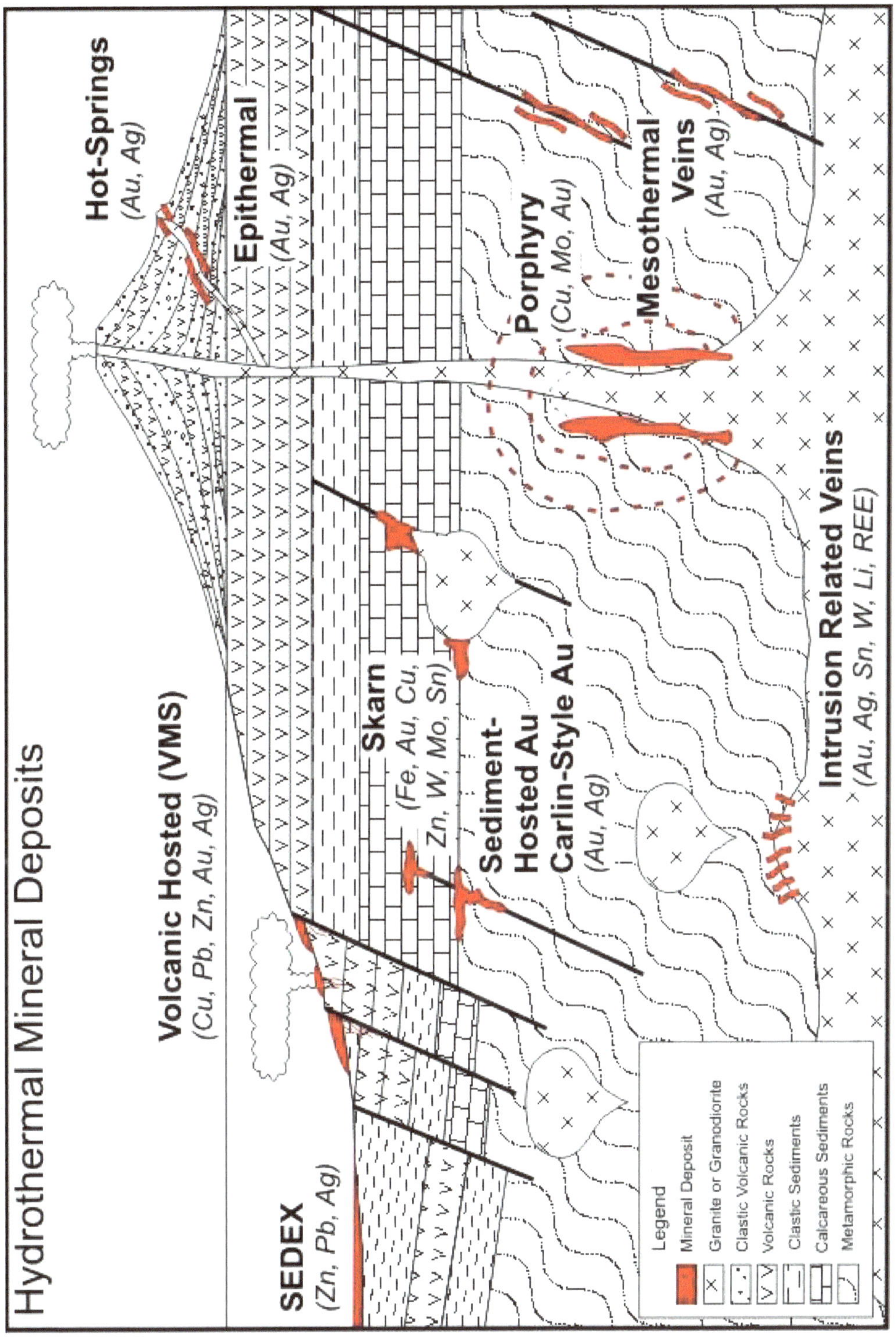

Figure 1-9: Hydrothermal Mineral Deposits, *mineral deposits come in many types and geometries, this diagram illustrates several of the hydrothermally formed types, and where, and under which conditions they tend to form in the Earth's crust. The type of deposit and its depth will greatly affect how the deposit is explored for and eventually mined. Millions of years of tectonic activity has brough many deeper formed deposits closer to the surface making their exploration and development possible.*

As an exploration geologist I am more interested in the fluid that leaves, because this is where all the goodies are. The incompatibles elements, those left in the melt during fractional crystallization, typically include water, carbon dioxide, sulfur, chlorine and/or fluorine, salts from excess alkali metals not incorporated into the silicates, and metal. Basically, this fluid is pure acid plus dissolved metal. Iron, lead, zinc, copper, silver, gold, mercury, arsenic plus many others readily dissolve in high concentrations of hydrochloric and sulfuric acid. This fluid, when above 300 C° contains an appreciable amount of dissolved silica. Hydrofluoric acid, when present increases the amount of silica in the fluid through two step reaction that inhibits silicon and oxygen bonding. (Chang & Meinert, 2008; Mitra & Rimstidt, 2009)

What this natural process has done is drastically concentrate the metal. Granodiorite, an igneous rock formed from melts commonly associated with ore generating fluids, has a composition of 4 to 9% metal, excluding Aluminum (Jung et al, 2015). For example, let's take a modest sized magmatic pluton, say $10km^3$; of that 5% is metal, mostly iron, and evenly distributed. Once the magma crystalizes, only about 5% of the total mental content will be trapped in the silicate minerals. The remainder stays in the ore-forming fluid. In our example, this means of a $10km^3$ pluton $0.5km^3$ is metal, of that $0.5km^3$ only $0.025km^3$ will be locked in silicates while the remaining $0.475km^3$ of metal stays in solution. The conditions that control how these remaining metals precipitate vary greatly; however, zonation or crude segregation of metals is common in many deposit types, further concentrating economic metals. (Robb, 2020) The process also chemically changes the nature of the fluid, usually sulfur becomes oversaturated, so that precipitates will not be in a silicate but rather a sulfide, or sometimes a carbonate, or chloride. All these are significantly easier to remove metal from economically. Weathering of precipitated ore minerals may continue to further concentrate economic metals, making extraction even easier. (Sillitoe, 2010; Robb, 2020) Metal deposits come in many different types and geometries. Figure 1-9 illustrates generally where and under which conditions within the Earth's crust several of these deposit types are formed.

In the most extreme examples, metal is concentrated into veins or massive sulfide zones that are >30% metal. Figure 1-10 is a photo of drill core taken from the multi-metallic South

Mountain project in southwestern Idaho. The composite (average) grade/concentration for this interval is 21.27% zinc, 12.1% iron, 1.00% arsenic, 0.77% lead, 0.30% copper, 0.1% cadmium, 230g/t bismuth, 220g/t antimony, 147g/t silver, and 8g/t gold. Of these, likely only zinc, lead, copper, silver, and gold will be recovered for market. (BeMetals 2020)

Figure 1-10: South Mountain Ore, Idaho, USA, *is an example of highly concentrated metallic ore. The massive sulfide zones often have a total metal concentration near 40%. The interval shown contains 21.27% zinc, 12.1% iron, 1.00% arsenic, 0.77% lead, 0.30% copper, 0.1% cadmium, 230g/t bismuth, 220g/t antimony, 147g/t silver, and 8g/t gold, with the balance mostly sulfur and about 10% quarts. Of the metals, likely only zinc, lead, copper, silver, and gold will be recovered for market. Large granodiorite intrusions to the southwest of the deposit are presumably the source of ore-generating fluids. Fluid reactions with the local marble produced this high-grade multi-metallic skarn/carbonate replacement style deposit. Photo courtesy of Thunder Mountain Gold inc., geochemical values from (BeMetals, 2020).*

There are still many complexities, because in virtually every instance, the conditions that create an ore body are a little bit different. Unsurprisingly, this results in different deposit types that will require varying engineering practices to mine and refine. Most of the training for geologists in the mining industry is geared toward understanding the array and variation of rock and ore-forming processes, learning to identify these minerals, and making accurate maps. Specialized techniques in geophysics and geochemistry are becoming requisite as most of the easily identified surface exposed deposits have already been developed. Engineers and metallurgists are usually tasked with the challenge of extracting the metal. This includes everything from designing mine infrastructure to executing the mine plan to figuring out appropriate metallurgical techniques for metal extraction and refinement.

The key takeaway is that each ore body is unique. Hopefully, this has helped explain a little of the "why" without putting you through a graduate course. For investors and traders, knowing some of the terminology and having a foundational understanding of where these commodities come from will help you better communicate with industry sources and understand reports and presentations. All this ultimately will help answer the important questions that revolve around assessing and managing risk.

Endowment

The total Earth endowment of precious metal is difficult to calculate, primarily because our ability to probe the crust in a comprehensive way is still significantly limited. We can, however, make reasonable assumptions based on observations, production records, and current global reserves. This provides us with satisfactory relative abundances. Global reserves should never be interpreted as *"this is all we have left;"* rather, it means this is all that we currently have ready to mine. Usually, new reserves keep pace with those being extracted. When they do get out of balance, it is usually temporary. These situations often create trade opportunities, and production vs. reserves is a metric that active traders in the space keep an eye on.

Another part of the question: *"Where does the metal come from?"* is much more literal. Does it come from the U.S., Africa, Russia, or somewhere else? Metal endowment is not evenly distributed; it is as variable as the terrains of our planet. Figure 1-11 displays the major operating mines of the world, colored by commodity type, and Figure 1-12 reports 2022 gold production by country. Location affects things like shipping, labor, tariffs, and political risk to name a few. Having a good idea of what metal comes from where, who uses it, and where all parties are located helps the intelligent trader identify opportunities. As these are efficient industries, many excellent opportunities arise from disruption to the supply chains. A little bit of advanced research into a specific market can help identify where the pressure points are, so if a crisis comes about you are prepared to capitalize on it.

***Figure 1-11: Mines of the World by Commodity**, several patterns can be observed when looking at the distribution of various metal mines globally. These reflect the geological events throughout Earth's history that have concentrated and/or exposed metallic minerals on the surface. The plethora of gold and copper mines along the Pacific rim of North and South America is an obvious one and is related to the subduction zones between the Pacific plate and North and South American plates. Source data (USGS)*

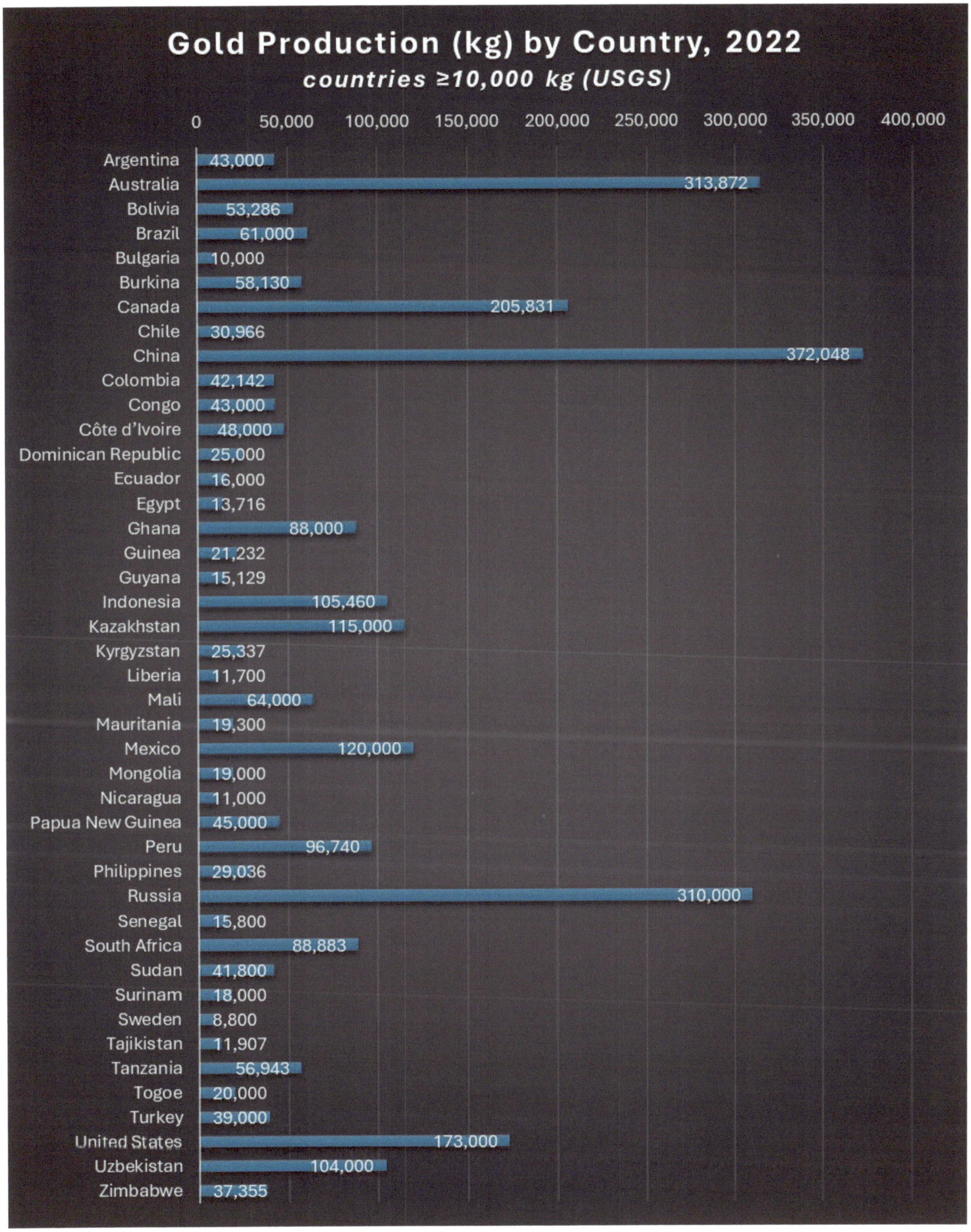

Figure 1-12: Gold Production by Country, 2022. (compiled from USGS data)

Chapter 1: Genesis and Endowment

Chapter Summary:

1: Heavy elements, including precious metals, are formed through major astrophysical events, including supernovas and kilonovas. They are rare, in part, because they are difficult to make on the elemental level.

2: As Earth differentiated, the majority of heavy elements were pulled toward the center of the planet. The crust and upper mantle, while not completely void of precious metals, have very low concentrations.

3: The natural processes of partial melting and fractional crystallization concentrate metals and bring them upward into the upper portions of the crust. These metalliferous fluids form various types of ore deposits, depending on local factors including geology and chemistry.

4: Metal endowment is unevenly distributed. This gives rise to both logistical and geopolitical considerations when developing the resource and when trading financial instruments tied to these commodities.

To end this chapter, I would just like to say how amazing our universe is. The next time you look at that gold ring on your finger remember, a star had to die not once, but twice so you could enjoy its luster. A true gift from the galaxy.

Notes

Chapter 2: Properties and Uses for Precious Metals

As with any service or product, serious investors owe it to themselves to do a little due diligence and understand that product's place in the economy. This chapter presents some of the basic properties of silver, gold, and platinum group metals, and explores uses in modern society for these materials.

Silver (Ag)

Silver is a soft, white, and lustrous metal that is malleable and slightly more resistant to corrosion than copper. It is unique because it has the highest electrical and thermal conductivity, as well as the highest reflectivity of any metal. Silver has a melting point of 961 °C and is found in two stable isotopes, Ag-107 (51.839%) and Ag-109 (48.161%). Interestingly, there are very few stand-alone silver mines in the world, rather most of the silver produced is a byproduct from mining other metals, like gold, copper, lead, and zinc. This is an important fact to remember when we discuss "streaming companies" and for understanding supply vs demand of silver. (Brittanica, 2024a)

Silver has many uses. Its electrical conductivity makes it an obvious choice for electronics, solar panels, and certain batteries. It is used to make high-end mirrors, in filtration systems, and for antibacterial applications. It was a primary component for x-ray and photographic film, though with digital instruments, that technology is becoming obsolete. (Brittanica, 2024a)

Silver is used in jewelry. Traditional sterling silver is 92.5% silver with the balance of copper. While alloying it with copper does make for a more scratch resistant and stronger piece, it is also more susceptible to corrosion than pure silver. Pure silver itself is still quite reactive, especially in warm moist environments, and any owner of silver jewelry has learned that care must be taken to protect against tarnish. Advanced alloys have been created that are highly resistant to tarnish, usually by adding germanium, palladium, zinc, and other metals instead of copper (Jewelry Informer, 2024). Silver has been used throughout history in coinage and as investment bullion. Silver is as much an industrial metal as a precious metal. This is important, because unlike gold, where most of what has been mined is still in possession by someone, silver is consumed. (Brittanica, 2024a)

Figure 2-1: Silver Forms, *1- Silver Nugget, 2- Alexander the Great as Zeus Ammon on a silver tetradrachm of Lysimachus, 297–281 BC, in the British Museum. Diameter 30mm. (Brittanica 2024a) 3-Argentite, Silver sulfide Ag_2S, Ucucchacua Mine, Peru (Tukos Minerals, 2024).*

Referring to Table 2-1, we observe that industrial uses for silver in 2020 eclipsed all other uses combined. This trend is expected to continue. As manufacturing efficiencies continue to reduce the amount of silver used in products, it becomes increasingly less cost effective to recycle them. Thus, more of the metal ends up wasted in landfills, while this trend exists with virtually all electronic products, it is especially true for solar panels, as manufactures are continually striving to make them cost competitive with traditional energy sources. For solar panels specifically, recycling compacity has been drastically outpaced by manufacturing capacity. Recycling cost is estimated at $20-$30/ panel whereas landfill disposal cost average $1-$2. (EPA, 2024: Atasu et al, 2021) Because of its lower price, silver has the lowest recycling rates compared to all other precious metals. It would take a significant rise in the price of silver to improve solar panel and other electronic recycling rates.

***Table 2-1: Global Silver Supply & Demand by End Use 2021**, (Silver Institute, 2022)*

World Silver Supply & Demand (million ounces)
(totals may not add due to rounding)

	2020	2021
Supply		
Mine Production	781.1	822.6
Recycling	162.2	173.0
Net Hedging Supply	8.5	-
Net Official Sector Sales	1.2	1.5
Total Supply	**953.0**	**997.2**
Demand		
Industrial	464.9	508.2
...of which Photovoltaics	101.0	113.7
Photography	27.8	28.7
Jewelry	149.8	181.4
Silverware	32.4	42.7
Net Physical Investment	205.0	278.7
Net Hedging Demand	-	9.4
Total Demand	**880.0**	**1,049.0**
Silver Price (US$/oz, London Price)	20.55	25.14

Source: Metals Focus

Gold (Au)

Gold is a bright yellow, extremely soft, and dense metal. It is the most malleable and ductile of all metals. To illustrate this, the smallest wire gold can be drawn into is about 5 microns. At that diameter, 1 oz of gold would produce a wire 50 miles long! This property has been exploited for thousands of years, pressing gold leaf over statues and other ornamental items. Gold has extremely high thermal and electrical conductivity and a melting point of 1064 °C. It is one of the least chemically reactive elements but will dissolve in solutions containing a mixture of hydrochloric and nitric acid, as well as in alkali cyanide solutions. The latter is commonly used in the mining process to leach gold out of host rocks. Chapter 1 mentioned that weathering process can concentrate elements. In gold's case, its density, malleability, and inert nature allow weathered particles from eroded gold deposits to accumulate in streams where they adhere or press together when they come into contact to develop into flakes and nuggets. These form placer deposits that, when at the surface are easily exploitable (think gold panning) and require little to no refinement. It is a relatively rare element. All the gold mined in the history of the world would weigh about 200,000 tons and fit in a cube less than 75 ft on each side. (Venditti, 2023) This, if evenly distributed across the global population, 8.24 billion, it would be equivalent to 5 gold rings per person, with each ring containing about 4.5 grams of gold.

Historically, coins, jewelry, and other artistic artifacts were made from gold. (Brittanica, 2024b) (World Gold Council, 2024) Evidence for human use of gold dates to before 6,000 B.C. (Yeend et al., 1989) Its common use in antiquity is in part, surprisingly, because of its availability, as ancient cultures were able to exploit several placer deposits.

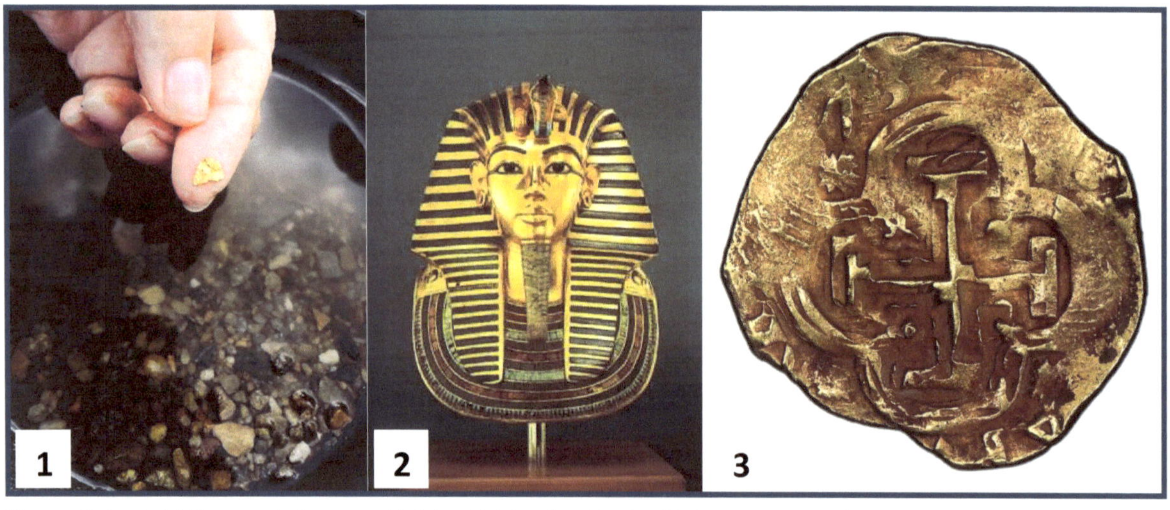

Figure 2-2: Gold Forms, *1- Large gold flake, Fairbanks, Alaska (Gold Daughters, 2024). 2-Tutankhamun, gold funerary mask found in the king's tomb, 14th century B.C.; in the Egyptian Museum, Cairo (Brittanica 2024b). 3-Spanish Doubloon, 1673-S M8 AU50, PCGS# 721390 (Collectors Corner, 2023).*

In modern society gold serves three primary functions: It is the metal of choice for jewelry due to its easy workability, resistance to corrosion, and in pure form being hypoallergenic. Jewelry makes up about 50% of the annual demand for the metal with Asian markets being the largest consumers. Another 40% is turned into bullion, which is purchased by central banks, electronically traded funds (ETFs), and the retail investment market. Gold is still universally accepted as a means of trade among central banks and an advantage of holding gold at this level is that it is politically natural. (Armstrong, 2024) Finally, about 10% of gold demand is for industrial uses. Though silver, due to its lower cost, superior electrical properties, and better wear resistance, is usually the better option for electronics, gold is used if the circuits and/or connections need to be corrosion resistant. It is also used in infrared shielding applications. About 0.25% is used in dentistry and other medical related applications. (World Gold Council, 2022) (Britannica, 2024b)

It is estimated that humans have mined 208,874 tons of gold throughout history, with 2/3 of that obtained post 1950. Reports from central bank stores and the jewelry industry indicate that a little over 85% of historically mined gold is still accessible. This makes sense knowing that the two largest markets are jewelry, which has high recycling rates, and bullion, which is traded but rarely consumed. (World Gold Council, 2023a)

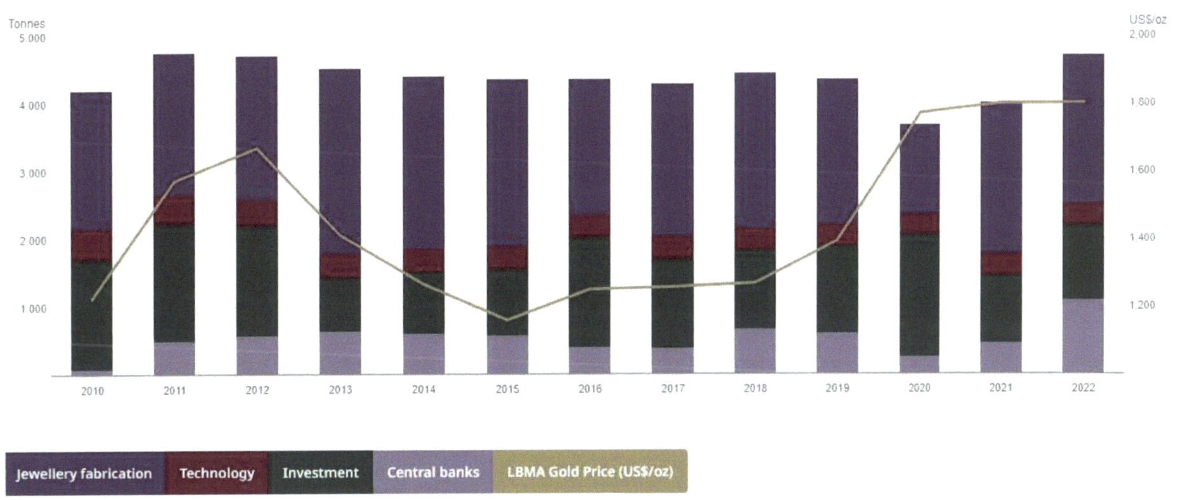

Figure 2-3: Gold, historical demand by sector vs price $U.S. (World Gold Council, 2023c).

Another note about gold, recycling rates tend to increase as the price of gold rises. This is not a surprise, but as more gold enters the consumer market, it creates the potential for more gold to be recycled. The added production from recycling will apply downward pressure to gold prices. Recent reports show recycled gold accounts for about 26% of total production, this is during a time of high prices. Times of global economic hardship, likely also increase recycling rates, as people desire to turn scrap and old jewelry into money. Figures 2-4 and 2-5 present recent production data. (World Gold Council, 2023b)

Tonnes	Q1'22	Q1'23		YoY % change
Total supply	1,165.1	1,174.4	▲	1
Mine production	843.1	856.0	▲	2
Net producer hedging	25.9	8.1	▼	-69
Recycled gold	296.2	310.4	▲	5

Figure 2-4: Gold Production, Mined vs Recycled Q1 2022 and 2023 comparison (World Gold Council, 2023b).

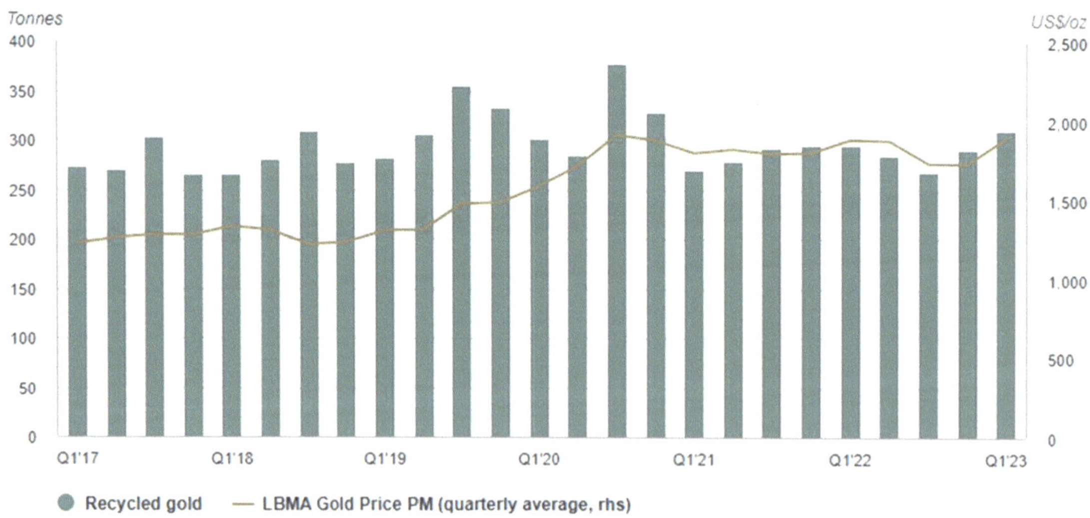

Figure 2-5: Recycled Gold Production vs Price $US, (World Gold Council, 2023b).

Recycling streams are constantly improving, so rest in peace (or maybe not in peace), that your ashes post cremation will be sifted. All gold, silver, titanium, and stainless steel will be recovered before your ashes are delivered to loved ones. In some cases, money received from human metal recycling is donated to charity, other times it simply helps your undertaker meet their bottom line. Knowing this may prompt a few questions as you are settling your affairs. Be assured, you aren't the only one who knows that hip replacement was expensive. (Common & Malik, 2018)

Platinum Group Metals (PGMs)

There are six platinum group metals: platinum, palladium, iridium, rhodium, osmium, and ruthenium. All six have similar chemical properties, and all have industrial uses. These metals have high melting points, palladium the lowest at 1552 °C and osmium the highest at 3033 °C. All have good resistance to chemical degradation, but their electrical conductivities are significantly less than silver, copper, and gold (Table 2-2).

Of the six platinum group elements, you will likely only own or trade platinum and palladium. The others do have some interesting uses; for example, iridium is used for the arc points on high-end spark plugs, many of which last 100,000 miles. The fact that platinum does not tarnish makes it a good choice for jewelry; however, its high melting point can make it difficult to work with. A "white gold" ring may contain some palladium and has probably been electroplated with rhodium. The latter adds scratch resistance and lustrous finish. All PGMs appear in different alloys used in long-wearing corrosion-resistant electrical contacts, with aerospace and military applications being the most common.

Table 2-2: Metal Properties, *note, elements with a low electrical resistivity will have a higher conductivity. Selecting a metal for a particular industrial use is always a tradeoff between physical properties and price. Data from (RSC, 2024) and (Total Materia, 2024).*

Metal Properties: Sorted from most to least electrically conductive

Metal	Resistivity Ω/m x10^{-8}	Thermal Conductivity W/mC°	Melting Point C°
Silver	1.7	419	961
Copper	2	380	1084
Gold	2.25	312	1064
Aluminum	3.5	193	660
Titanium	4.2	22	1670
Rhodium	4.3	150	1964
Iridium	4.7	59	2447
Tungsten	5.6	170	3414
Nickel	6.9	91	1453
Ruthenium	7.1	120	2333
Osmium	8.2	88	3033
Lithium	9.28	88.1	181
Iron *(native)*	9.6	80.2	1538
Palladium	10	75	1552
Platinum	10.6	74	1769
Lead	22	35	328

Table 2-3: Platinum, supply and demand by sector, *the industrial demand for platinum significantly exceeds its demand by the investment and jewelry sectors. For this reason, platinum and other PGM prices are much more sensitive to industrial cycles than either gold or silver. Table from (Cowely, 2022).*

Supply '000 oz	2020	2021	2022
South Africa	3,222	4,611	4,204
Russia	699	638	-
Others	1,015	948	1,018
Total primary supply	**4,936**	**6,197**	**-**
Demand '000 oz	**2020**	**2021**	**2022**
Automotive	2,045	2,353	2,820
Jewellery	1,656	1,478	1,447
Industrial	2,474	2,949	2,627
Investment	1,022	-28	-92
Total gross demand	**7,197**	**6,752**	**6,802**
Recycling	-1,702	-1,659	-1,628
Total net demand	**5,495**	**5,093**	**5,174**
Movements in stocks	-559	1,104	-

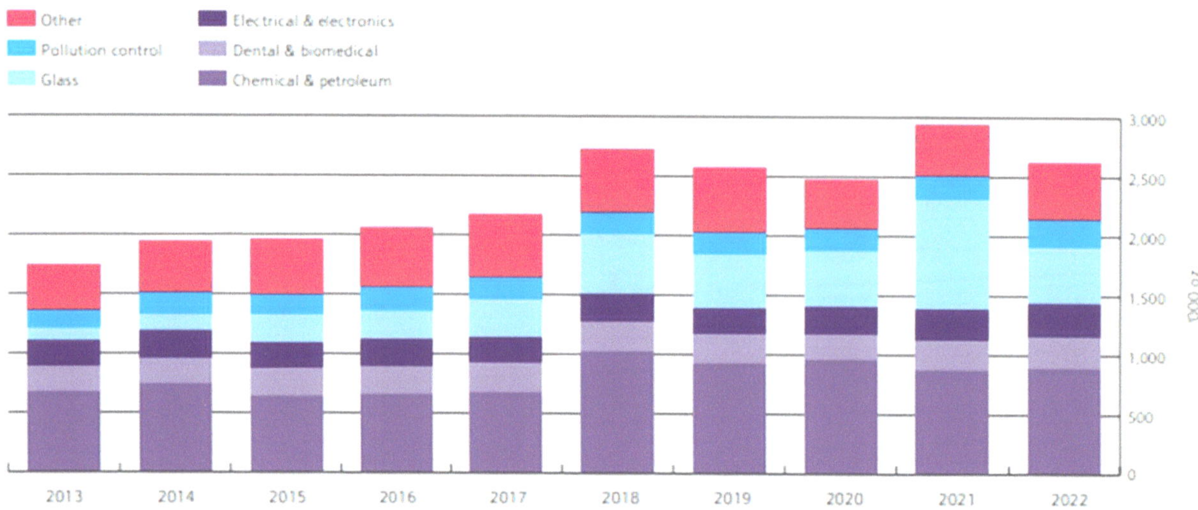

Figure 2-6: Industrial Demand for Platinum, *due to their unique properties, PGMs are critically important elements for many sectors. Outside of the auto industry, the largest consumer is the petrochemical and refining industry. Virtually every gallon of refined fuel and plastic has touched a PGM at some point in its process stream. Chart from, (Cowley, 2022).*

Figure 2-7: Standard (copper Ni plated) Spark Plug vs Iridium. *The high melting temperature and low reactivity of PGMs have led to many uses. One in particular that touches the average person is spark plugs. 1- A new and used standard copper with nickel plating spark plug. The used plug being replaced has about 30,000 miles of wear. 2- A similar pair of iridium spark plugs; however, in this case the used plug has over 100,000 miles of wear! The substantially higher melting temperature and lower reactivity of iridium allow the electrode to better withstand the constant 2900 °C arcing. Iridium spark plugs do cost about 3-4 times as much as standard spark plugs, but that is 3 less times you need to pay your mechanic to maintain the engine. Image modified from (Carcody, 2020).*

Chapter 2: Properties and Uses for Precious Metals

Platinum, palladium, osmium and to a lesser extent rhodium and ruthenium are all used in industry as catalysts. In chemistry a catalyst is a substance, usually used in small amounts relative to the reactants, that modifies and increases the rate of a reaction without being consumed in the process.

In general, two requirements of most chemical reactions are 1) heat, as it takes energy to change from one molecular configuration to another, and 2) the ability to exchange electrons. Platinum group elements are well suited to both. First, their high melting points allow them to remain stable as heat is added to the reactants. Second, having high atomic numbers, their inner four electron shells are full, but with incomplete outer electron shells. This means they have electrons available that will loosely bond with one of the reactants until the other reactant comes into contact and bonds strongly into the new molecule, disassociating with the PGM metal in the process and leaving it unchanged. Having this "halfway point" in the reaction reduces the overall amount of energy required for the reaction to take place. Without exploiting these reactions, modern society would not exist as we know it, as they touch fuels, foods, plastics, electronics, transportation, manufacturing, textiles, and construction to name the major ones.

Not surprisingly, due to chemistry, certain PGMs are better suited for particular reactions than others. As always, there are expense and availability considerations in industry, so in some cases, a less efficient catalyst may be used if it works well enough and is available. We can observe all these factors in action by looking at the automotive industry and the use of catalytic converters. Figure 2-8 explains how catalytic converters work.

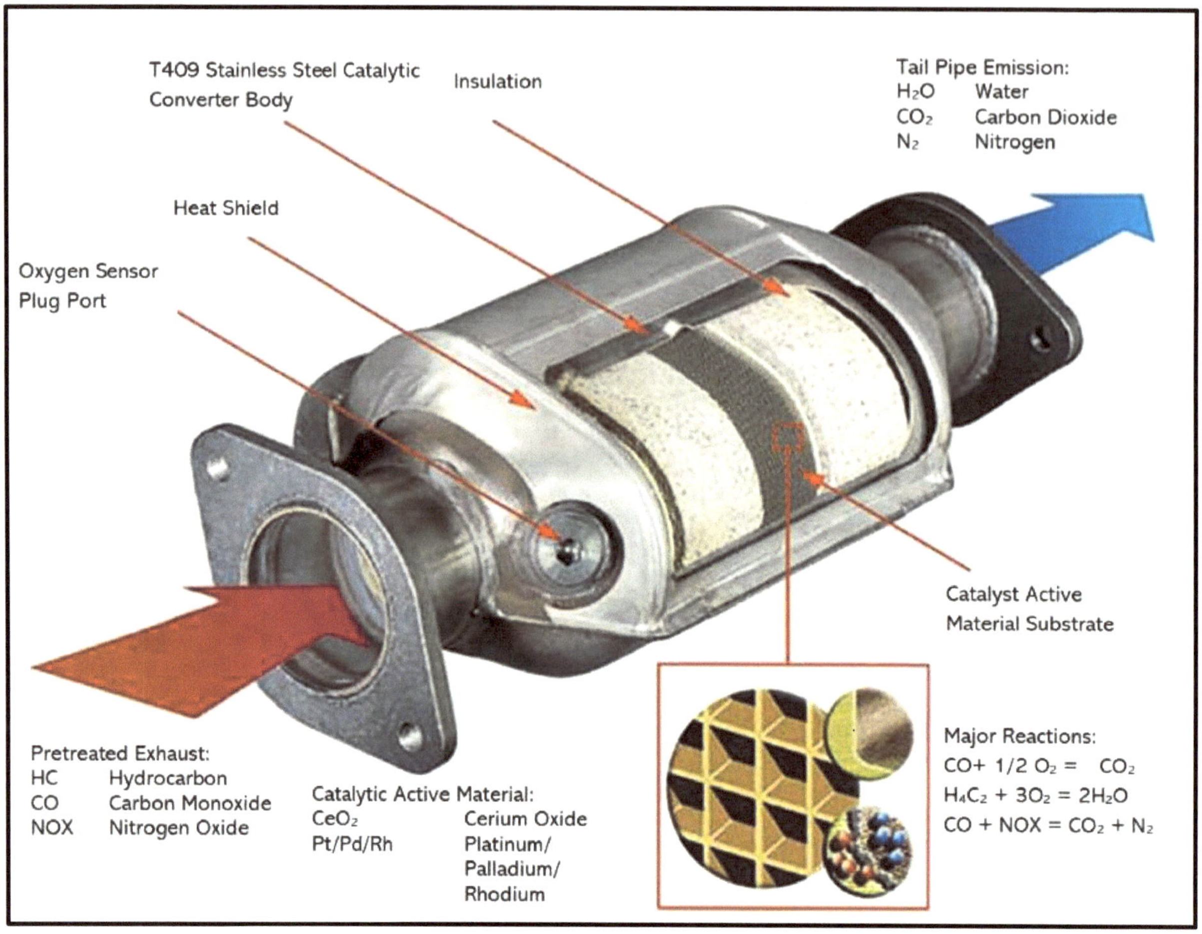

Figure 2-8: Design and Function of a Standard Catalytic Converter: *Hot pollutants from incompletely combusted fuel pass through a porous honeycomb-structured medium, that has been impregnated with micro drops of PGMs. These catalyze reactions that convert the pollutants to harmless compounds including carbon dioxide, nitrogen, and water vapor. Image modified from (Bryant, 2021).*

Platinum is the best catalyst for reducing harmful gas emissions from internal combustion engines. For this reason, it tends to be used for diesel engines. Others, most commonly palladium, are sufficient for gasoline engines. This is an interesting case, as 14 years ago the auto industry was trying to replace platinum as the catalyst because it was the more expensive metal. They were successful in switching to palladium for gasoline engines, which tend to have lower emissions than diesel engines, due to the lighter and more refined fuel. This increased demand significantly drove up the price of palladium until it exceeded that of platinum. (Coghlan, 2021) The rise was so dramatic, it became one of the largest metals surprises in modern history, Figure 2-9.

Despite platinum now being significantly less expensive and a better catalyst, in the US they have not switched back to platinum. This has to do with tooling and supply chains. The US has only one producing palladium/platinum mine, the Stillwater mine in Montana. Which produces 2-3 times as much palladium as platinum. With the other largest producers of PGMs being South Africa, Russia, and China (Table 2-3), it makes sense that US automakers have chosen to stick with what can be produced domestically. (Coghlan, 2021)

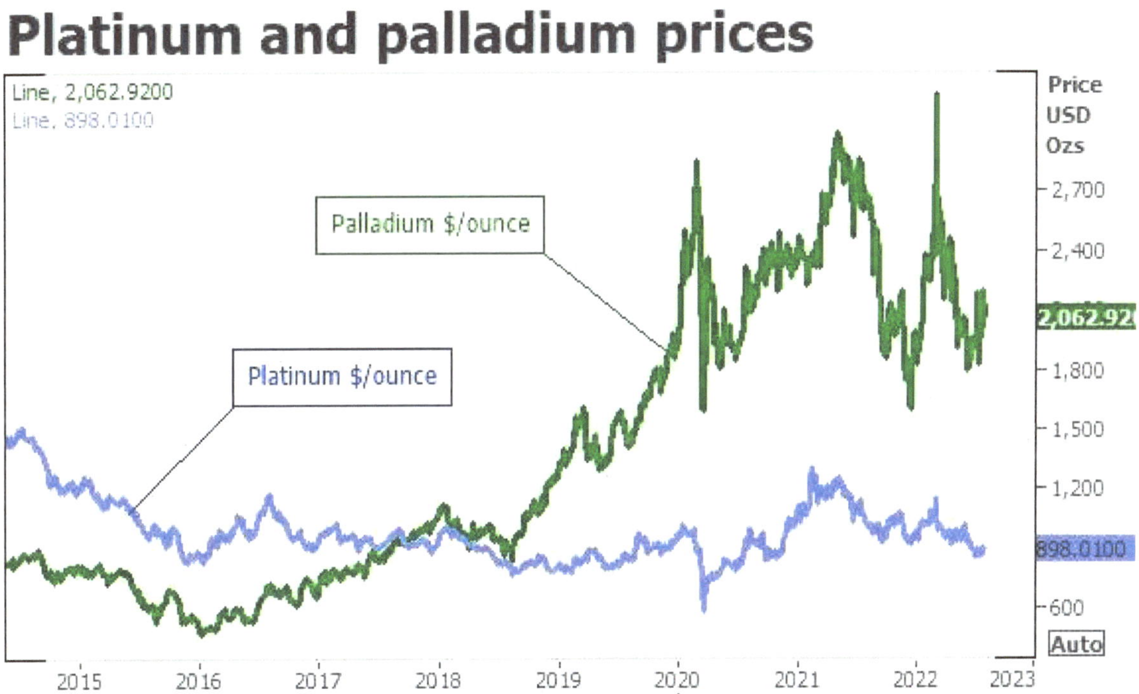

Figure 2-9: Platinum vs Palladium $U.S. Historical Chart: *Aggressively increasing global and domestic emission regulations has led to a significant rise in the consumption of PGMs, which has had an effect on costs, palladium in particular. Despite platinum being a better catalyst for catalytic converters, global auto manufacturers switched to palladium in the mid twenty teens, in part, because of its lower price. This increased market drove the price of palladium far above that of platinum. Due to the larger domestic supply of palladium in the U.S. domestic manufacturers are yet to switch back to platinum, instead prudently valuing a more secure domestic supply chain over commodity savings. (Cowely, 2022; Coghlan, 2021; Chart from (Shivaprasad & Hobson, 2022).*

Indeed, considering these are choices the executives would have been making in 2019, and the world subsequently experiencing supply chain disruptions from both the Covid-19 pandemic (2020 to 2022) and the Russia-Ukraine war (2022 to present), we can say they chose well.

A key point with PGMs is that their price is mostly influenced by their industrial applications, which is not surprising given industrial uses significantly outweigh demand from the investment and jewelry sectors (Table 2-3 and figure 2-6). That said, they will still participate in price appreciation when gold and silver move, but do not expect those movements to directly correlate. The auto industry is one of the two largest consumers of PGMs. Active investors and traders in this space keep an eye on global auto production, as well as PGM stockpiles and current mining production.

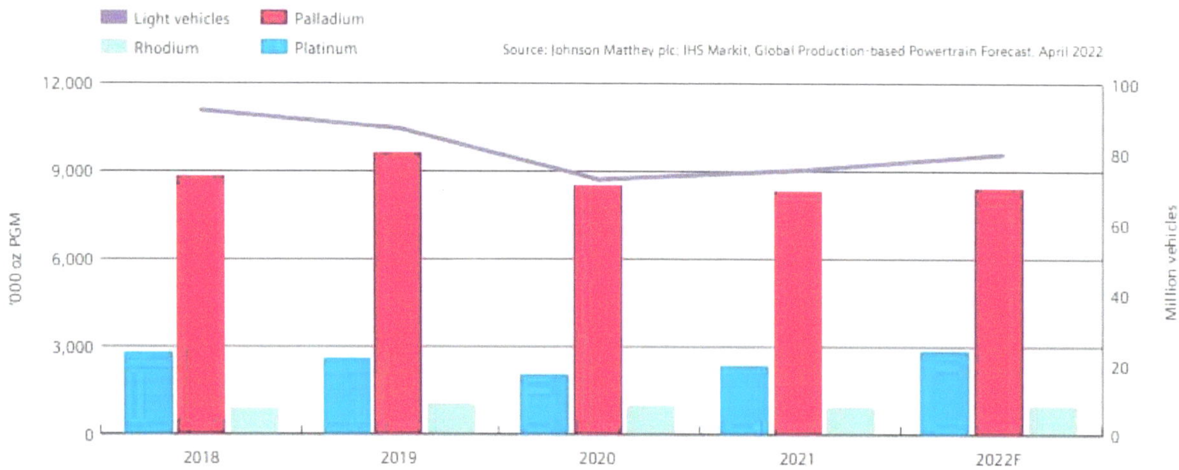

Figure 2-10: Platinum Group Metals Demand vs Global Light Vehicle Production: *PGM prices are more influenced by industrial and manufacturing demand than gold and silver, because their consumption in these sectors is greater than in jewelry and investments. The auto industry is one of the largest consumers. Investors and traders of PGMs pay attention to auto production rates and global production. Comparing this chart with figure 2-9 helps one see how PGM prices are related. (Chart from Cowely, 2022).*

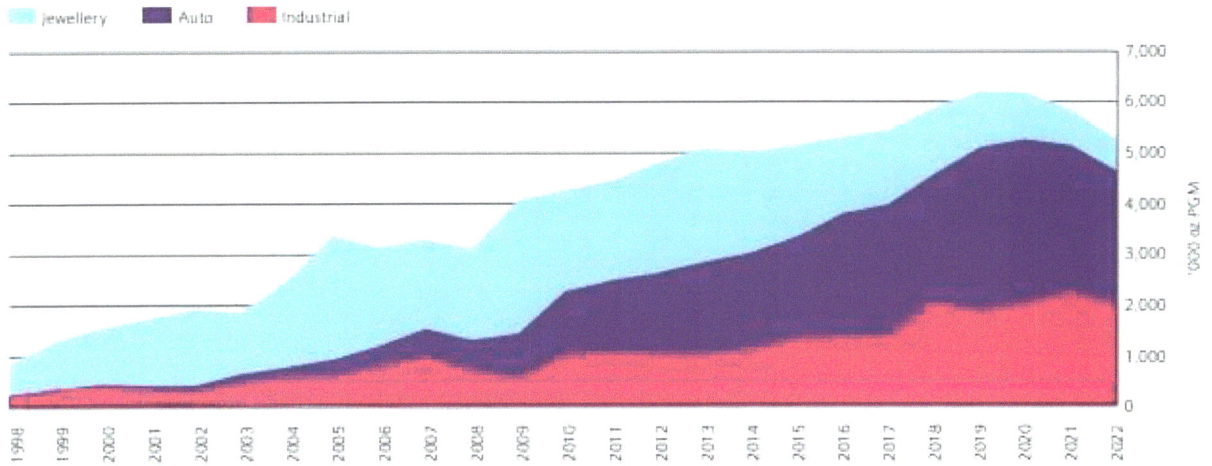

Figure 2-11: Platinum Group Metals Demand by Sector in China. *As China has transitioned into an industrial nation so has their demand for PGMs increased. Also, in the late 1990's the majority of consumption was in the jewelry sector while currently it is dominated by the auto and industrial sectors. Chart from (Cowely, 2022).*

PGMs are an integral part of the refining and petrochemical industry. Platinum is used to catalyze reactions with naphtha feedstocks to produce high octane gasolines (Curry, 1957). Polypropylene, nylon, and polyethylene terephthalate (PET plastics, think type 1 water bottles) all require PGMs as part of their upstream production process (Cowely, 2022). Knowing what countries are consuming PGMs, how they are consuming them, and where they are getting them can give a trader valuable insights, not just on the movement of metal prices, but also to a region's overall economy, trade opportunities for companies selling downstream products, and identifying where the opportunities will be if there is supply-chain disruption. Figures 2-11 and 2-12, for example, give valuable insight into current PGM consumption in China but also can be used as supporting evidence that the growing trend of Chinese manufacturing is not only growing but will eclipse western production in the near future.

Knowing this, China's recent push on electric vehicles (EV) makes sense. With EVs you eliminate the need for PGMs in both catalytic converters and fuel refining. China has abundant lithium deposits but no PGM deposits. China's policy is not about protecting the environment but instead reducing geopolitical risk and protecting their PGM supply chain for aerospace, military, and technology applications. (Shaikh, 2025; WPIC, 2025)

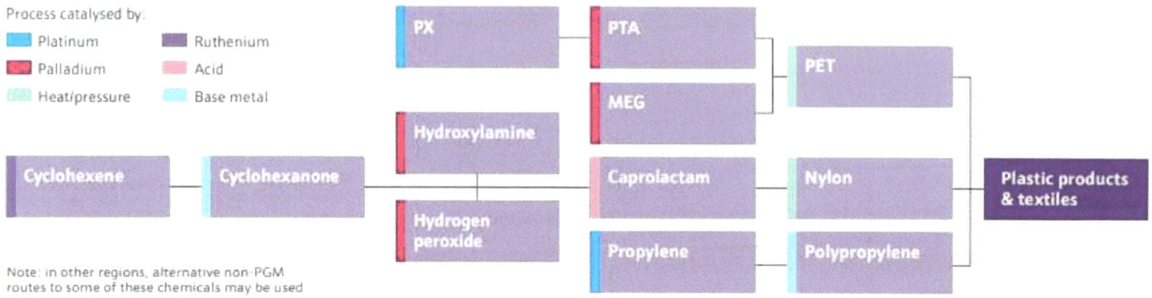

Figure 2-12: Platinum Group Metals, Use in Chinese Upstream Petrochemical Processing of Plastics. *While there are a few exceptions when we look at global processes, what this chart illustrates well is that the creation of virtually all plastics will require a PGM catalyst at one stage or another of their manufacturing. Chart from (Cowely, 2022).*

Another key point with PGMs is that their endowment is significantly more constrained than both gold and silver. Respectively, 75%, 54%, and 82% of the world's platinum, palladium, and rhodium reserves are contained in the Bushveld complex of northern South Africa. As the world's largest layered mafic intrusion, the Bushveld is also a prolific producer of chromium, vanadium, tin, nickel, copper, and cobalt. This large mineral rich province currently has over 30 active mines and predevelopment projects. (Deseta, 2020)

PGMs are not only constrained geographically but also corporately. Ninety-eight percent of global PGM reserves are controlled by just five companies (Table 2-3). Each of these companies owns several mines on different continents, and PGMs are not their only commodity. In the US, we are home to the palladium-platinum producing Stillwater-East Boulder mines in Montana. While this deposit is significantly smaller than the Bushveld complex, it does boast the highest grade of all active PGM mines (figure 2-13). It is owned by Sibanye-Stillwater, a South African company.

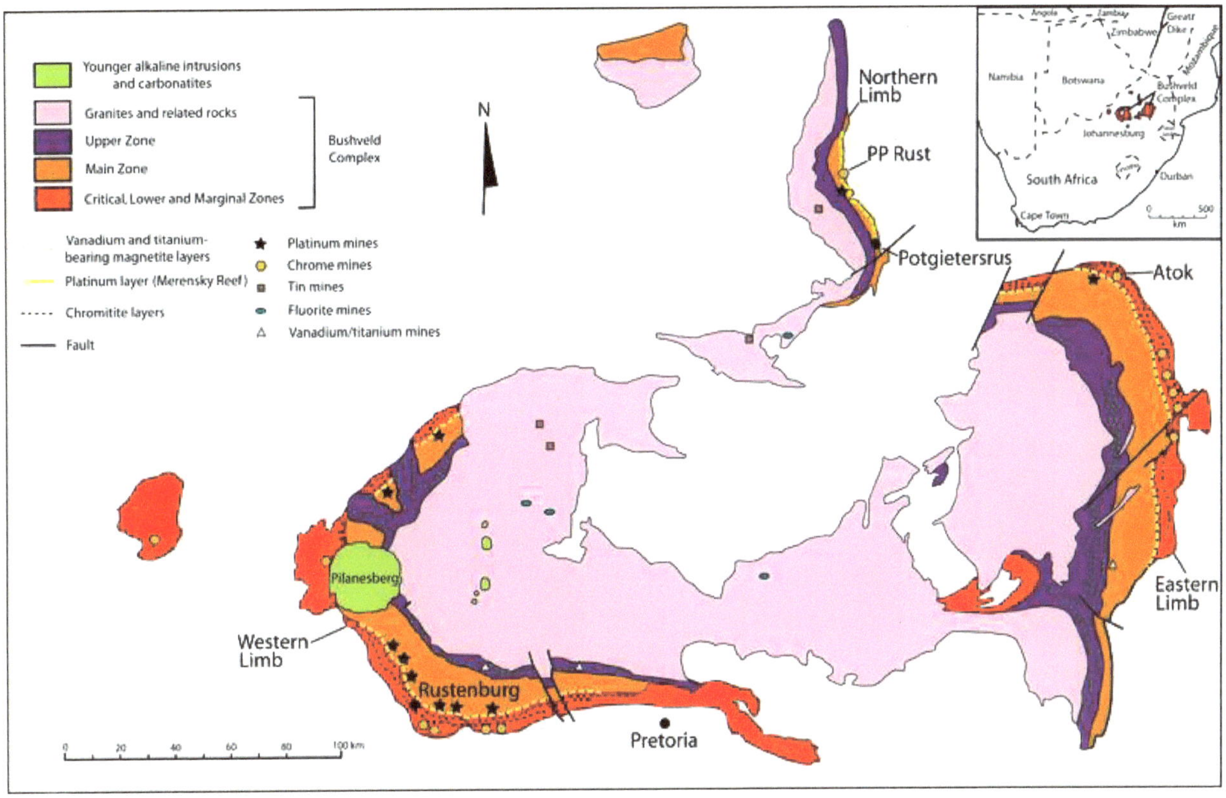

Figure 2-13: Bushveld Complex, South Africa, *the world's largest layered mafic intrusion, Bushveld hosts 75%, 54%, and 82% respectively of the world's platinum, palladium, and rhodium reserves. Currently more than 30 active mines and predevelopment projects, both open pit and underground, are active within its bounds. (Deseta, 2020) Map from (Taylor et al, 2009).*

Table 2-4: Platinum, 5 largest companies by production: *These 5 companies control 98% of the worlds PGM reserves. Data compiled from **(**Besta, 2020).*

Company	2020 Pt production (oz)	Ticker	Flag
Anglo American Platinum	2,050,000	NGLOY	South Africa
Impala Platinum	1,310,000	IMPUY	South Africa
Sibanye-Stillwater	1,080,000	SBSW	South Africa
Northam Platinum	900,000	7JR.BE	South Africa
Norsk Nickel	700,000	-	Russia

Being both geographically and corporately constrained, and considering the importance of PGMs in modern manufacturing, the investor/trader needs to be aware of unique risks when purchasing PGMs or related securities. After seeing the sensitivity of this relatively small but globally important market, it does not take much imagination to see potential geopolitical and supply-chain crises. Indeed, if diplomats and politicians were aware to what extent their economies are intertwined, they might play more nicely with each other. Undoubtedly, as the world becomes more technologically dependent on PGMs, this will make for some interesting geopolitics, and opportunity!

Figure 2-14: Palladium-Platinum Ore, Stillwater Complex, Montana, USA: *Sulfidic serpentinite platinum-palladium ore. This ore sample grades to around 2.5 ounces of Pd-Pt per ton of rock, with a Pd-Pt ratio of about 3:1. (Photo and description from John, J., 2008).*

Chapter Summary

For the investór and trader, all three of these metals (Silver, Gold, and PGMs) present different opportunities for different reasons. I have given the underlying basics of each that are not expected to change significantly in the near term. Be aware, however, that there is constant evolution in these spaces, and those who best understand these commodities and use cases will be most able to predict and notice the subtle cues of a changing market.

Key Points

1- Silver is the most electrically and thermally conductive metal. It is the ideal choice for electronics.

2- Silver is the most common of the precious metals and is usually a by-product of mining other commodities.

3- Silver's industrial demand is larger than demand of both jewelry and investment bullion combined. It also has the lowest recycling rates.

4- Gold is soft, dense, has excellent conductive properties, and is extremely corrosion resistant.

5- Gold has been exploited for over 7,000 years! Its properties allow it to concentrate in placer deposits that were used by ancient cultures.

6- Gold has low consumption rates, therefore, 85% of mined gold is still available.

7- Demand for gold comes primarily from the jewelry and bullion sectors.

8- Gold has high recycling rates. About 25% of current production comes from recycling.

9- Platinum Group Metals (PGMs) have high melting points and excellent corrosion resistance, which make them good catalysts.

10- PGMs are primarily industrial metals. Their prices strongly correlate to their industrial demand.

(continued)

11- Virtually every aspect of modern society is dependent on the catalytic reactions facilitated by PGMs.

12- PGMs are geographically and corporately constrained. Five companies control 98% of PGM reserves.

13- The Bushveld complex in South Africa accounts for more than half of all global PGM reserves.

Notes

Chapter 3: Key Principles and Common Misconceptions

Introduction

As an exploration geologist part of my job is risking capital to find mineral deposits. This often includes drilling exploration holes. I wish I could say all holes drilled were successful, but the fact is many disappoint. This is not a necessarily a loss, as commonly we learn the most from the "dead" holes. Dead holes force us to shift our paradigm and rethink our model because the assays don't lie. They tell us unapologetically that we were wrong. Medicine, construction, and other fields similarly give professionals clear signals when something isn't right. Probably the most important lessons to learn in trading and investing are 1- recognize when you are wrong and 2- do not hesitate to take corrective action. These are often expensive lessons. Those who do not learn from these lessons usually must find a way to "succeed" doing something else.

Unfortunately, there are several misconceptions when it comes to the precious metals that cloud the reasoning of participants in these markets. This chapter explores several with the goal of dispelling myths and finding truth. As I eventually learned, much of the truth is contradictory to what many of the so called "experts" say.

Gold and Silver are money - or are they?

Two key fundamentals to understand for all markets are the concepts of 1) money, and 2) assets. Money in its purest form is no more than a means of exchange, a unit of accounting. For it to function as money it must satisfy the ***double coincidence of wants*** in all cases, meaning that it must be universally accepted. Its function is to create efficiency in markets that would otherwise rely on various forms of barter. Money, because of this added value to an economy, also carries its own price. Once the nature and purpose of money are understood, it does not really matter what it is made of. It doesn't need to be backed by anything other than the confidence that it can be exchanged at the expected valuation. Historically, all kinds of items have been used as money, including shells, paper, small ingots, coins, and leather among other things.

Assets are on the opposite side of money. These include "hard assets", gold, silver, wheat, oil, buildings, pipelines, real estate, companies (and their stock), but also include intangibles, like intellectual property. Often, they are items that are used and consumed, such as fuel, food, construction and manufacturing materials. Each is priced in terms of money.

In times of economic decline, money is in shorter supply than assets, thus money's value rises against assets giving it greater purchasing power. Or said another way, in times of decline, people are willing to sell assets for less money. Conversely, in times of economic growth, money is in greater supply than assets, and people are willing to pay more for assets. The two behave like a seesaw, oscillating back and forth through time (Figure 3-1). This is a primary component of economic cycles. The use of currency dates back to at least 3000 B.C., with the use of shells as money in China (Kusimba, 2017; Figure 3-2). As an investor you need to keep the concepts of money and assets and their relationship to each other straight; otherwise, you will be buying when you should be selling. (Armstrong, 2015a)

Figure 3-1: Assets vs Money. *Both assets and money command a price in the marketplace; however the relative valuation toward each other fluctuates. Barring other influencing factors, in times of economic decline, money will be in greater demand, and it will have greater purchasing power over assets. Durring times of economic growth, however, assets will be in greater demand and will bring a higher price. Understanding the nature of money, assets, and their relationship to each other is one of the foundational priciples of economics. Modified from (Armstrong, 2015a).*

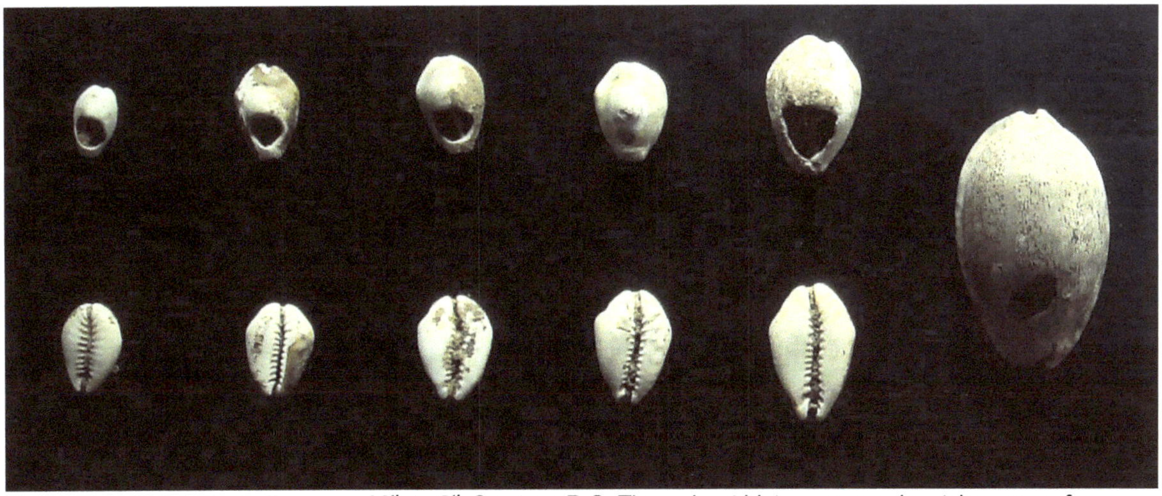

Figure 3-2: Chinese shell money 16th to 8th Century B.C. *Throughout history, money has taken many forms and shapes. To function as money, it must satisfy the double coincidence of wants, meaning that it is universally accepted as a means of exchange. Money is not backed by any physical asset, but rather by the confidence of the people within its economy of use. Photo from Japan Currency Musuem, 2008.*

While the concept of assets vs money is relatively straight forward, there is some confusion concerning the role of gold and silver, as throughout history these have alternatively been used as both assets and money. Upon investigation, we notice that during times gold and silver were money, they behaved like money, in regard to their relationship with assets. Likewise, when they are assets, they behave as assets. Figure 3-3 plots gold against the Dow Jones Industrial Average (DJIA) from 1920 to 1960. During this period, the US was on the gold standard, with a 1 oz gold piece valued at $20 in the 1920's. In the late 1920's the U.S. experienced an economic boom. With WWI and the Spanish flu behind them and a rapidly expanding auto industry, assets demanded high prices; however, the value of gold stayed level, because it was used as money. When the market crashed in 1929, initiating the great depression, assets fell in price, but again because gold was used as money, its value remained relatively unchanged. The abrupt rise in the value of gold we see on the chart occurred when President Franklin D. Roosevelt (FDR) confiscated gold in 1933 at $20.67/oz and then revalued it at 35/oz in 1934. (History.com Editors, 2020) Figure 3-4 displays the period from 1960 to January 2024. In the late 1960s and early 1970s the gold standard began to break down. Redemption of dollars for gold by the public ended in 1933, but now governments were severely limited. External gold market valuations did not match the official one. Despite several revaluation attempts between the US and international partners the standard collapsed in 1973 and was officially abandoned in 1976. (Elwell, 2011)

Figure 3-4 allows us to observe gold's behavior before and after it was demonetized. Post 1930, instead of stable patterns attributable to currencies, we now see volatile swings similar to that of commodities.

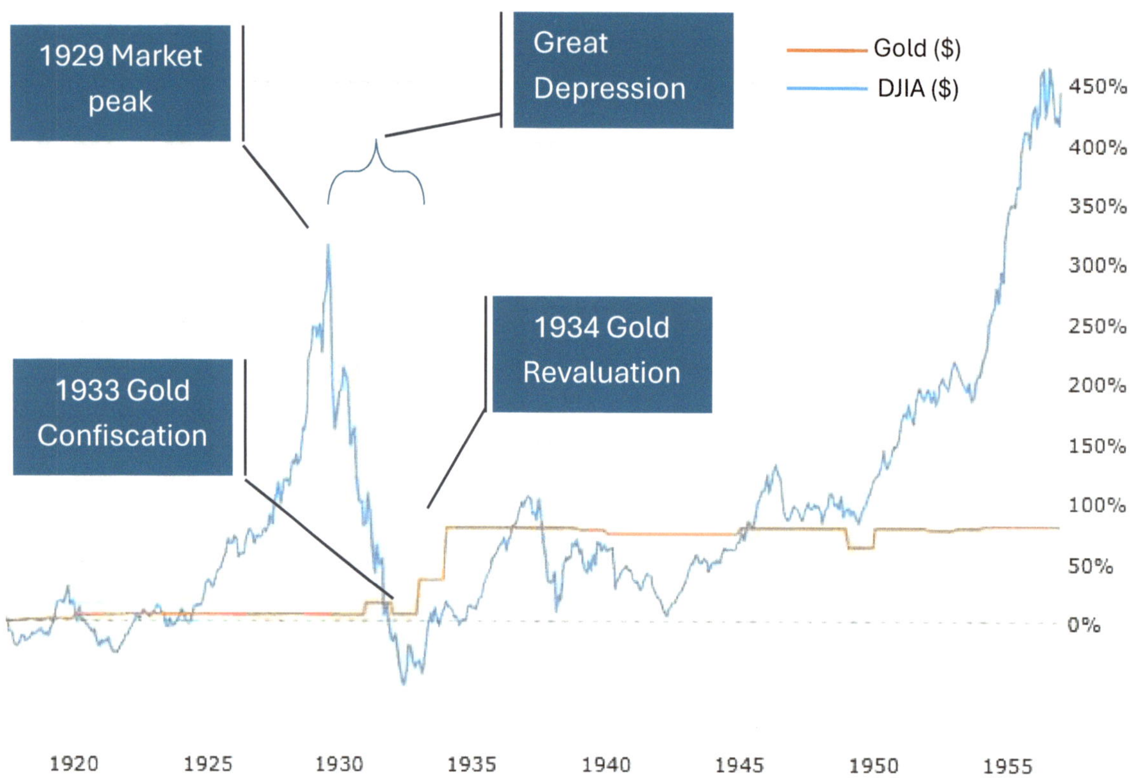

***Figure 3-3: Gold vs Dow Jones Industrial Average (DJIA)*, % gain/loss 1920 to 1960.** *In the chart, the orange line represents gold and the blue line the DJIA. Gray verticle bars represent periods of economic recession. The US was on the gold starndard for this entire period, with the notible event of gold confiscation in 1933 and revaluation in 1934. Notice how the DJIA moves up and down relative to gold, which more or less stays flat. The DJIA is behaving like assets would be expected to in regard to money; it becomes drastically more expensive between the 1925-1929 auto bubble and then drops even more dramatically between late 1929-1933, durring the great depression. Chart modified from Macro Trends, 2024.*

During the 1970s, a portion of gold's volatility was likely due to traders trying to find its level. It is not uncommon for a new market to have high volatility; however, by 1980 gold began showing its sensitivity to fiscal policy and geopolitics, making a major but short lived high soon after the USSR's invasion of Afghanistan. Like most assets in mid-1980, it responded to high interest rates by dropping in value. Similar to the DJIA, gold suffered a major decline as part of the 2008-09 world financial crisis, its recovery, however, significantly outpaced the DJIA. With many retail investors hesitant to go back into the share markets, they used gold as an alternative. Gold made a major high in late 2012. The subsequent long-term correction, in part, was fueled by a significant oversupply and was exacerbated in spring 2013, when Cypress sold $523 million of its gold bullion, equal to about 3.6% of annual gold production, to cover debts. The fear was other small economies would be forced to do the same, which would completely flood the gold market. (Reuters, 2013) The DJIA didn't peak until 2020 just prior to the Covid-19 pandemic.

As seen in Figure 3-4, gold ceased to behave as money in the United States post 1973 and has subsequently followed a commodity pattern. Outside of extraordinary geopolitical or fiscal policy effects, which can and do happen, expect the value of gold to decline in periods of economic contraction and rising interest rates. Two macro events supporting the price of gold currently despite rising interest rates are 1) the potential of the Ukraine War becoming a larger international conflict, and 2) the declining confidence in sovereign debt, Europe especially. Unfortunately, many continue to misunderstand golds relationship to money even at high-ranking leadership levels. For example, some U.S. States have enacted laws allowing gold and silver to be used as legal tender again. (Carpathian, 2024) However, these transactions will never work with the stamped value on the coins or gold notes because the intrinsic value of the metal (a commodity) is fluctuating. The value of the metal (priced in dollars) and the value of the item (also priced in dollars) will be measured before a transaction can be made. The only thing these states have accomplished is the incentivization of "in kind" transactions.

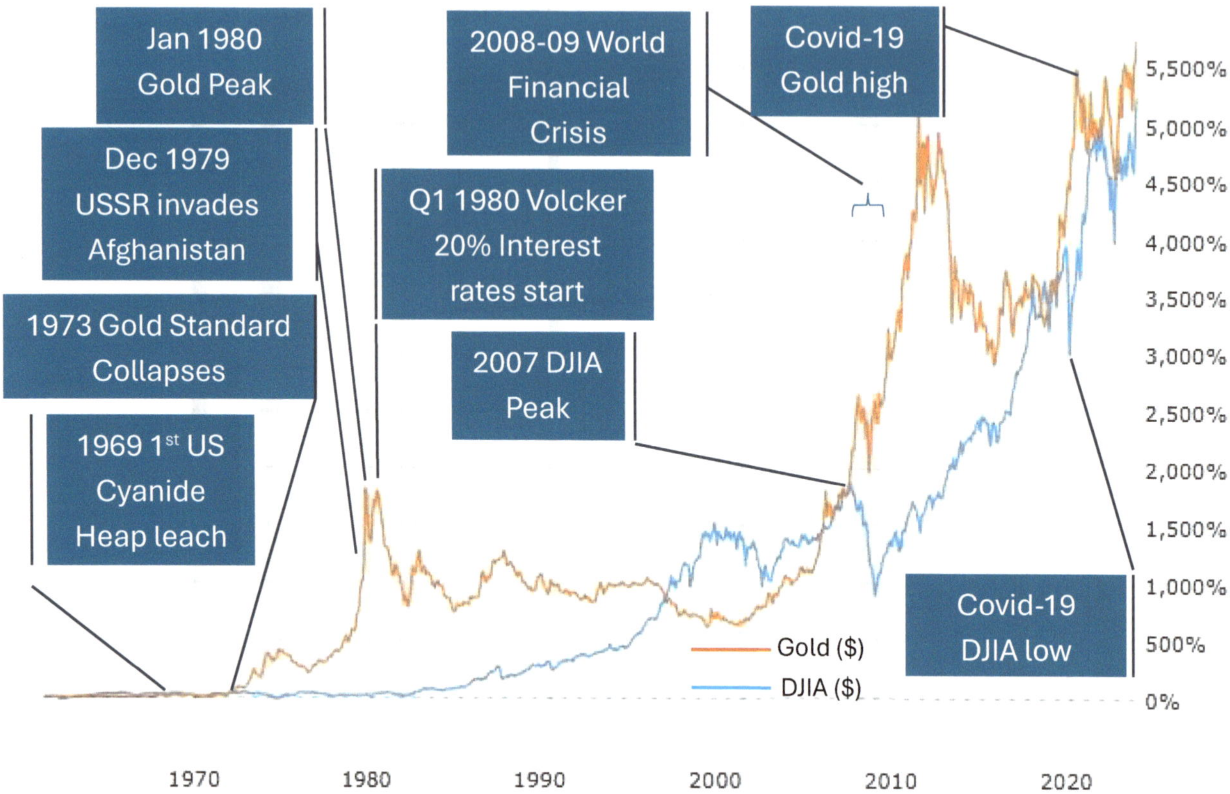

Figure 3-4: Gold vs Dow Jones Industrial Average (DJIA), % gain/loss 1960 to 2024. *In the chart, the orange line represents gold and the blue line the DJIA. Grey verticle bars represent periods of economic recession. The US was on the gold starndard until it collapsed in 1973, though officially it didn't end until 1976. Before 1973 gold's behavior was stable (it was money), however post 1973 its pattern resembles that of a commodity, but with a particular sensitivity to geopolitical risk and fear/lack of confidence. Probably the best examples of gold's fear sensitivity are: the 1980 high after the USSR's Afghanistan invasion, rise in the wake of the world financial crisis, and initial high at the beginning of the Covid-19 pandemic. Though off the chart, the current all time high of $4,370/oz in December of 2025 is amidst a backdrop of the Russia/Ukraine War, excessive soveriegn debt, and global trade/terrif tensions. Chart modified from (Macro Trends, 2024).*

Interestingly Rome went through a similar transition where their silver denarius began having a high intrinsic value, but between 64 and 270 A.D. successive emperors continued to reduce the purity and size of the denarius until it lost almost 100% of its silver content. This debasement of the coinage effectively created a denarius with a lower intrinsic value than its monetary value. In other words, it became strictly money. The process took a lot longer than for the U.S., likely because they had to physically make their money whereas most of the money in the modern economy is created through debt instruments. (Desjardins, 2016)

The Gold Standard and Currency Pegs

Many incorrectly believe a return to the gold stand is the answer to all our woes. Metal standards in functionality have very few differences from currency pegs, for explanation purposes it is easier to start from the currency side.

With a currency peg a country decides it wants to "peg" or set a fixed rate of exchange between its own and another country's currency. The primary reasons this may be beneficial involve trade and currency risk. If you are a small country and importers are trying to bring commodities to your markets, but your currency is volatile compared to others, importers face the risk of losing money as the exchange rate changes. They may choose not to deal in your markets or charge higher prices to protect themselves against these risks. Creating a stable exchange rate makes it less risky for them to trade with you. Likewise, your countrymen will find it easier to export their products. This can add stability to supply chains and allow long-term investments in outside markets. Many Caribbean countries peg to the U.S. dollar. A significant portion of their economies are tied to tourism, mostly from U.S. residents, and this greatly facilitates more tourism and related investment. Many middle eastern oil producing countries also peg to the U.S. dollar, as oil primarily trades in dollars it is easy to see their logic. (Banton, 2022; Zucchi, 2023)

While efficient trade is good for an economy, the use of a currency peg to achieve it has its negatives. First, the peg must be maintained. A country cannot set an arbitrary rate, because markets value a currency by their confidence of the issuing country's economy. That confidence includes such things as total productive power of its population, debt management, assets, natural resources, and political environment. Even though it is pegged to one currency, it is still floating against all others. If a peg is in place, it must be maintained, meaning the central bank uses foreign reserves to buy back quantities of their currency from the market during times when the home currency is losing value relative to the peg currency. Conversely, when the peg currency is losing value, the central bank must sell quantities of their currency to decrease demand, lowering their currency's value until it is back in line with the peg currency. In times of stability this is usually manageable. In volatile market cycles, the central bank may not be able to keep up with market pressures, and the peg will break. Panama has maintained its peg with the U.S. Dollar since 1904, while others like China in 2005 were forced by market cycles to adopt a "soft peg" that floats within a narrow range and is easier to manage. It took the Swiss Franc less than 4 years to break its peg with the Euro which happened in January 2015. (Pylas, 2015; Finance Monthly, 2015) Since the global economy moves through market cycles, it can safely be assumed that all currency pegs will break at some point. To avoid this, Kuwait in 2007 pegged to a basket of currencies. This solution provides the same trade benefits but stabilizes external market pressures. (Armstong, 2015b; Banton, 2022; Zucchi, 2023; McGinley, 2022)

A Second negative that must be understood is when a country pegs its currency to another currency, they expose their currency to the same risks as the pegged currency. These risks can involve trade, economics, currency manipulation, and politics among others. (Banton, 2022)

A third risk is the peg is set too high or too low. Too low creates trade tensions, hurts foreign business, and stifles domestic living standards. Too high promotes overconsumption of imports, and when the peg fails, it results in inflation. (Banton, 2022)

The gold standard was essentially a peg, but to gold instead of a foreign currency. It is a common misunderstanding that it was our government's choice to move away from the gold standard. In truth, market pressures had already created such a disconnect that by the time the U.S. officially ended the gold standard in 1976, the dollar had already effectively been on a floating system for more than two years, figure 3-4. (Elwell, 2011)

Like currency pegs, precious metal standards are subject to external market pressure. The U.S. has had a rather involved history regarding a precious metal(s) standard. From 1792 to 1834, the U.S. had a bimetallic gold/silver system. The set ratio was 15:1 silver to gold. This ratio, compared to international markets slightly, overvalued silver and undervalued gold domestically. Unsurprisingly, most gold fled the U.S., being sold for greater returns abroad and leaving the U.S. with a de facto silver standard. In 1834, to solve this problem, the official ration for U.S. coinage was changed to 16:1 silver to gold, this reversed the trend, as now silver was undervalued and sold abroad while gold accumulated, resulting in a mostly gold standard from 1834 to 1862. During the U.S. Civil War and for over a decade after (1862 to 1879), the gold standard was abandoned and the country used fiat currency (the original greenback), locally issued bank notes, and private tokens, figure 3-5. Much of the 1870's involved debates about bringing the U.S. back onto a metal standard and reestablishing conversions of dollars for precious metal. (Elwell, 2011)

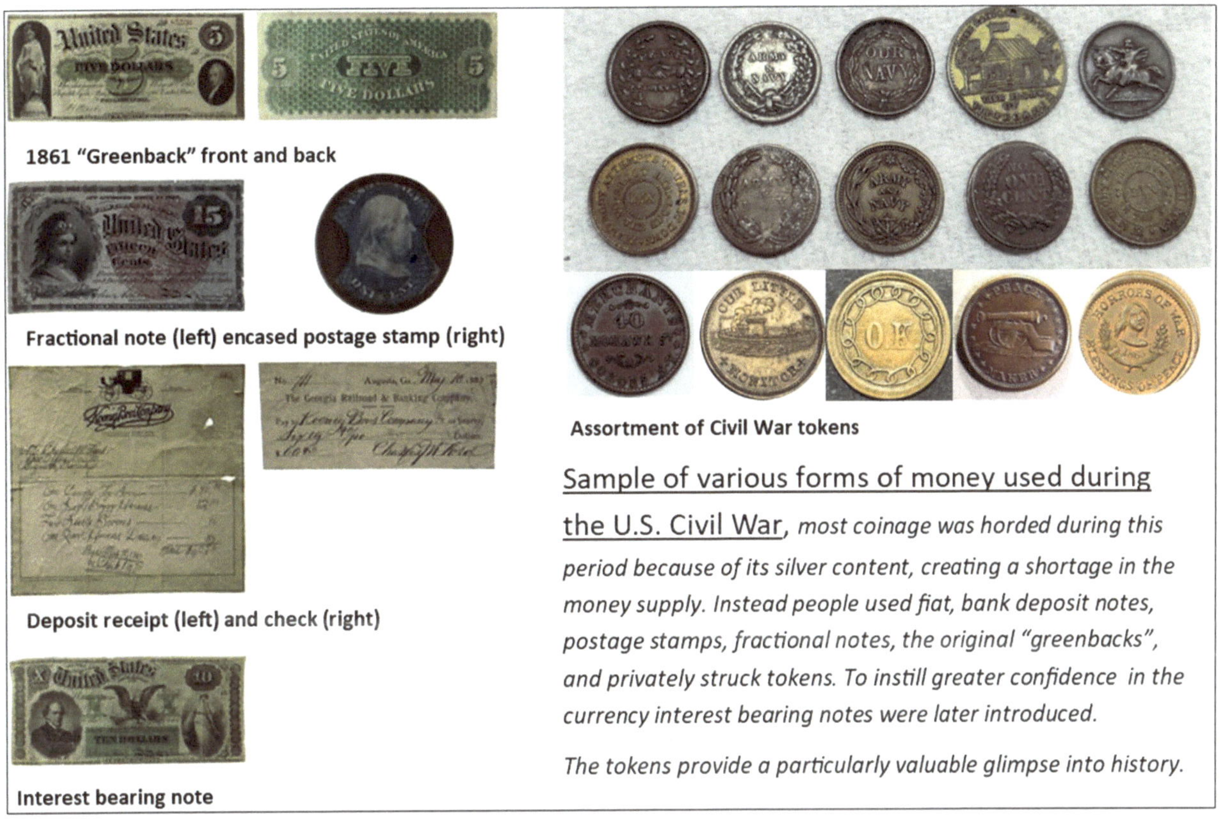

Figure 3-5: Sample of U.S. Civil War Era Money. *Durring the Civil War and for almost a decade after (1862-1879) the U.S. abandoned its gold standard. Rapid printing of fiat led to high inflation and hoarding of silver/gold coinage, commerce disruptions due to the war also locally limited the money supply. This period demonstates how a economy may respond when dealing with both high inflation and a limited money supply. (Federal Reserve Bank of Atlanta, 2024), images compiled from (Federal Reserve Bank of Atlanta specimins collection and numismatic information and auction sites including: R. Howard Collectibles, NCGcoin.com, numinista.com, numismaclub.com).*

Significant political divisions formed around the preference for either silver or gold over the other as a metal standard. The Coinage Act of 1873 effectively demonetized silver and put the U.S. on a gold standard, the main reason was to help standardize trade with France, also on a gold standard, and other international partners. By some, the act is still referred to as "The Crime of

1873." The mint still produced silver coins as a revenue-generating activity. They would buy silver at market price and issue coins bearing a higher monetary price. While these coins had some intrinsic value, there was no official "backing" of the monetary value. The Gold Standard Act of 1900, for the first time, created a gold reserve for the backing of paper notes. (U.S. Mint, 2017; Elwell, 2011)

Banks, however, experienced challenges. Technological advancements now allowed the timely clearing of transactions between banks, including those in different regions. Checks were the new common mode of these transactions. The gold standard system was inelastic. The U.S., still being a largely agrarian society, experienced banking pressure and often "runs" during planting and harvest times. This seasonal demand was pushed to the extreme when the 1906 San Francisco earthquake and fires drew massive amounts of capital from the rest of the country for rebuilding. This resulted in the Panic of 1907, a banking crisis that led to significant banking reforms and creation of the Federal Reserve (FED) in 1913. The Federal Reserve provided banks a place to borrow cash during these high demand times. The twelve reserve banks would set regional interest rates; thereby attracting capital to regions of the country that needed it most. It could also create elastic money by purchasing corporate debt, allowing businesses to keep operating. Unlike current methods of national burrowing, corporate debt would expire and was thus less inflationary. As part of its original mandate, the FED was tasked with maintaining the gold standard. This proved problematic in 1930, as external gold markets were causing gold prices to rise. The U.S., after the 1929 crash, needed cash to keep the economy moving; however, lowering interest rates and expanding the money supply would cause gold reserves to move offshore. In an effort to preserve gold reserves and the gold standard, FED banks maintained or even raised interest rates for the first several years of this crisis. This event evolved into the Great Depression. The standard was not maintainable at its current rate which led to the gold confiscation and devaluation of 1933-34 (Figure 3-3). After confiscation, gold was no longer redeemable for cash by citizens; however, a quasi-gold standard system that allowed for exchanges between central banks lasted until 1973, when the gold standard collapsed completely, (Figure 3-4). (Elwell, 2011, Armstrong, 2022; Moen & Tallman, 2015)

Contrary to many a "gold bug's" opinion, the U.S. gold standard was about facilitating international trade not preserving currency value. Also, it seems managing the metals standard proved problematic and contributed to domestic crises. If the U.S. wanted to again move to a peg for facilitating international trade, the only attractive scenario would be pegging to a basket of several assets which could include major currencies and possibly some commodities like gold and oil. This would satisfy a diverse set of trade partners, afford flexibility in maintaining the peg, increase U.S. exports, and avoid the political risks commonly associated with pegging to one asset only. Assets and weighting would need to be selcted with care and require the sophisticated duty of managing the peg. This would involve the Federal Reserve to maintain significant holdings of all assets in the basket and participate in the open markets to keep valuations in range. Once congress can balance the budget it would probably be worth doing. (Armstong, 2023b; FasterCapital, 2025)

Gold is up when the market is down, or is it?

When I was new to precious metal markets, I often heard "When the market goes down, gold goes up." The truth is, however, with the exception of only a very few instances in history, this is simply not true. In fact, most of what we hear in regard to the relationships between markets is not true. Table 3-1 is a correlation matrix showing gold and several other markets using daily closing values from August 28, 2000, to January 26, 2024. There are several conclusion we can draw from these data.

Our first conclusion is that gold does not have an inverse correlation with the stock market, but in fact has a moderate <u>positive</u> correlation with both the Dow Jones Industrial Average and the Nasdaq. When looking at individual sectors it has an even greater correlation with real estate, energy, utilities, industrials, materials, and healthcare, while its weakest correlations are with financials and telecommunications. Gold and silver are the only two markets to have any significant inverse correlation with interest rates. Data from Table 3-1 make sense, considering the earlier discussion of assets versus money. Generally, all assets rise and fall together, though at different rates. That gold behaves similarly to hard asset intensive sectors is no surprise, nor are gold and silver's relationship to interest rates and financials, considering metal investments do not pay interest.

Table 3-1: Gold Correlation with Other Markets, period Aug 2000 to Jan 2024. *Calculated from data compiled by Yahoo Finance, and the US federal reserve. Correlations utilize daily closing valuations of SPDR sector EFTs along with gold, silver, Dow Jones industrials, and Nasdaq indexes. Three key obsevations are that gold has a moderate corelation with the general market with somewhat stronger correlations for hard asset intense sectors, and that while gold and silver have a weak inverse correlation with interest rates the same is not observed with the market indexes. Also, silver has weak market correlations with most sectors.*

	Gold	*Silver*	*DJI*	*Nasdaq*	*XLU*	*XLP*	*XLB*	*XLI*	*XLV*	*XLE*	*XLRE*	*XLK*	*XLF*	*IYZ*
Gold														
Silver	0.87													
DJI	0.75	0.42												
Nasdaq Comp	0.74	0.42	0.98											
XLU (utilities)	0.81	0.47	0.98	0.95										
XLP (staples)	0.81	0.47	0.98	0.96	0.99									
XLB (materials)	0.82	0.52	0.98	0.97	0.98	0.98								
XLI (industrials)	0.77	0.44	1.00	0.98	0.98	0.99	0.99							
XLV (healthcare)	0.76	0.41	0.99	0.98	0.98	0.99	0.98	0.99						
XLE (energy)	0.78	0.64	0.71	0.63	0.74	0.74	0.78	0.74	0.71					
XLRE (real estate)	0.82	0.72	0.92	0.91	0.93	0.91	0.91	0.89	0.91	0.39				
XLK (tech)	0.72	0.39	0.96	0.99	0.93	0.93	0.95	0.96	0.96	0.63	0.89			
XLF (financials)	0.49	0.16	0.92	0.91	0.86	0.85	0.88	0.90	0.89	0.56	0.91	0.90		
IYZ (telecom)	0.58	0.35	0.78	0.74	0.79	0.79	0.75	0.78	0.75	0.56	0.27	0.66	0.69	
FED (discount rate)	-0.38	-0.39	-0.01	-0.06	-0.06	-0.12	-0.05	-0.02	-0.05	0.05	0.08	0.02	0.29	-0.18

0.85-1	strong correlation
0.7-0.849	moderate correlation
0.55-0.69	weak correlation
0.35-0.549	very weak correlation

1= perfect correlation

-1= perfect inverse correlation

0= absolutely no correlation

A second conclusion that debunks common myth, is that low interest rates lead to a higher market. For many of the sectors, the correlation to interest rates is near zero. For financials, it is 0.29, reflecting that banks do make a little more on loans when rates are higher, whereas, companies that have high debt utilization are more likely to benefit in periods of low rates, as do other companies in periods of high rates. We must be comfortable with the idea that markets do not move on rates alone and should probably stress less every time the Federal Reserve adjusts the discount rate.

Finally, it is interesting that silver has a much lower correlation than gold to stock markets. Later discussions about silver and how it is used by society will explain this observation. While gold, and to a lesser extent silver, have positive correlations to stock markets, seeing in which sectors they behave most alike and most differently is quite beneficial. That gold and silver have significantly lower correlation values with the Dow Jones and Nasdaq than almost all other sectors, merits allocation to metals in portfolios, this less-correlated diversification is one of the primary reasons cited by fund managers when adding positions linked to these assets. Comparing Table 3-1 with Figure 3-4, we see both gold and the DJI fell in the 2008-09 world financial crisis. Gold had a much quicker recovery. In the 2020 COVID-19 crash, again both gold and the market fell; however, gold fell less and made a very quick peak as the market was bottoming. What supports gold is the fear factor. If you need to be mobile with your wealth and do not trust cash, gold is the best solution. When studying the charts and table in this chapter, we see gold responds strongly to war, prospect of government collapse, and other global crises.

Gold as an Inflation Hedge?

A common misconception is that gold is a hedge against inflation. Figure 3-6, a 100-year inflation adjusted gold price chart, dispels this myth rather efficiently. We see that the all-time high in real terms, with respect to inflation, was the 1980 high made shortly after the USSR invaded Afghanistan. Despite all the inflation between 1980 to September 2024 gold failed to make a new high in inflation adjusted terms. At the time of this writing gold recently exceeded the high in both nominal and inflation adjusted terms reaching $3,674.27/oz on September 12, 2025. For comparison, Figure 3-7 presents a 70-year inflation adjusted oil price chart. While fuel prices at the pump may seem high, in reality, on an inflation adjusted basis the price per barrel is more average.

Both commodities (gold and oil) share a similar explanation for the decline in real prices, which to a significant extent involves technological advancement. In gold's case cyanide leach recovery and larger and more efficient earth moving equipment have made extremely low-grade deposits profitable. In some cases, gold grades as low as 0.065 g/ton are justifiable (SSR Mining, 2018). Gold also has high recycling rates, with 85% of the gold ever mined still accessible by the economy (World Gold Council, 2023a). This high production and accumulation of gold make it difficult for gold to achieve new highs in real terms without a significant catalyst. The current global outlook has provided this catalyst, moving forward as we have a combination of potential economic and geopolitical crises brewing. These include the Russia/Ukraine War, Isreal/Palestinian conflict, trade tensions, and a sovereign debt crisis on the brink of erupting.

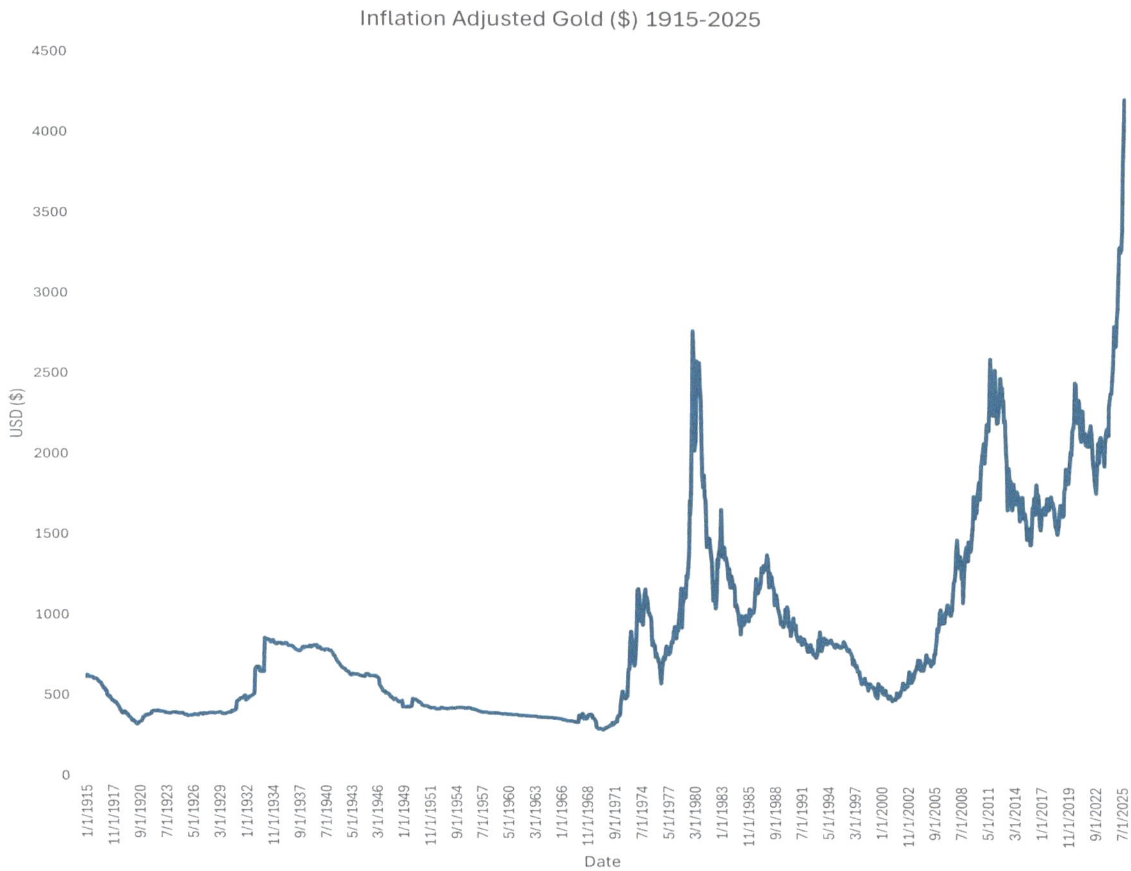

Figure 3-6: 100-year Inflation Adjusted Historical Gold Prices. *In real terms, we did not exceed the 1980 high in gold made soon after the USSR's invasion of Afganhistan until Sept. 12, 2025. The new 2025 highs are amidst a backdrop of concern that the Ukraine/Russia war will expand to NATO, international trade disputes, and looming concerns of a soveriegn debt crisis. While geopolitical events usually are the catalysts for high valuations, two major fundimentals have also played a part in this 40+ year gap between fresh highs in real terms. First is technological advancement. Cyanide leach technology in combination with significantly more efficient mining systems and equipment. This has made very low grade deposits now profitable to mine. About 2/3 of historical gold production has taken place post 1950. Second is that gold has low consumption and high recycling rates. About 85 percent of all gold ever mined is still accesable by the economy. These all apply downward pressure on prices. If the current geopolitical crises expand we could potentially see even greater highs in real terms, but if/when they subside, the expectation is for gold to continue to decline in real terms. (Macro Trends, 2025a (chart data); World Gold Council, 2023a).*

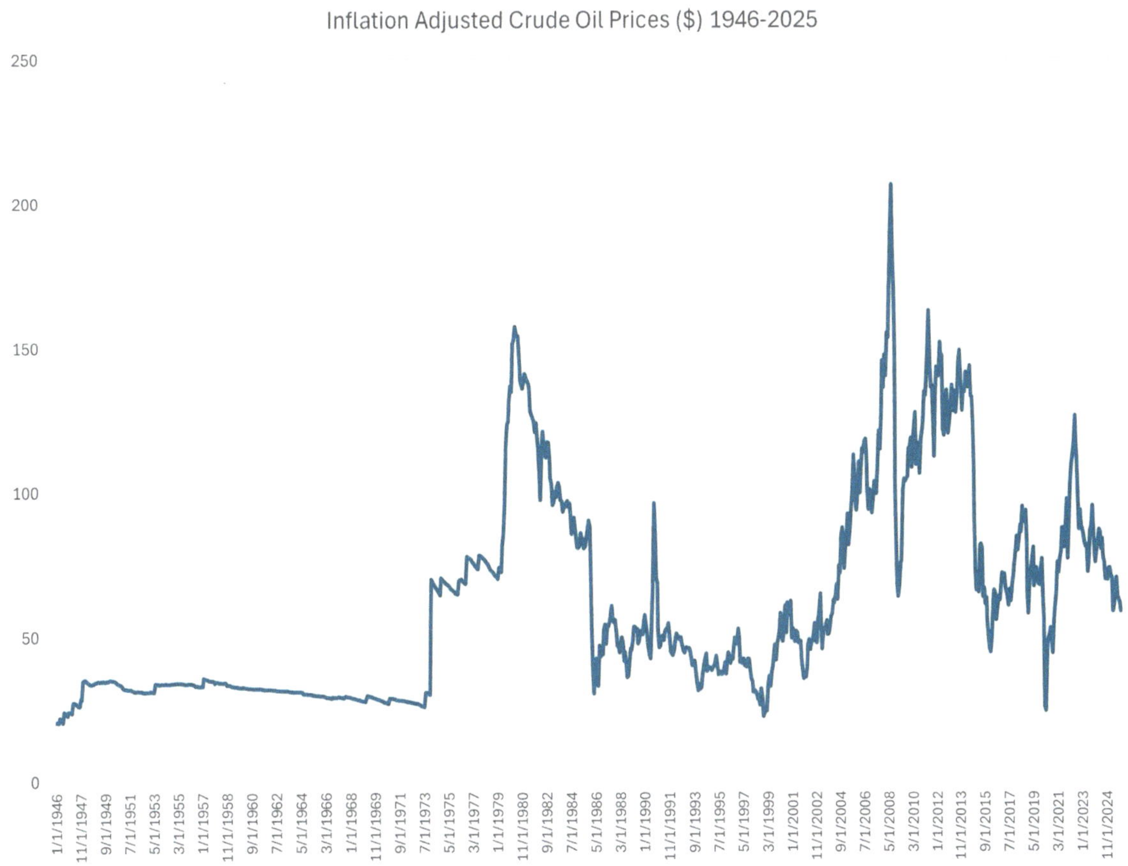

Figure 3-7: 70-year Inflation Adjusted Historical Oil Per Barrel Prices. *In real terms oil peaked with the economy in 2007. It reached an all time low durring the early days of the 2020 pandemic, where it even traded negative for a few hours. Since 2007, oil prices have experienced downward pressure due to technological advancement, making production more efficient, hydraulic fracturing, for example, has turned great swaths of the U.S.A. into highly productive oil fields. With gold making new highs in real terms while other commodities are declining highlights how it is moving on geopolitical events. (Crooks, 2015, Chart: Macro Trends, 2025b).*

Oil also has benefited from technology, hydraulic fracturing has opened vast new oil and gas fields in the U.S. from reservoirs that were once thought impossible to produce, allowing the U.S. to once again become one of the largest global producers (Crooks, 2015). Unlike gold, however, oil is consumed, so we will always require new reserves and production, but as alternative energies and electric vehicles gain adoption this will take pressure off oil prices. It is likely we have already lived through "peak oil". Interestingly, and maybe ironically to the environmentalist, the electric vehicle will likely strengthen the coal industry at the expense of the petroleum, as alternative energies alone will not be sufficient to support the mass electrification of the automobile. The resulting lower fuel prices will be a boon to the air travel and transport industries.

This same trend of decreasing in cost in real terms exists in most commodities including things like computer chips. Figure 3-8 charts the prices in real terms of several agricultural products. Efficiencies in one sector often increase the efficiencies in related sectors. The key to all of this is energy, as it impacts everything else.

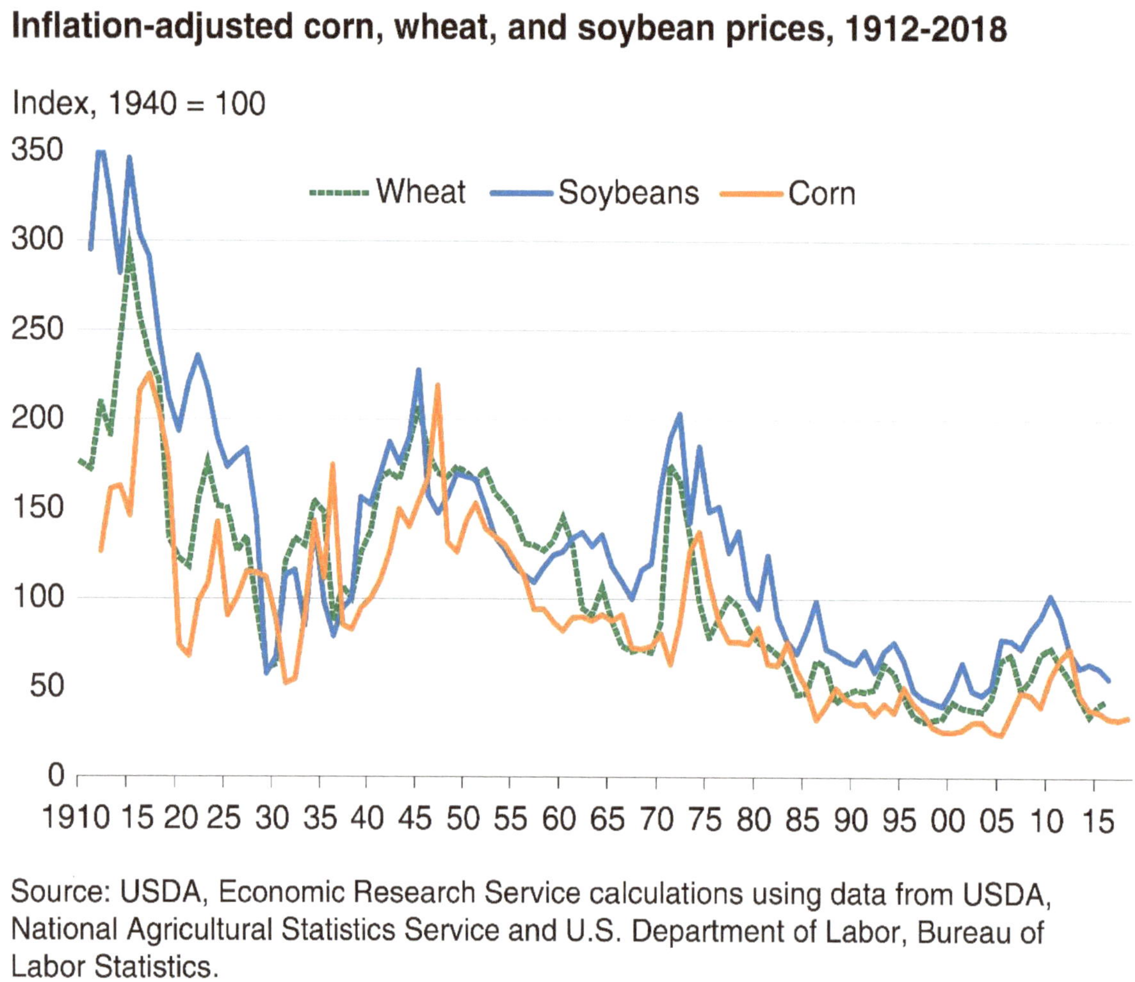

Figure 3-8: Inflation-adjusted corn, wheat, soybean prices. *Advent of the internal combustion engine drastically increased humanities ability to farm, both by making it easier and by being able to realocate ground previously used to feed draft animals to human food production. Post WWII efficiencies, primarily in the petroleum/petrochemical industry but also the mining industry, have continued to decrease the real costs of many agricultural products. (Chart: USDA, 2024)*

Chapter 3: Key Principles and Common Misconceptions

In agriculture, most people understand that lower fuel prices make it less expensive to work the fields, but few realize that natural gas is central to the production of ammonia nitrate, which is both a fertilizer and the key component of ANFO (Ammonium Nitrate/ Fuel Oil) the primary explosive used in most surface mining operations. Phosphate (another fertilizer) is usually mined then treated with either heat or wet processes depending on the level of desired refinement.

Greater energy availability in addition to more gold has resulted in more metal in general, as well as more food, more and larger housing, more cars, more aircraft, more travel, more access to education and healthcare, more science, more advanced weapons, more social spending, more infrastructure, and more government. Really, just more everything. As sectors scale, they almost universally become more efficient, there is one major exception. Figure 3-9 illustrates the inflation adjusted per capita spending of the U.S. Federal government, instead of trending downward and becoming more efficient per unit (person), has continued to rise to the point where spending will soon eclipse GDP. The trend is likely the result of two major factors. First, the government doesn't produce any goods or services in the traditional sense, and those that it does provide are not funded by sales, but taxes, so there is no competition or internal driver to promote efficiency. As the bureaucracy grows, it simply needs more staff to manage. Second is spending that extends beyond the domestic economy. Sectors with significant government interaction tend to follow a similar pattern, health care in the US is one notable example.

The extent to which gold hedges inflation is a derivative of the total energy and labor inputs required to produce it. Simply, as technology increases the efficiency of the inputs required to produce gold, it decreases gold's effectiveness as an inflation hedge. If gold is not a hedge against inflation, what is it? As economist Martin Armstrong succinctly said, "Gold is the hedge against government". Gold responds most when people lose confidence in their government. This is often the case with wars, regime changes, and other major geopolitical events (Armstong, 2019). At such times, affected currencies experience extreme volatility, money seeking safety tends to migrate to more stable currencies and gold as it is the most portable commodity. As governments limit the portability of gold, this diminishes to a certain extent its attractiveness.

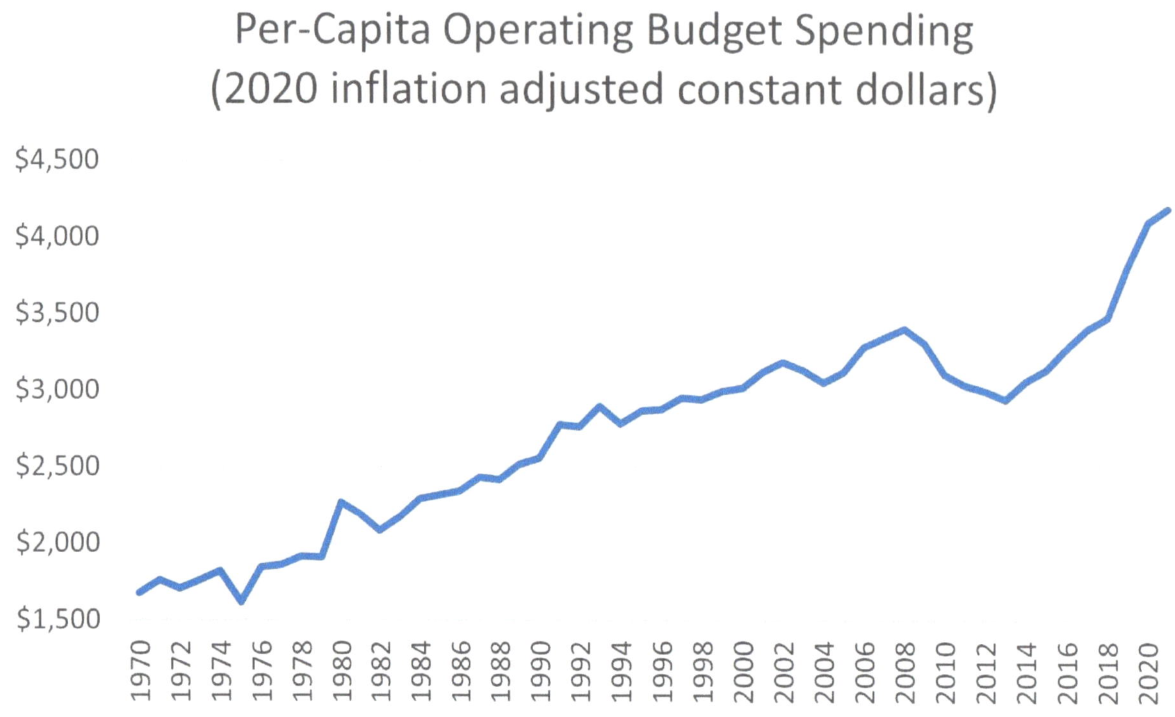

Figure 3-9: Inflation-adjusted US Federal Spending Per Capita. *Unlike almost every other economy of scale, government becomes more expensive per unit. The likely explanation is because government dosen't produce goods and services in the traditional sense. Those that are produced are funded from taxes, not sales, so there is little to no competitive pressure to drive improvement and efficiency. The other imput likely supporting this trend is spending that extends beyond the domestic economy. (Chart: Mercier, 2022)*

Gold is a global market, and one must think in terms of local currency. For example, an affluent individual in a small nation may choose to keep a significant portion of their wealth in gold instead of the local currency. If their country experiences a coup or goes to war the local currency may decline significantly in value against that of gold, yet gold in terms of major currencies may still be relatively unchanged. The person arguably could also have purchased cash dollars to achieve the same goal. Since about 70% of US dollars trade outside the US, for gold to experience a real rise against the dollar will require events that cause global, not just U.S. populations to lose confidence in the dollar. The key to identifying a true bullish or bearish trend in gold would be comparing its performance against several major currencies. Only if the trend is manifesting in several currencies will you know it is real and not just constrained to one currency, locality, or supply chain. (Armstrong, 2020)

Ratios

Gold and silver prices, like those of all commodities, are subject to supply and demand. However, gold and silver in particular have been related since the early days of civilization, both in their mode of production and with their use as money for significant periods in history. There are four ratios that help us understand the relationship in these metals and the part they play in the modern economy. The most important thing to remember about this topic is that each of these ratios is dynamic.

Gold : Silver Production & Accumulation Ratios

In chapter one we briefly discussed the nuclear physics and chemistry behind why gold is less abundant than silver, but do we actually know how much less? The answer is not really. What we know about the amount of gold and silver on Earth is a function of what has been mined and what are in known reserves. The ratio of the production of gold vs silver is driven by the metallogeny and chemistry of deposits currently under development, and it should not be surprising that this changes as some deposits are depleted and others begin production. The significant increase in silver production beginning in Q4 2004 and peaking in Q4 2015, displayed in figure 3-10 coincides with Peñasquisto, San Cristobal, Cannington and several other mines either coming online or increasing production. As mentioned in chapter 2, silver is often a by-product metal, through this same period metallurgical technology has improved, and it is now more cost effective to recover silver from lower grade polymetallic ores. In the last century the silver to gold production ration has been between 3 and 9, and it may have reached as high as 44 to 1 during the 17th century, primarily due to the significant increase of Mexican mines during the time. (Angelo, 2017)

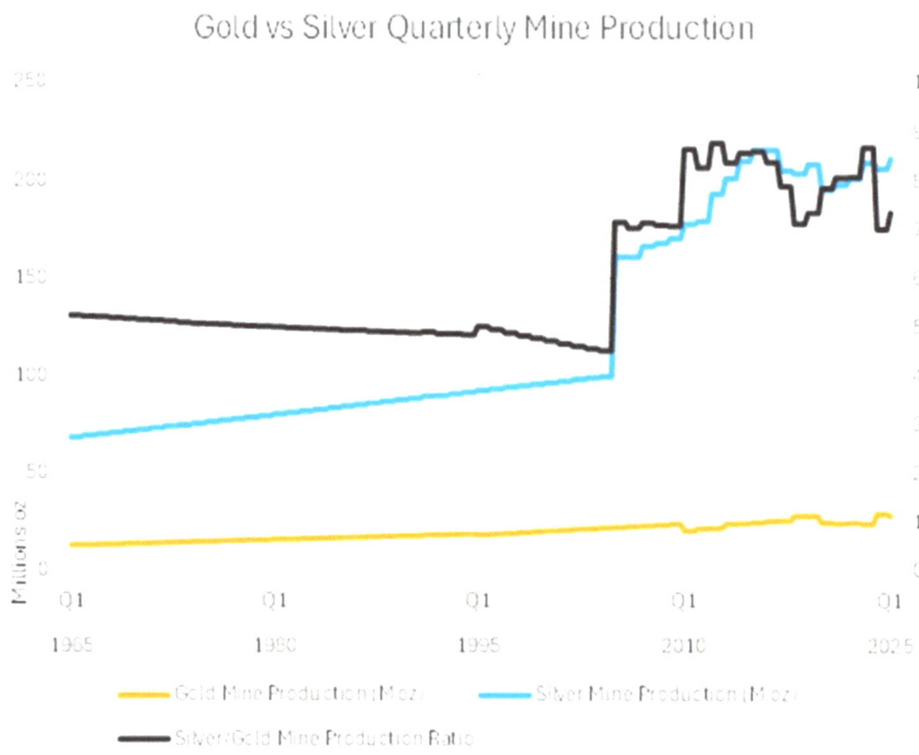

***Figure 3-10: Gold vs Silver Quarterly Mine Production.** The amount of silver vs gold produced is significantly affected by the metallogeny and chemistry of currently producing mines. In recent years about 8 to 9 times more silver is produced each year than gold. (Forbush, 2025)*

Another interesting metric is the amount of gold vs silver in the world. For this discussion we are concerned with the amount of bullion or investment metal. An estimated 6,716,021,254 oz of gold has been mined in human history, of which 85% is believed to be directly accessible by the economy. (World Gold Council, 2023a). Of the 5,708,618,066 oz that hasn't been lost to time, an estimated 1,653, 819,000 oz (29%) is in the form of investment bullion, the balance is primarily in the form of jewelry with a small percentage in electronics. It is more difficult to give a similar statistical breakdown of silver, but currently about 2,116,600,000 oz of silver bullion exists. Despite production of nearly 9 times as much silver as gold there are only about 512,781,000 more ounces of physical silver than gold or in other words, about 1.28 oz silver for every ounce of gold. The point is that gold accumulates while silver is consumed, while the trend is slowing (figure 3-11), it still makes one wonder if or rather when the amount of physical gold bullion will eclipse that of silver.

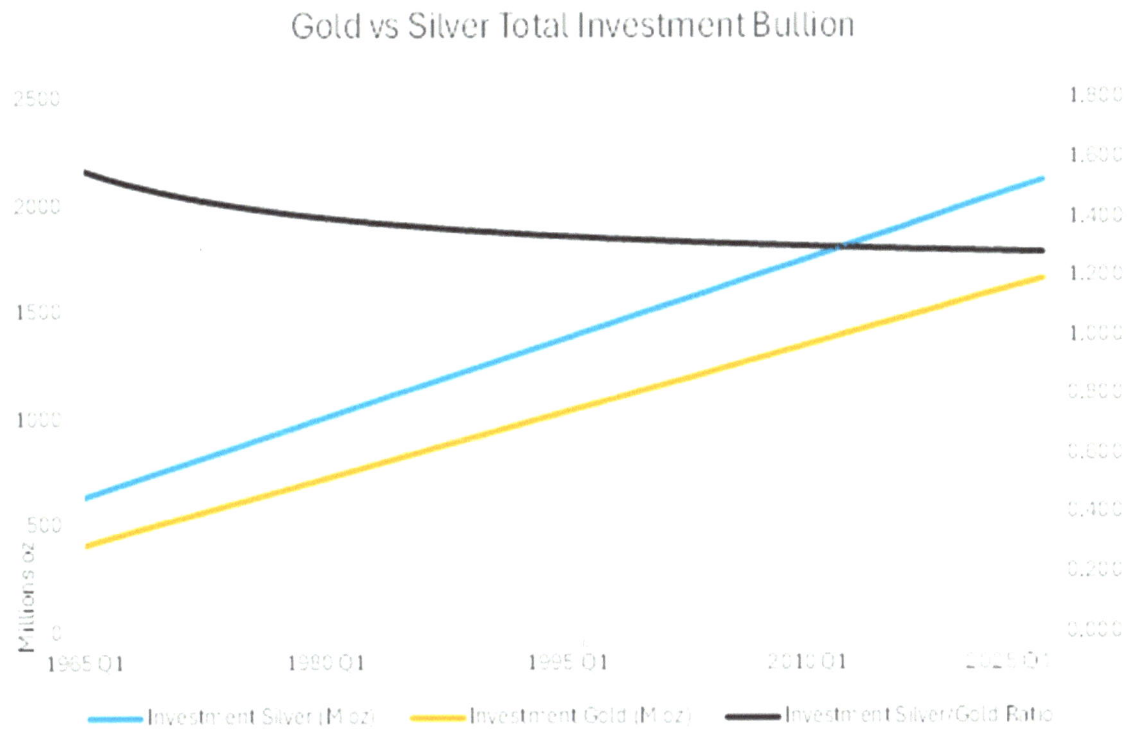

Figure 3-11: Gold vs Silver Investment Bullion. *Despite annual production of 8 to 9 times that of gold, silver being as much an industrial metal as a precious one is consumed, whereas gold accumulates. Currently there is only 1.28 times as much silver bullion than there is gold. The trend is slowing due in part to greater silver production in the last 15 years, but the amount of physical gold bullion may eventually surpass that of silver. (Forbush, 2025)*

Gold/Silver Price Ratio

The gold/silver price ratio is used frequently by precious metal investors and traders. When the ratio moves to one extreme or the other it is often a signal that one of the metals is over or undervalued compared to the other. Traders may use it when creating pair trades or simply seeing when the ratio is at an extreme, will do further research to see which metal price is more likely to move significantly and bring the ratio closer to average. Longer term investors use it to help time physical purchases. Viewing figure 3-12, the price of gold exceeding 120 times the price of silver per ounce in Q3 2024, silvers looks undervalued. Observing quarterly silver prices and a rising wedge pattern, this is normally a bearish pattern, but given the high ratio silver may extend its gains helping normalize the ratio. The spread in the ratio has mostly been due to gold's rise in response to geopolitical turmoil, escalation of which could drive gold even further. Easing those tensions would likely initiate a decline bringing the price ratio back to a moderate level.

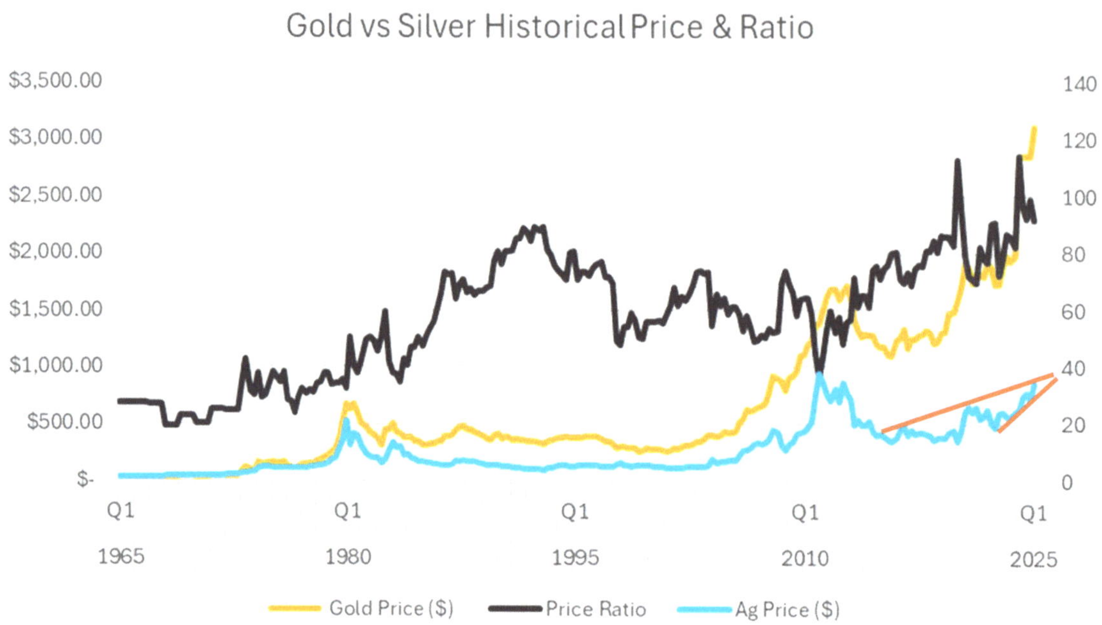

Figure 3-12: Gold vs Silver Historical Price & Ratio. *The gold/silver ratio is a popular metric used by precious metal traders and investors to help predict movements in metal prices. When it moves to one extreme or the other it often signals that one of the metals in over or undervalued relative to the other. Used with other forms of technical analysis, charting techniques, and understanding of current events a trader can gain confidence in the continuation or forecast a change in trend of metal prices. (Forbush, 2025)*

Gold vs Silver Market Cap

A final metric to understand is the market cap. As previously noted, gold accumulates while silver is consumed, and in regard to investment bullion there is only 1.28 oz silver for every ounce of gold. Also, gold is currently about 100 times the value of silver per ounce. This translates to a gold market capitalization of about $5 Trillion vs a $375 Billion market cap for silver. To put this into perspective, the estimated total value of all global assets (stocks, bonds, real estate etc.) for 2025 is $515 trillion, and all the gold bullion in the world accounts for just under 1% of it. This is one reason why many large institutions avoid precious metals all together, it is much smaller than say currency markets. This is also the reason why big money prefers to trade gold when it does invest in precious metals, as the higher market cap can support more investment and reduces risk. In contrast, silver is retail driven. Both gold and silver take up about the same amount of space, so large holders of physical metal, like central banks, will prefer gold as it is a more concentrated value for the same shipping, storage, security expense. This is not to say the smaller silver market cap has not attracted market manipulators, the Hunt brothers in the late 1970s being the most well-known example. This also in part explains the late but pronounced moves into highs when compared with gold, as when the buying frenzy reaches the retail investors, they all come in at once into a relatively constrained market. Lastly, it illustrates why silver prices will be more sensitive to supply/demand mismatches on the industrial side, as there is less bullion available to pull from in a shortage and it is easy to flood the bullion market in times of greater supply.

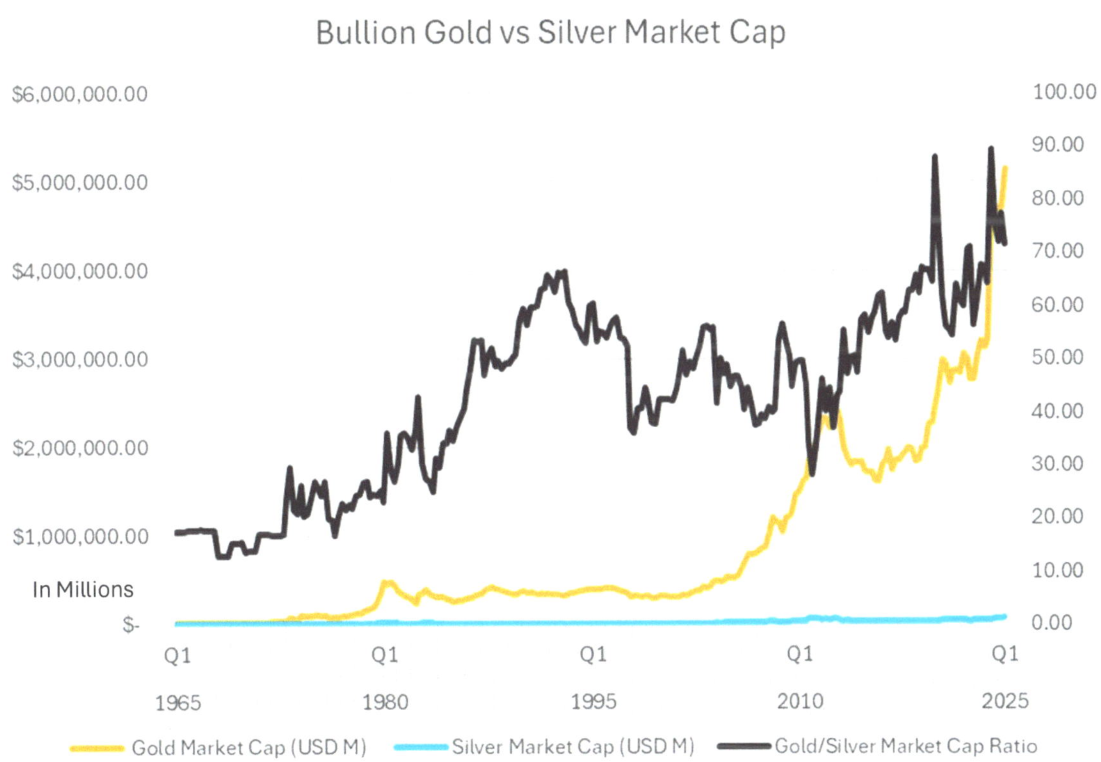

Figure 3-13: Bullion Gold vs Silver Market Cap. *Investment gold has a current market cap of about $5 Trillion, vs a $375 Billion market cap for silver. Big money requires large markets and primarily will trade gold, silver is more retail driven. The smaller market cap also makes silver prices more sensitive to supply/demand mismatches that occur in its industrial consumption. (Forbush, 2025)*

Confidence

A final principle to understand is confidence in regard to money. When a population is confident of the issuer's financial strength, they are more willing to accept their money as payment for goods and services, regardless of the intrinsic value. The U.S. is currently the world's reserve currency not because people like America, but because the U.S. has never canceled its currency. A nickel from the 1860's has the same monetary value as one minted yesterday, though its collectable value may be much higher. In a world where several major economies have changed or canceled their currency in the last 100 years that adds a lot of confidence to the U.S. dollar. Paper or even electronic dollars have no intrinsic value yet in countries all over the world individuals are willing to accept dollars because they are confident dollars will hold their value and be accepted in turn. Larger players hold dollars to more easily access the U.S. economy. This is not new, even economies peripheral to Rome imitated Roman coins, and this was so other merchants would have confidence in their coinage and allow them access to Rome's economy (Vagi, 2013; Armstrong, 2015c)

As people loose confidence in the issuer of a form of money or its acceptance they will naturally gravitate to another form of money that either has higher confidence/acceptance by market participants or has a higher intrinsic value. The efforts we are witnessing by some market participants trying to use gold or other high intrinsic value methods of payment reflect the eroding confidence in today's fiat currency. These same people are seeking to exchange their money for assets while the money still has buying power. It is a sudden loss of confidence that is usually the cause of hyperinflation. In a large economy it is difficult to create money fast enough to significantly affect the money supply, but if there is a sudden loss of confidence, a large money surplus is almost immediate. Understanding this, arguably the most important role a politician can play in a country's success is the execution of sound economic policies that keep debt ratios low, and economic activity high, thus maintaining confidence in the currency.

Chapter 3: Key Principles and Common Misconceptions

Summary

1. Gold and silver throughout history have at times been money and at other times commodities. Today they are commodities and behave as such in the markets.
2. A gold standard has little difference from a currency peg. Both must be maintained and be expected to break at some point. Often, they cause as many problems as they solve. In short, a gold standard will not save our country from all its economic woes, but constraining government spending to realistic budgets might.
3. Gold is not inversely correlated with the US share markets but rather shares a moderate correlation, whereas, silver has a weak correlation. Gold, being a hard asset, not surprisingly, correlates better with the real estate & energy markets.
4. Gold is not the ideal hedge against inflation (as often advertised), and in real terms has a declining trend similar to many agricultural products. Gold is, however, the preferred hedge against government.
5. Gold/Silver production, physical bullion, price, and market cap ratios help us understand the presence and function of these metals in our economy and some of the fundamentals behind their price movements.
6. The acceptance of any form of money is a derivative of a population's confidence in the issuer. It is a sudden loss of confidence in an issuer and by default their money that causes hyperinflation.

Notes

Chapter 4: Owning Physical Metal

Introduction

Owning physical metal is often how people begin investing in precious metals (PMs). The four most common forms of physical metal are jewelry, silverware, bullion (coin and bar shaped pieces), and junk silver (old coins made out of silver but in such poor condition as to have no or little collector value). While the secondary jewelry and silverware markets are lucrative areas for some, these spaces require a high degree of expertise and a lot of determination and effort to find deals. This is unsuitable for the average investor, though I think everyone should have at least five gold rings (mentioned in chapter 2), simply to own their share of the gold in the world. Most, however, will not have adequate time or desire to develop the skills, knowledge, and contacts to be successful in the jewelry/silverware space.

On the other hand, there are situations when dealing in jewelry, silverware, and other forms of crafted gold and silver form a critical part of an investment or business model. These could include ownership of a pawn shop, auction house, or a secondhand jewelry or recycling business. In these and similar cases it is important to proactively seek advice from niche experts and dealers.

Privacy, why people buy bullion

Bullion products are typically the gateway for precious metals (PMs) investors. PMs are unique among investment assets, as these are what you buy when you don't want anyone to know what you have. Stocks, bonds, bank accounts, insurance policies, real estate, crypto, firearms, even vehicles all have your name, social security number, and/or other identifying information attached in some way. The only way the government would know you own PMs is if you bought it with a credit card or crypto or self-reported.

One of the primary reasons people buy bullion is privacy. It is one of very few concentrated tangible assets that is "off the grid" and this is its greatest advantage. In the U.S. 11.6% of the population admits to owning gold and/or silver. Interestingly the demographic most inclined to ownership is millennial aged males (Bauder, 2020).

Storage

Being a good of concentrated value, storage is often a challenge. You must not only have a space but a secure and protected space. There is a reason the U.S. Treasury's bullion repository in Kentucky is adjacent to Fort Knox (home of the U.S. 1st Army Division).

If kept in a safety deposit box or a storage facility, it will cost some fees every year. Bullion does not pay interest or dividends; it just sits there, and at some level there is always an expense. This is another of the primary reasons most institutional investors do not buy physical PMs; storage and security for the quantities they would be interested in are impractical.

Keep in mind that banks do not insure items kept in a safety deposit box. Granted, the likelihood of them being stollen is low, but if they are, you have no recourse other than a capital loss for taxes, even then you will likely need to provide proof of purchase documentation. If you choose to use a safety deposit box, I recommend a local credit union, as fees are generally lower, and proximity/access is better. Safety deposit boxes have their own risks. If you violate lease terms (non-payment) or there is a lien filed against you, the institution could drill the box and remove the contents for the creditor. During a bank failure or buyout, your access may be limited and may require you to close the deposit box within a certain number of days before contents are removed. In most cases, the property is moved to a depository center to await a formal claim. Also, what if you die? Do you have a will with instructions for the contents? In this situation, the contents of unknown safe deposit boxes are often forfeited to the government. While the chances of these thing are low, if applicable, it exposes your assets and information to significant risk of loss. (McGuinn, 1991; Peeler, 2021; Pearson, 2018)

Private depositories offer secure storage with insurance. When using one of these facilities, realize, you are exposing yourself to custodial risk. In a recent case, a depository owner stole $75 million worth of PMs from depositors, and (surprise) they had not purchased insurance as advertised. The depositors lost everything. (DiStefano, 2023) This, again, is a rare occurrence, but custodial risks are higher than at a brokerage, because these types of facilities are not regulated. Remember that physical PMs are "off the grid" and there will not be a paper trail or electronic log of transactions, unless you keep one.

Some sites will tell you to "bury it in the back yard." Don't. I had a math teacher in high school tell me about a friend of his who bought 800 oz of silver and buried it in his back yard. Fifteen years later after he had closed on the sale of his house and was preparing to move, he realized that he had poured a concrete patio over the top of his buried silver. Doesn't sound like a fun weekend to me.

Depending on the property, home safes can be a great deterrent from would be thieves. Be sure they are bolted down, as the floor metal is often thinner than the sides. I had a neighbor to whom thieves knocked over his gun safe, then cut out the bottom to gain access while he was on vacation.

I have seen several examples of people modifying their homes by adding hidden spaces in walls, a loose floorboard, or secret room behind a shelf. These options can be a practical, relatively low-cost solution that does not draw attention.

If you decide to keep it under your bed with your guns and ammunition (very normal in Idaho), you need to understand that its value (along with that of the firearms) is not covered by renter's or homeowner's insurance policies. If you are robbed or your house burns down, the answer is simply, "sorry." That said, most insurers will let you purchase riders to cover a portion of physical PMs you keep at home.

The investment bullion actually is

"Gold is the hedge against government." -Martin Armstrong

As governments become more stressed, they tend to become more aggressive with taxation or, in extreme cases, even asset confiscation. It is a tell-tale sign they are going broke. Historically, the most common cause of this is war, but political change, overspending, and other variations of fiscal/social mismanagement can also be causes. If your government is near a default, then physical assets are the best thing you can have, as currency will lose value drastically once confidence in the currency is lost. What has always made PMs a good choice for this scenario is that they require relatively little space compared to other commodities, are not as sensitive to spoiling, and are portable (unlike real estate). When a government stabilizes, all surviving physical assets then find a price in the revalued, or potentially new, currency. Conversely the old cash and debt instruments become seriously devalued or potentially worthless. While an extreme scenario, history has demonstrated it isn't uncommon. As a government nears financial collapse, one could expect real estate to be taxed at ridiculously high rates, and pensions, retirement accounts, and savings are all potential targets for confiscation. This is usually under a pretense of war or another crisis for the "national good." Confiscation of assets from the citizens of Cypress in 2013 is a recent example (Dabilis, 2013).

In extreme cases, a government may also set controls limiting the movement of capital out of a country. Technology and airport security make such authoritarian actions easier to enforce when applied to physical assets such as PMs. This could cause downward pressure to metal values in affected regions. As traders and governments become aware of political and custodial risks, they will move their gold to "safer" jurisdictions. Large gold shipments are often precursors to major events, such as the 1929 crash or 2010-12 European debt crisis. For comparison in 2025 we saw 400 tons of gold move compared to 700 tons and 500 tons during Covid-19 and the 2008 Financial Crises respectively. Again, *"gold is the hedge against government,"* because it holds value during a dramatic drop in currency values, and if they don't know you have it, they can't come after it.

Units

Mass

All precious metals trade both domestically and internationally in troy ounces. A troy ounce is 31.103476 grams, which is slightly heavier than the avoirdupois (AVDP) or standard ounce which is 28.349 grams. By 1527, the UK, was using the troy ounce as the official unit of measure for gold and silver. The U.S made it official in 1828. (Chen, 2024a) Some coins and bars say troy ounces and others simply "oz," but it should be understood as troy oz.

The standard is named after Troyes, France, which in the Middle Ages was a major trade city in Europe. The troy pound is twelve troy ounces, dissimilar to the AVDP pound which has 16 AVDP ounces. Given that the city of Troyes dates back to Roman times and that several Roman units were factors of 12, many believe troy ounces to be related to, if not directly derived from, the Roman system. For example, the Libra (Roman pound and source of the abbreviation lb. and British £) divides into 12 Uncia (ounces(s)). (GoldSilver, 2024; Chen, 2024a).

The world is slowly transitioning to using metric grams instead of troy ounces. While metric is more convenient (especially in exploration), 1 ppm ≈ 1 gram/ton for example, many investors and traders prefer that precious metals have their own units, as it sets them apart from other commodities. It is also fun to know that gold and silver may be the only commodities in the modern world to have traded in the same units for more than 2000 years.

Fineness

While many systems of metal purity or fineness have been used throughout history there are two common systems today. The first and arguably simpler is the Millesimal System. It expresses fineness in units of parts per 1,000, therefore, a fineness of 1000 would be 100% pure. U.S. coin silver (90% Ag and 10% Cu) would have a fineness of 900 and British coin silver (85% Au and 15% Cu) would have a fineness of 850. There is no description of what the other alloying metals or impurities are, the fineness describes only purity of the primary precious metal. This system is primarily used for bullion products and often traders and investors will colloquially refer to a piece's purity by the number of 9s. For example, the purest gold ever produced was six nines fine, or had a purity of 999.999 or 99.9999%. This was produced by the Perth mint in 1957 (Thomas, 1989).

The Karat (U.S. spelling) or Carat (U.K. spelling) is the other system often encountered. It is the more historic system and is still used in the jewelry industry. This system is a ratio of parts per 24. For example, 18 karat gold= 18 parts gold/ 24 parts total mass. Again, there is no required description of what the other 6 parts are made of. In England, the carat was divisible into four "grains" and a grain further divisible into four "quarts". Thus, a gold alloy of 127/128 fineness or 99.2% purity could be described as 23-carat, 3-grain, 1-quart gold. In this system 24 karat gold is considered pure and would be equivalent to 999 or three nines fine in the Millesimal System. The Karat/Carat system is not to be confused with the Carat system for weighing pearls and gemstones, which is not a ratio of pureness but rather a unit of mass.

The Millesimal System is gradually replacing the Karat/Carat system even in jewelry, in part because refining methods have improved, because jewelry alloys have become more sophisticated, and it is easier to describe these additives with the new system by disclosing the parts made of alloying metal. For now, investors and traders need to be familiar with both systems. In Europe 18k gold may be stamped 750 using the newer system, meaning 75% gold.

It is extremely difficult to refine metal to 100% purity, hence 24k or 999 traditionally was considered pure, as it was the best technologies of the time could produce. Today most bullion products will be 999.9 but pay attention as there is some variation among producers.

Buying PMs Bullion

To buy bullion it is necessary to understand the meanings of spot price and premium. The spot price is the reported value for the commodity being traded. It is the price paid by the largest buyers, such as refiners and smelters, and will fluctuate throughout a trading session just like any other market. Spot price is the base price for any commodity-related product or service. Premium is the price paid above the spot price. Always expect to pay some premium. For PMs, premiums includes the cost of turning a 1000-oz, 95 to 98% pure doré bar, commonly produced by a mine, into a smaller 99.999% pure bar or coin. It also includes a commission that a dealer charges as their profit. Generally, smaller sized bullion carries a higher premium than larger sizes. This is logical, because it takes more energy to make a thousand 1-oz coins out of a doré than ten 100-oz bars; also, when the dealer makes bulk sales, he doesn't need to make as much profit per unit. This is just the metals version of buying your mustard at Costco.

Both spot price and premiums fluctuate, and shortages of popular products can increase their premium, just as oversupply from the mines might decrease the spot price. Sometimes they move in tandem; other times they do not. The premium can be calculated by subtracting the spot price from the total price for the products of interest. Most online dealers make this convenient by having the real-time spot price posted on their home page. Many dealers will give discounts or free shipping if the purchase exceeds certain thresholds. Of primary concern is the <u>total cost</u> or the combined spot, premium, and shipping costs. Often, it is not critical to time a purchase perfectly in regard to spot price, if you can get a deal on premiums and/or shipping.

Bullion is not something to trade frequently and expect to make a profit, as premiums and shipping costs add to the total purchase price. Also, when selling the dealer receives a commission. Often, the dealer will quote you the spot price, however, depending on the product and quality it is customary to ask for a price above the spot price. For example, 1-oz silver coins in brilliant uncirculated condition will demand a higher premium than the same rounds in tarnished condition or 10-oz bars in new condition. If you counter with a price, say a $1/coin over spot but still $2.5/coin below retail, the dealer may take it if he is confident that he can quickly resell the coins. A humorous experience I had regarding this:

I went to buy silver rounds. The man ahead of me at the dealer's shop sold the dealer 10 silver rounds, for which the dealer paid about 3 dollars under retail and maybe $0.50 over spot for the rounds. I came up to the counter next and said:

"I would like to buy silver rounds."

"How many he replied?"

"Twenty."

"I only have these 10 that just came in, but they are yours if you want them."

He charged me full retail, earning $2.5/round or $25 for about 10 minutes of work. Not a bad business if the process can be repeated consistently. Had the man who sold the coins and I each known the other's objectives, we could have agreed upon more favorable terms in the parking lot. These opportunities are rare, of course, and hence, the dealer served his purpose in the economy and received his due.

Back to trading bullion. Many online dealers post the prices they are willing to pay for common or popular products; this removes the haggling aspect. To have profitable bullion investments, it is necessary to wait for significant moves in the price of the PMs and/or the prices dealers are willing to pay. The moves have to at a minimum equal the total price you paid which includes the spot price, premium, to/from shipping, and commissions.

Choosing your dealer

Like brokers and dealers for other services, options and quality will run the gamut. I think most people would agree we want to avoid those who have been sued for fraud. These commonly include those who advertise in utility magazines, and on TV, especially to seniors in the same time slots as Medicare supplement plans. (Shadel & Eaton, 2016)

Even when these companies use appropriate sales practices, the types of marketing they use to reach their audience are expensive. This often drives the premium paid over 30%; and 30% in the negative is not where to start any investment. On the buying side, the refiners advertising on TV to buy old jewelry often pay less than what could be gained by finding a refiner yourself. Of course, it makes sense to understand the type of jewelry owned by asking questions like: *"Is it 14 or 18 carat gold?" "Is it solid or gold fill?" "What is its weight?"* If you can't answer these questions before you put it in the special envelope and mail it, you probably deserve to be conned. The takeaway: **Don't buy mail order or on TV - Ever!**

The best dealer is often one found locally. There is a coin shop near me that I frequent for my collectables, but they also deal in a few bullion products. Their premiums are usually par, if not slightly better, than those of online dealers, and they are just down the street, so I do not pay shipping. I also like that I am helping support a local business. Explore a bit and find the good dealers near you. Local coin clubs can be a great resource for finding the most reputable local dealers. Later in this chapter, I will provide a list of regional and national dealers that I have dealt with and the niche of each.

Bullion Products

The product variety, especially in the silver market, has drastically expanded in the last decade. Though I will focus on silver products; other PMs exist in similar products but with fewer options and variety.

Bars

For starters bars come in various sizes, most commonly 1, 5, 10, 50, 100 oz. These can be either milled (very sharp and crisp appearance because the bar is mechanically cut); poured (a more natural rounded shape as molten metal is poured into a mold and cools); or shaped into a figurine (skulls were all the rage in 2016; hope you didn't miss it!).

Bars typically have lower premiums than rounds or coins, but the premium goes up as size comes down. Some bars have decorative artwork that may cause them to be more popular and, therefore, demand a higher premium. Some bars are old and produced from mints that are no longer in business.

Such bars often carry much higher premiums, because they have become quasi collectables. Older and serialized bars produced by the Silvertown and Engelhard mints are good examples (Silver Gold Pill, 2020). If you are not interested in the collectible value, you should avoid purchasing these bars.

Figure 4-1: Examples of common silver bars in circulation today. *Silver bars today come in several formats 1, 5, 10, 50, and 100 (troy) oz bars are the most common. Milled bars have crisp sharp edges and are machined, poured bars are formed in a mold as molten metal cools and have more natural rounded edges. Finally, figurines with standardized weights are also popular. The process of collecting bullion is coloqually refered to as "stacking" and the collection itself called a "stack." This particular stack is 1200 oz. The photo comes from one of the many You Tubers who periodically like to display their collection for public view (image: BigstackMcgee, 2022).*

Rounds

Rounds are coin shaped pieces of bullion, like bars, they do not have a face (currency) value stamped into them and can be produced by anybody. Most common are 1-oz rounds, but 0.5-oz, 2-oz, and 5-oz rounds do exist. "Trade unit" might be stamped on 1-oz rounds. This is a throwback to the 1870's trade dollar. Essentially Asian trading partners preferred the Mexican peso or 8 Reale because of its higher silver content compared to the U.S. dollar. Dollars we reluctantly accepted and always at a discount and purchasing Mexican Pesos to trade with came at a steep premium. From 1873-78 the U.S. produced 1-oz silver pieces called "trade dollars" that were minted for internation trade and became a common means of exchange in the orient. This also provided an outlet for the oversupply of silver in the U.S. coming from the Comstock lode and other prolific western silver mines. (Duncan, 2012) The use of "trade unit" on silver rounds today is synonymous with 1 troy ounce.

Certain brands of rounds may demand a higher premium than others. Many private mints produce sets. Chinese lunar calendar sets, for example, are popular and can become quasi collectables demanding higher premiums.

Bars and rounds generally have good secondary markets, where dealers often sell "used" bullion for a discounted premium. These pieces usually have some minor dents, scratches, and tarnishing. Used products are an efficient way to reduce premiums. If one's goal is to simply have something to trade or barter during a crises without regard for collectable quality, this is a good option.

As many issuances have gradually moved towards collectible, people have become very picky about their silver. Most new products now come sealed in plastic to prevent tarnishing. A word of advice: *"If it comes in plastic, leave it in plastic."* Upgrading and putting the piece in better plastic is an option. This helps get a better price when sold, if the piece has become collectible.

Figure 4-2: Small collection of 1-oz silver rounds in circulation today. *Silver rounds come in several formats 0.5, 1, 2, and 5 (troy) oz rounds are the most common. Anyone can contract a mint to produce rounds, because they carry no monetary value, only intrinsic or metal value. Often rounds are produced by companies or other organizations to commemorate events. Private mints try to use asthetic designs that will help the product sell and may even produce a series of designs, if the design or series becomes popular it may eventually become collectable. The photo has examples of these scenerios: Thunder Mountain Gold Mine (lower left) is a company produced commemorative, 2012 chinese lunar Year of the Dragon by APMEX (lower right) quasi collectable, Trump coin (center right) future collectable? Generic rounds (top row), two rounds are stamped as trade units (secound row center left & bottom row center), "trade unit" is synonoumous w/ 1 troy ounce. (image: GeoTech LLC, 2024. All rights reserved.)*

Chapter 4: Owning Physical Metal

Bullion Coins

Bullion coins are usually coin-shaped pieces that are produced by a national mint and have a monetary value stamped on them. A familiar example is the American Silver Eagle. It is a 1-oz silver coin produced by the US mint since 1986 and has a 1-dollar value stamped on it. In theory you can use it as a $1 bill, if you are dumb enough to do so. Currently, they sell for almost $40. Despite having a monetary value placed on it, these are not considered money by the treasury, they are "numismatic products" and there is nothing illegal about melting them down. It is expected that many will be melted down eventually. (Public Law 99-185, 1985) Several countries mint this kind of coin and sell them to raise money.

Usually, the stamped monetary value is significantly less than the silver value, though Canada has notable exceptions. For instance, they have a 1-oz silver coin stamped with $100, and they sold them for $100. The silver at time of minting was worth $20-25, allowing the mint to profit the difference. Because the coin has $100 value on it, upon sale you should not take less than $100 for it and provides you protection against loss should the price of silver fall.

Bullion coins, when produced by larger countries, are usually engraved/stamped by their national mint. American Silver Eagles, Canadian Maple Leaves, Australian Kookaburras, British Britannias, and Chinese Pandas are examples. However, many smaller countries cannot afford to own and operate a mint, instead they contract with a private mint to produce their coins. The Sunshine Mint in Idaho, USA produces almost half of these "world coins." The Scottsdale Mints is another U.S. based private mint that serves a similar clientele. Coins produced by these companies are minted and shipped directly to national suppliers, and many will likely never see Africa, South America, or the Pacific Isles, from where they supposedly came. They sure look nice though.

The important point is that these almost always carry a higher premium than rounds. This is one of the crossovers between the bullion and collectable coin markets. In fact, many of the mintages, or total number of a particular coin produced, are limited to less than 25,000, with the intention that they will become collectable. This type of coin should be maintained in as perfect condition as possible in order to continue to demand a high premium. Airtight coin capsules and storage tubes are good options. It makes sense to pay attention to mintage numbers and understand that some designs will be more popular than others. A popular design, combined with low mintage, often causes a coin to appreciate faster than rounds due to this "collectible premium". This can also work against you. If few people like a design, it's resale price will fall until it is similar to that being paid for rounds.

Figure 4-3: Collection of 10 1-oz silver bullion coins dated 2017, each from a different world mint. *Bullion coins are sponsored products of a country's government. They carry a monetary value (usually significantly less than the metal value) and are sold to generate revenue. Larger contries with their own mints strike their own coins; whereas, small contries contract with another national mint or a reputable private mint (more common today). Several of the above coins were struck at national mints; however, the elephant, gorilla, and marlin where struck at private mints per contract for Somalia, Congo, and the Cayman Island, respectively. Mintages of many bullion coins are intentionally kept low, as they are intended to become collectable. Several of the coins are a series, where the design changes every year. The Kookaburra and Elephant releases are highly anticipated each year by collectors. (image: GeoTech LLC, 2024. All rights reserved.)*

Buying Considerations

Consider the objective before buying. If the goal is to purchase the most metal possible for the least money, large format bars from the secondary market are the best option. If you are prepping for a zombie apocalypse and plan to use the pieces for trade, you should buy small rounds and bars. Once again, use the secondary market to reduce premiums. It is advised to focus on smaller formats, as these facilitate small day-to-day transactions. If you desire to physically examine your purchase from time to time, instead of letting them indefinitely sit in sealed tubes hidden under the bed, you might prefer to go with the coins and build a collection.

Junk Silver

Junk silver consists of old coins that no longer circulate but still have value because they have a high silver content. U.S. half dollars, quarters, and dimes from 1964 and earlier are made of what is called coin silver. This also includes the silver dollars our grandparents talk about. In the U.S., coin silver had a composition of 90% silver and 10% copper. Silver is a soft metal; copper was added to increase wear resistance, with the tradeoff of less tarnish resistance. British coin silver was 85% silver, 15% copper. Other coins may have differing silver compositions depending on coin type and issuer. If making a junk silver purchase be sure to research the coin type involved, knowing the metal content is paramount when discussing price.

Usually, the quality of junk silver coins is such that they have hardly, if any, collectable value; in many cases the images have worn away almost completely. Junk silver is for many the preferred option for crises situations. Because silver is the least expensive of the PMs and the coins are fractional, it would be the easiest alternative method for trade and commerce for small transactions.

U.S. coin silver has been a popular investment, in part because the coins are still legal tender, the U.S. being one of the few nations to never cancel their currency. A 90% Ag 1928 dated quarter will still spend for 25¢ even if the value of its silver content drops below that. Meaning if the price of silver collapsed, they would still have the monetary value. With the inflation experienced over the last two decades increasing the spread between monetary value and metal prices, the silver in a pre-1965 quarter is worth about $6 today, this is less of a concern. Being fractional and in small units, junk silver is an ideal means of exchange in a crisis situation when compared to larger format bullion products that would be difficult to make change with. For this reason, many bullion owners also have an allocation in junk silver. It can typically be purchased through the same dealers as the bullion products.

Figure 4-4: Example of U.S. "junk silver" coins. *These are old coins that used to be in circulation but were removed because their intrinsic or metal value exceded their monetary value. Many of the coins pictured are actually in better condition than typical "junk" coins, which in many cases it is difficult to distinquise the designs. U.S. pre 1965 half dollars, quarters, and dimes are made of "coin silver" (90% silver & 10% copper). Junk silver is popular with investors who are concerned about protecting their ability to make everyday purchases in a crisis. Being fractional and in small pieces they would be much more conveinent for making small transactions and change than larger format silver. (image: Tseytlin, 2017)*

U.S. fractional silver coins have not been manufactured since 1964 and many are hoarded for reasons mentioned above. This has led to a steady increase in both demand and premiums. Another product worth mentioning is the Valcambi CombiBar™. This is a bullion bar that is breakable into smaller, down to 1-gram, units. The divisibility allows them to facilitate transactions that require fractional precious metal. Each division bears the assay and a serial number and is recognized by all traders and manufacturers of bullion. These divisible bars come in gold, silver, platinum, and palladium. Premiums tend to be higher than similar sized non-divisible bars but lower than small bars or rounds. They are a good balance for a buy and hold investor who wants to save some on premiums but are still divisible in the event the investor finds themselves in a situation where they need to trade in smaller increments. This and similar products serve the same market as junk silver. By volume, I expect the divisible products will one day eclipse junk silver as we continue to move further away from the time silver was used in coins.

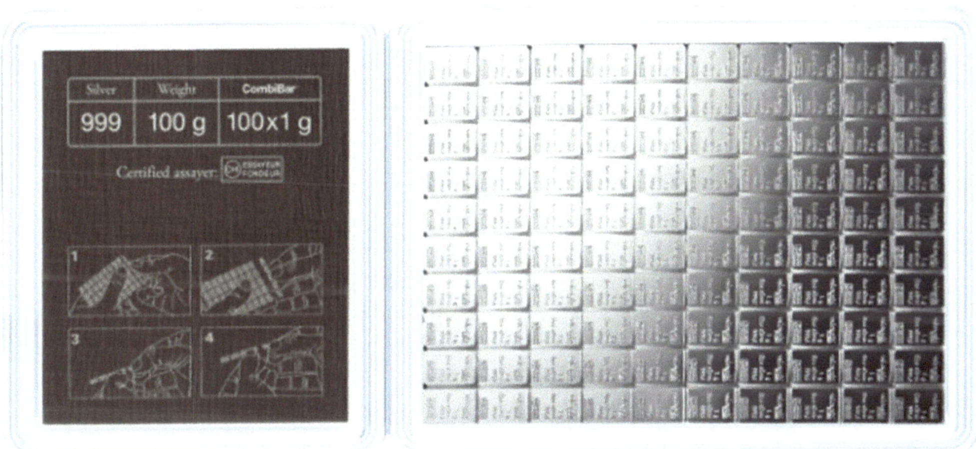

Figure 4-5: Valcambi CombiBar™. *This is a high purity bullion bar designed to be easily divisable to 1 gram units. It appeals to those seeking fractional precious metal investments. While the example pictured is silver, Valcambi also produces divisable bars of gold, platinum, and palladium. (Valcambi, 2025)*

What type of bullion should you buy? It is up to you, really. As long as you are paying attention to price and market trends and understand what you are buying and why, it is hard to go wrong in the long run with any of these formats.

Time-cost averaging is arguably the best buying strategy for bullion, at least for beginners. Buying each month or every other month over time levels out ups and downs in the market. Another strategy is to buy in retirement, using a portion of money taken from forced mandatory withdrawals of a traditional IRA or 401K. Instead of going back into the market through a brokerage, retirees with a short investment window may choose to simply buy bullion to later use or gift it to heirs.

Other investors get a sense of security having bullion in their possession as protection against crises (zombie apocalypse/bank failure/invasion/hard times). In a sense, it is the deep reserve portion of their emergency fund. As discussed above, this has both associated risks and expenses.

Frauds and Fakes

As long as there has been trade, there have been cheats. Historically, this has been done both by individuals and governments. Common forms have included shaving or nipping off portions of coins, making coins out of less valuable metal, or reducing the size/metal content of a coin.

Most modern attempts are variations of the same. Some notable examples from recent history include gold bars that have been drilled and less expensive tungsten metal poured into the cavities, or gold poured/plated around a tungsten core. Tungsten has a similar density to gold. This has allowed these types of frauds to get past testing methods commonly used by dealers, which usually involve weight and dimension measures, or acid tests, in which impurities of base metals will react. More recently, use of X-ray fluorescence (XRF) machines has become commonplace. These instruments are good for measuring purity and do so quickly, with analysis usually taking about 3 minutes. XRF has displaced traditional acid testing in many applications and will quickly identify replicas or fakes made of impure alloys. For example, mixing zinc and copper in the right ratio will yield a form of brass near indistinguishable in color from that of gold.

In this case, weight and measure tests, XRF, scratch test (gold is soft), or an acid test would all be effective methods. The x-ray spectra however do not penetrate deeply, so if the fraud is a core of tungsten with thickly plated gold the instrument will only assay the surface. This is also important when testing silverware, as many brands were silver plated not solid silver.

Figure 4-6: Fradulant 10-oz gold bar with tungsten fill. *Image of fradulent gold bar with a significantly less valuable tungsten core sold to a jewlery dealer in Manhattan, NY in 2012. Tungsten has a density similar to gold, which make sophisticated fakes like this one difficult to detect. This bar was seriallized and purchased from a reputable international dealer. Larger format gold is most securly purchased from mint direct dealers. Smaller format gold has a lower risk of this kind of fraud as the size makes it more difficult and less cost effective to produce. (Wile, 2012)*

Counterfeit, or replica, coins are often advertised as genuine, most commonly in the numismatic space but increasingly with bullion. Technology has advanced such that some counterfeits are nearly indistinguishable from authentic pieces, and most dealers have been fooled at least once. There are simple steps that bypass most of these risks.

First, smaller format gold is very difficult to fill with a tungsten core and, therefore, less likely to be fraudulent. Second, focus on common bullion products from reputable mints, and buy from dealers that source directly from those mints. These products have the diameters, thicknesses, and weights published. For added peace of mind, test the diameter and thickness with a digital caliper, and also the weight with a digital scale capable of measuring a minimum of 0.00 oz. Also, test with a rare earth magnet (very strong). Precious metals are not magnetic; only iron, iron alloys, and in some cases chromium are magnetic. These tools can be bought for less than $50 total investment. It is also good to compare with a piece you know to be genuine, sometimes lettering or slight design variations are a give-away. If a piece doesn't pass inspection, return it to the dealer. Reputable dealers take fraudulent pieces back. If buying from a local dealer, ask (before you complete the purchase) if they can analyze a piece's purity. Many dealers now have this capability with either portable or bench top x-ray fluorescence machines, which perform a non-destructive analytical test for metal content. Avoid buying bullion on eBay, the fee structure is such you won't find any deals there anyway. Also, avoid anything out of China, as that has been the source of most counterfeits for well over a decade. (Fahey, 2014; U.S. Gold Bureau, 2012)

Efforts to counter fraud include diagnostic tests, serial numbers, chain of custody documents, advanced engraving techniques and other resources. The website Fakebullion.com, for example, has built an impressive database of fakes that have been found. You can use images to compare. The Sunshine Mint has developed advanced engraving techniques and sells inexpensive decoder lenses that allow you to verify the bullion piece. For many buyers this makes their products preferred over others, and they now carry a small premium. Finally, Gold Coin Ballance™ makes a unique 3 in diagnostic tool compatible with several common gold bullion coins. It allows you to test diameter, thickness, and weight (using a fulcrum). The risk of fraudulent coins has been around as long as the coins themselves; however, if a buyer is aware and prudent, using both a network of reputable dealers and several of the techniques and methods mentioned, they have little to worry about.

While color should be the least trusted of all diagnostic tests, it is always the first observed. Color should always be used negatively, meaning if it doesn't look right the piece should definitely be tested if not avoided all together. Not affirmatively, where a piece looks OK in regard to color, so we are going to forgo everything else. As a mineral exploration geologist, I can safely say my eye is trained better than 99% of the global population in regard to subtle differences in color, texture, and luster. Most of the others are jewelry professionals. I <u>never</u> trust color exclusively.

That said, buyers should have an idea of what colors precious metals and their common alloys have, in both their polished and rough forms. If for no other reason than to be a better-informed consumer. Figure 4-8 is a color comparison of the most common precious metal alloys. If you have a chance, look at several known pieces with a hand lens or low power microscope.

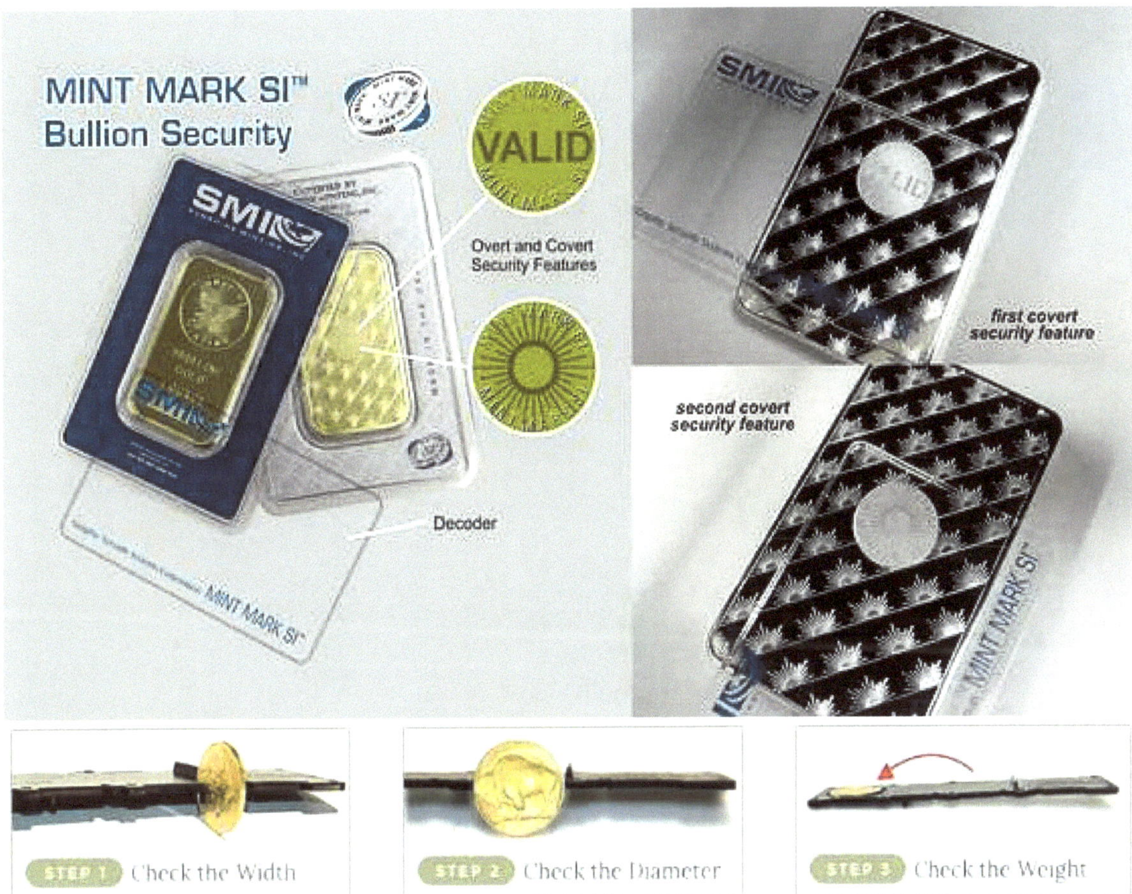

Figure 4-7: Tools to detere and detect fraudulant bullion. *Micro engraving (top 3 images) and Gold Coin Ballange™ (3 lower images) are two methods to help protect bullion investors. The Sunshine Mint has adopted advaned microengraving techniques that allow them to place coded images on their products, serving the same purpose as a watermark on currency bills. When you look at the bullion through a security lense that can be inexpensively purchased from them, you can varify the validity of any Sunshine minted product. This feature has made their products prefered by many bullion investors. The balance is a clever measuring device compatable with several of the more common gold bullion products. The single tool allows you to conveniently test the diameter, thickness, and weight of compatible products. (SMI, 2024; goldcoinbalance.com, 2024)*

Figure 4-8: Color guide to precious metals and their common alloys. *Pure metals have a distinct color, but impurities or alloys will change that color. Pure gold is a bright yellow, while copper has a reddish hue, alloys of the two are in-between. Similarly, the white metals grade between white (pure silver) and gray (nickel). Karat specifications dictate how much of the precious metal must be present, this protects the consumer and standardizes the industry in regard to purity and value. It does not however constrain what the composition of the remaining fraction must be. Manufactures are often creative tweaking these, even to the extent of adding uncommon metals into the alloy to achieve various properties which can include improved tarnish resistance, workability, wear resistance, or aesthetics among others. It is not uncommon for a wedding band today to contain 6 or more metals alloyed together. This can cause a noticeable color variance within the alloy type depending what base metal(s) are used and in what proportions. This is one reason why color alone is one of the least usable diagnostic properties. Understanding how the different metals in an alloy affect the color and physical properties empowers consumers. (Egan, 2024)*

Jewelry, Not a Bullion Investment

Jewelry should not be viewed as a bullion investment for two reasons. First, bullion is by definition of high purity and in fixed masses to facilitate trade. Jewelry is not in fixed masses and usually has much lower purity than bullion. Traditionally sterling silver was 92.5% silver and the balance copper; 18 karat, 14 karat, and 10 karat gold each had progressively more copper (Cu), but Cu was the only addition. Most jewelry today is an advanced alloy of precious and other metals to achieve specific properties, often having 2-4 additional metals in the alloy. Knowing the true composition, however, can be complicated, because as more modern jewelry finds its way into recycling streams, the stocks many independent jewelers use become a mix of whatever alloys were recycled. Usually trace to small percentage amounts won't drastically change the alloy's properties and are not worth the effort of additional refinement. The appropriate amount of precious metal is simply added to make it the legal Karat grade or fineness. Today knowing the composition of a piece without access to manufacturer supplied documentation usually involves an XRF analysis because most jewelry alloys now contain several metals. My wife's 18-Karat white gold wedding band for example has almost a dozen different metals. To illustrate Table 4-1 provides 5 common "white gold" recipes used in the jewelry industry today.

The second reason not to view jewelry as an investment in bullion is the premium. With jewelry you are buying wearable art, a significant if not majority proportion of the price you are paying is for the labor involved in creating this art. Intricate pieces are more labor intensive and thus have a higher premium over metal value. Also, many pieces have set gemstones. Resale values usually ignore this and will pay you close to the spot price for the metal, and any gemstones are removed and handled separately. Transactions with jewelry will always be more complicated than bullion and involve an appraisal process. For these reasons investments in heirloom jewelry should be treated both in strategy and care as a collection. Later chapters will give more specifics on collectable investments.

Table 4-1: Common White Gold Alloys, *modern jewelry alloys often incorporate several metals to achieve different colors and physical properties. (Smerten, 2001)*

```
(Au = 24ct gold.  Pd = Palladium. Ag = Silver. Cu = Copper. Ni = Nickel)

Palladium White Gold Alloys:
18ct White:   75% Au + 10% Pd + 10.5% Ag + 2.5% Cu + 2% Ni

14ct White:   58.5% Au + 10% Pd + 28.5% Ag + 1.5% Cu + 1% Ni

Nickel White Gold Alloys:
18ct White:   75% Au + 14% Ni + 5.5% Cu + 5.5% Zn (Zinc)

14ct White:   58.5% Au + 14.5% Ni + 20% Cu + 7% Zn
         or    58.5% Au + 15.3% Ni + 25.8% Cu + 0.4% Zn (Harder alloy)
9ct White:      37.5% Au + 17.5% Ni + 27.6% Cu + 17.4% Zn

Palladium-Nickel White Gold Alloy:
18ct White:    75% Au + 15% Pd + 5% Cu + 5% Ni
```

Precious Metal Alloys

As mentioned in chapter 1, owning your proportional share of the world's gold would be the equivalent of five rings. While jewelry is not the focus of this work, most will own a few to several pieces, and will benefit from the following discussion and its broader implications.

When not used for bullion, precious metals are usually alloyed or mixed while in their molten form with other metals. This achieves desired properties for required applications. A valuable principle to understand is that whenever two pure substances are mixed into an impure substance, the liquid phase of that substance is expanded, meaning the boiling point will be higher and the melting/freezing point will be lower. For example, pure silver has a melting point of about 962 °C but sterling silver (92.5% Ag and 7.5% Cu) has a melting point of 893 °C, about 9% lower. This principle has broad applications in the modern world, everything from the ethylene glycol/water mixture for the coolant in your car to the flux on welding rods. See table 4-2 for select precious alloy melting points.

The metals also impart different properties to the alloy when added. This category of materials science continues to discover and develop ideal alloys for virtually every application and can cause some disruption in sector demand of metals as new alloys are developed. For example, silver has the best electrical conductivity of any metal but is susceptible to corrosion, for this reason it is primarily used in electronics except for when corrosion resistant contacts are needed. Gold has been the traditional substitute in this case, but gold is expensive. Many of the new corrosion resistant silver alloys are displacing the use of gold in this area of electronics manufacturing.

Table 4-2: Melting points of common precious metal alloys, *alloys will have lower melting points compared to pure metals (compare to table 2-2). As many of these alloys allow for some variation in metal content, their melting points are reported as ranges. Data from (Cooksongold, 2025).*

Alloy	Melting Point °C	Melting Point °F
Sterling Silver 0.925	893	1640
Coin Silver	879	1615
Silver-Palladium	651	1204
940 Argentium Silver	875	1607
Gold-Germanium	356	673
18k Yellow Gold (Au/Ag/Cu)	905-960	1661-1760
14k Yellow Gold (Au/Ag/Cu)	830-870	1526-1598
18k Rose Gold (Au/Cu)	875-900	1607-1652
18k White Gold (Au 75.1%/ Pd 13%/ Ag 11.85)	1200	2192
14k White Gold (Au/Pd)	1020-1100	1868-2012
9k White Gold (Au/Ag/Zn)	910-940	1670-1724
9k White Gold (Au/Ag/Pd/Ni)	915-950	1679-1742
Platinum-Iridium (85/15%)	1820	3308

Another general principle to understand is that alloys will be stronger than the native metal. This is due to the metals lattice structure. Element atoms are different diameters, when two metals are alloyed together the resulting lattice structure is now more complicated than either of the original structures. In simplest terms, it is now physically more difficult to shift atoms around within the lattice. As a result, the alloy has improved hardness and strength and with some exceptions also lower ductility and malleability compared to the native metal. This principle is critical to modern manufacturing and engineering making lighter weight, stronger, and more efficient equipment, machines, and aircraft. It is still just as useful in jewelry, making soft and weak metals stronger, so they are more erosion resistant and have improved tensile strength allowing finer and more intricate designs, or greater load capacity for gemstone heavy pieces. For example, pure gold, or 24 karat gold, is so soft and weak it erodes quickly and generally is not suitable for everyday wear like wedding bands. But when alloyed with copper, both strength and hardness increase.

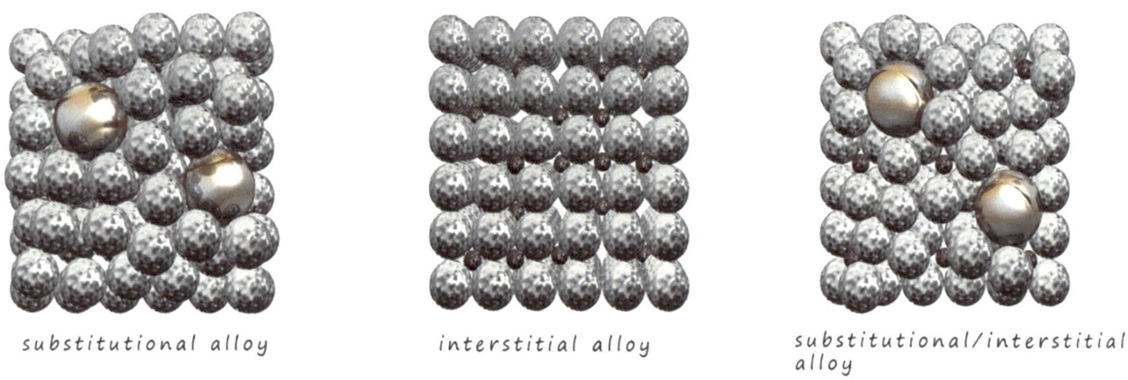

Figure 4-9: Example of alloy lattice types, *each element has a specific atom radius, pure or native elements will have a simple lattice structure compared to compound. This is usually associated with strong interatom bonds. For metals, the native form will have the highest melting point and highest degree of malleability and ductility. When a metal is alloyed, the lattice structure becomes more complicated, often with drastically different sized radii now incorporated into the lattice. There is now more distance between like atoms which reduces the bonding force between them. This manifests as a lower melting point for the alloy compared to the native metal. The alloy lattice will also have fewer internal shear planes, this increases the tensile strength and harness of the alloy compared to the native metal but also reduces its ductility and malleability. (Image from GCSE, 2025)*

In jewelry alloys are created to control several properties, many of these are aimed to improve the workability of the metal by controlling the melting, annealing, and soldering temperature, as well as avoiding "fire scale" an unaesthetic oxidation layer created when soldering or heating sterling silver. Pure platinum, for example, is difficult to work with because of its exceedingly high melting temperature, but platinum alloys are much more manageable because of their lower melting points. Jewelers prefer to use alloys of different tensile strengths, hardnesses, and malleability depending on the piece and its intended use. Cast pieces are usually out of harder alloys, but tend to be more brittle, while chain links on necklace pieces would require a balance of malleability and ductility with high tensile strength. As mentioned, alloys with high tarnish resistance are in demand, several have been created over the last decade, many of them proprietary. Other alloys are created to increase or decrease the precious metal content while retaining workability properties to help manufactures meet different consumer price points. Finally, hypoallergenic alloys have been developed for consumers with allergies. It is reported that 10-15% of people have a metal allergy, usually to one or more metals including nickel, cobalt, chromium, copper, titanium, and to a lesser extent silver. (MedBroadcast, 2025)

Table 4-3 lists several metals and how they are used in precious metal alloys. If we have become this sophisticated with our jewelry alloys one can imagine where we are in terms of aerospace and defense applications.

Table 4-3: Elements Alloyed with Precious Metal, *this list summarizes the most common elements alloyed with precious metals in the jewelry industry and the properties it is used to improve. This is not an inclusive list of alloys of precious metal for industrial applications. For example, silver alloyed with 3-4% graphite will improve its already superior electrical conductivity. In jewelry making the primary properties of concern are melting, annealing, and casting temperatures; hardness, malleability, tensile strength; tarnish and "fire scale" resistance; intrinsic value of metals and reducing allergic reactions. (Grice, 2008; Chen, 2024)*

Element	**Alloy Application**
Aluminum (Al)	Tarnish resistance in silver
Boron (B)	Tarnish resistance in silver
Cadmium (Cd)	Tarnish resistance in silver
Chromium (Cr)	Tarnish resistance, strength, hardening
Copper (Cu)	Improves hardness & tensile strength, adds red for "rose gold"
Germanium (Ge)	Corrosion resistance, hardening, & reduce fire scale in silver
Iridium (Ir)	Hardener for platinum
Nickel (Ni)	Bleaching & hardening in "white gold"
Niobium (Nb)	Preferred substitute for those with allergies to silver
Palladium (Pd)	Bleaching, hardening, hypoallergenic, tarnish res., intrinsic value
Platinum (Pt)	Replace Cu in sterling silver for tarnish resistance & intrinsic value
Rhodium (Rh)	Electroplates PM alloys for color, durability, & allergy reduction
Ruthenium (Ru)	Hardener for platinum
Silicon (Si)	Tarnish resistance in silver, better gas absorption for casting
Strontium (Sr)	Tarnish resistance in silver
Tantalum (Ta)	Tarnish resistance
Thallium (Th)	Tarnish resistance in silver
Titanium (Ti)	Tarnish resistance & strength
Rare Earths	Y, La, Ce in tr amounts. Harding & tarnish resistance in pure silver.
Zinc (Zn)	Tarnish res., improves ductility of Cu/Au alloys, antimicrobial

Where to buy (and sell) PMs

Here is a list of several dealers I have used and their niches. I would also encourage you to investigate local options, and it would not surprise me if you find some really good ones. **Don't use eBay for bullion. There are too many fakes, and auction commissions usually make the legitimate bullion uncompetitive.** Low value numismatics and graded coins can be purchased through reputable sellers on eBay with low risk.

Coloradogold.com: This is a family (literally just 3-4 people) of precious metal brokers. They have very little overhead. For large orders (>200 oz silver or equivalent), they will in most cases be able to get you the best price, which often includes insured shipping. They are more cumbersome for small orders and have less product availability, but if patient they can probably find whatever you are looking for. For selling, they offer commission free trades if you originally bought the product through them; otherwise, they charge 1% plus shipping. They will not deal in numismatics, and do not accept credit cards.

APMEX.com: This is the largest of the big 3 online retailers. They tend to have higher premiums, but their on-hand selection is superior to all others. This dealer is a really good option for bullion coins, especially the international ones. Sometimes they have deals on secondary market products. They have a fair amount of numismatics. They take credit cards and even several cryptos. All places that take cards will pass on the 3-5% merchant fee the credit card companies charge them. For some, the fee is worked into the price; others post the fee as an additional expense. They offer an ACH payment method to keep transaction fees low.

Money Metals Exchange: This is another of the big 3 online retailers. Premiums are comparable to other online retailers. Their niche is they offer secured and insured storage. I have been in the vaults (top of the line) and at a nondescript location. This is one of few good options for custodial storage of bullion. They take cash, cards, and the broadest assortment of cryptos.

Oxford Assaying & Refining: This is a reputable dealer for buying PMs scrap, old jewelry, and even gold flake or concentrates produced by small miners. They also produce and sell bullion products. When selling scrap jewelry, your goal is to receive spot price at best. Most jewelry is impure, so they will pay only for the weight percentage of the actual PMs and maybe a little less to cover partial cost of refining. They can mint custom products for you.

Monarch Coin Corporation: This company is a Utah-based bullion and rare US coin and currency dealer. It tends to have slightly lower premiums than large internet retailers and a good selection of bullion products.

First Majestic Silver Corp.: This is one of very few mining companies that has its own line of retail bullion products. Offering multiple shapes and sizes, everything is stamped with their name. Some of the lowest premiums you will find and, unsurprisingly, because of that they are often sold out. If your goal is strictly to acquire bullion, then this is an excellent option.

JM Bullion: This is the last of the big 3 internet retailers. They have an overlapping selection with the other two internet retailers but some unique products as well. If you are in the market for a particular item in small quantities, shopping the big three is how you start, as all have high inventory turnover.

Sunshine Minting Inc: You cannot buy their products from them directly but do so through the other retailers. However, if you want to have bullion products made, this is a top tier supplier to the industry, minting many of the world bullion coins you see in the marketplace.

Kitco.com: This company provides news and commodity quotes for the metals/mining sector, but they also have a retail business. They have a broad selection of products. For sellers, the real-time quote and cart is (at present) the only one in the industry and has fair prices.

An additional note on selling. As with buying, you need to shop around. Pay attention to your total cost of selling, which includes spot price, shipping, and commissions (amount below full premium) you will receive. Check your local options, without shipping expenses, that may be best. All internet dealers offer a quote. Feel free to negotiate; often the initial quote is not their best price. Do not expect them to pay their listed price for buyers, as they need to make a profit, and there is not a lot of margin in these businesses. Kitco.com and Coloradogold.com can both be good options depending on the format, size, and volume. Finally, like a used car, you are likely to get the best price out of a local buyer. The important things are to choose an avenue that suits your comfort level and to pay attention to total cost. If you don't like an offer, you don't have to take it. Shop around or try back, until you find an agreement that works.

The crypto for bullion trade

Many of the online dealers now accept payments in major crypto currencies for bullion products. While I wouldn't recommend investors go buy crypto for the sake of doing this, for investors that already are active in crypto this can present an opportunity in the form of a modified pair trade. In pair trading you pick two instruments (stocks, indexes, or commodities future). Usually, the expectation is that they will behave differently, and the goal is to profit from the fluctuation in the relative values of the two. This is typically done by shorting one instrument while going long on the other. Even if both instruments end up moving in the same direction if one moves more dramatically than the other there is a probability of profit.

In this case, crypto is significantly more volatile than PM's. When crypto holdings reach a high the ratio between it and the bullion is likely at a high also. Instead of exchanging the crypto into cash (which involves transaction and trading fees and potentially taxes) the investor could buy bullion directly with their crypto. When the crypto price falls their value (now in the form of metal) has been preserved.

Some of the particulars you need to pay attention to are which cryptos the bullion dealer will except, timing, on chain transfer/exchange fees, and as before, premiums and shipping costs. Also understand that you are potentially giving up some of the privacy benefits of bullion when you buy this way as all transactions are permanently stored on the blockchain.

Money Metals Exchange currently accepts the most cryptos out of the online dealers. Their web site even invites you to call and discuss if they would be willing to accept payment in a crypto not currently listed. Both APMEX and Money Metals Exchange require using Bitpay. Make sure to account for any fees on the crypto side of the transaction and that you are comfortable with them.

Being your own custodian

In most cases, by owning physical PMs you will be your own custodian. This absolute control is a key motivator for many buyers. You will need to select appropriate storage and possibly insurance for your investment. Record keeping is where most owners fall short. At a minimum, keep records that include:

1. Purchase and sale transaction dates and broker/vendor used.
2. Amount paid for each pieces
3. Condition, if relevant
4. Total cost (shipping, insurance, commissions)
5. Where which pieces are stored.
6. Additional expenses (storage, transport, humidity control etc.)
7. Inventory of all pieces, including serial numbers if applicable.

Records, including the above information will help track the value of your PM investment, aid when preparing to sell, and calculate capital gains for tax mitigation. It also helps protect you in case you suffer a financial loss through burglary or need to make an insurance claim for another reason. In most cases, a spread sheet or even a handwritten ledger is sufficient. An organized file of receipts is also useful. The risk of forgetting about some of your PMs is actually higher than them being stolen. Records will help you keep track of it.

Summary

1. Owning precious metals can be uniquely satisfying. It provides a combination of control, privacy, and mobility unavailable in other major asset classes.
2. Most who own physical PMs should focus on bullion. Jewelry, silverware, numismatics and other collectables can be lucrative but require significantly more time for research and are less liquid.
3. PMs are the "Hedge against government".
4. There are costs and risks associated with the various storage options. For this reason, most institutional investors do not bother with physical PM investments. They are primarily for the retail customers.
5. Size and form will affect premiums paid. Investors should consider their objectives, and focus on the best aligned products.
6. Be aware of fraud and fakes. Take appropriate measures to protect yourself from each, including the use of only reputable dealers/brokers.
7. Jewelry should not be considered as a bullion investment due both to the complexity of metal alloys and non-uniform weights. Investments in precious metal jewelry are best if treated as collections.
8. Use a broker/dealer appropriate for the type of products you are interested in. Pay attention to total cost, both for buying and selling.
9. The crypto for bullion trade can be appropriate for investors already well versed in crypto. Time purchases when the ratio between the PM and crypto is at a high. Pay attention to total cost, and understand these purchase sacrifice a degree of privacy.
10. Keep good records for protection, convenience, valuation calculations, selling, and taxes.

Notes

Chapter 5: Precious Metal Securities: Part 1, ETFs, Gold Bonds, and Sukuk

Introduction

A horde of physical metal isn't for everyone, as discussed previously, there are some drawbacks and risks associated with storage. That said, I have yet to see anyone who hasn't enjoyed owning some bars and coins. When you feel the coolness of a small pile in your hands it is almost impossible for the giddy little buccaneer inside not to come out.

Precious Metal (PM) securities provide unique opportunities and risks when trading in the metals markets. We will discuss Exchange Traded Funds (ETFs) in this chapter and mining stocks in the next. Bonds and warrants also exist, but these are often solicited investments that are more difficult for the average investor to find and trade. In truth, bonds are less common in the minerals sector than other sectors and are usually only issued by the largest mining companies. Warrants, though more common, will be thoroughly addressed in a chapter on derivatives.

Precious Metal ETFs, ETNs, and other closed-end funds

Exchange-Traded Funds (ETFs) are designed to track a particular market or index. To accomplish this, the fund often has a weighted basket of stocks that trade in the index it plans to follow. For commodity ETFs (including PM ETFs), instead of stocks futures/options contracts are used, as well as possibly PM-related stocks & warrants and even some physical metals. Because PMs are concentrated high value commodity, and less bulky to store than things like grain, some funds choose to own exclusively physical bullion. **GLD** is a good example.

No matter the asset mix, market prices of the fund reflect a combination of the underlying value of futures contracts, securities, physical PMs, and investor sentiment. The Net Asset Value (NAV) is the value of assets divided by the shares. Because ETFs trade like stock, the price of shares can be lower or higher than the NAV. When share prices get too far from the NAV, purchases and/or sales of physical metals or securities are made by the Authorized Participant (AP). This person/entity is usually a large market maker tasked with managing the fund. In GLD and most other funds only the AP's shares are redeemable for physical bullion. (Sieroń, 2016) Investors and traders of these funds often consider whether the fund is trading at a discount or premium when buying or selling shares.

An important thing to understand is that an ETF or closed end fund will be structured as its own company, even if it is a subsidiary of a larger financial institution. The fund will be the actual owner of the underlying assets. This is the important difference between ETFs and Exchange Traded Notes (ETNs). ETNs do not hold any assets, they are unsecured liabilities of the issuer that track an index or price of a commodity. This structure allows them to track the index with little to no deviation. However, in the event of a liquidation, there are no underlying assets to liquidate, and shareholders are dependent on the financial strength of the issuer. (STC, 2022)

PM exchange traded securities are structured several different ways. This is due to taxation and the complexities of U.S. securities regulations, in which the SEC handles securities, and the FTC handles commodities. Each regulator has its own set of rules that can be very different and sometimes conflicting. PM funds need to navigate this; hence, their organizational and legal structure can take many forms depending on their objectives. In fact, I have yet to encounter any two funds that have been structured in the same way. This puts more responsibility on the investor/trader, because each structure comes with its own advantages, risks, optionality, and expense. When researching, it is helpful to first identify objectives before investigating particular funds. Once goals are established it is easier to identify funds with structures that meet those objectives. A fund with a structure that deviates too far from what is trying to be accomplished or presents an unacceptable risk factor given the investor's tolerance level or timeline should be avoided, and another fund pursued.

The Sprott Physical Silver Trust (PSLV) is a good example of a uniquely structured security. It is designed as a closed-end trust. It buys silver in proportion to invested assets. This structure gives shareholders claim to the underlying silver assets proportional to their share value. This means in the event of default; the metal belongs to the shareholders not the external financial institution. (QuandaryFX, 2020) To date this is the only metals ETF I have traded structured in this way, and that extra security is what makes it so popular. This security also allows you to redeem shares for physical silver, so long as you meet the minimum 10,000 oz redemption requirement and are willing to wait a month for processing and delivery.

There are also leveraged ETFs, that use derivatives to amplify by 2X and 3X percentage movements seen in the commodity price. These are popular, as often metals go through long periods of limited volatility, and these funds allow traders to increase their opportunity for gains due to amplified swings. These carry unique risks, as is often said about such funds: *"it's bad enough to be wrong, let alone three times wrong."* You also have to worry about time and volatility decay, and they may not track as closely as expected to commodity price movements. This is usually an effect of entrance timing and expirations on underlying derivative contracts. Understand, it is something you have no control over, and details of the derivatives held are not reported. Leveraged ETFs merit their own book. Simply said, these are for experienced traders. A novice or intermediate level trader will want to practice with them in smaller quantities and/or simulated trading until they know what they are doing. Medeiros, 2017 provides a balanced high-level view of leveraged ETFs, their risks, and how they can be used. While the goal of all these securities is to give exposure to price movements of the commodity, as said before, the investor or trader should not expect their price movements to be directly proportional to metal price movements. In addition to the underlying contracts backing the security, fund expense fees and market sentiment can also affect the share price, because it still is its own security. Generally speaking, they will follow a similar rising or falling trend, and while major disconnects can and sometimes do happen it is rare, however, minor to moderate disconnects can be quite frequent, and you should account for this in your risk management strategy.

The major advantage of ETF/ETNs is that they allow you to enter and exit the market quickly and inexpensively. Most online brokers no longer charge commissions on trades. Traders can set limit orders and stops to control entrance and exit points and provide downside protection. ETFs backed by futures contracts and leveraged funds typically have options markets. Because these funds are heavily traded, investors can use relatively conservative out of the money covered call option strategies. Since these funds do not pay dividends, investors can use call options to generate some income if they own a minimum of 1 "lot" or 100 shares. Each options contract for either calls/puts is for 100 shares. For example, if you owned 1,000 shares of a particular stock you could write 10 option contracts. Trading options is also its own book (and there are dozens). A good starting point with options is provided by (Downey, 2022). With ETFs and option strategies, we are simply applying trading skills commonly used with other equities to the PM market. When engaging in this type of trading you will need to have at least rudimentary skills in charting and technical analysis. Fundamental analysis is also helpful, but with precious metals being globally priced commodities the focus should be on macro-economic trends and geopolitics. Charting and technical analysis is easy enough to teach oneself through research, reading, and practice. Many brokerages offer advanced charting capabilities for users, and you should take advantage of these tools. Fundamental analysis will require understanding the common misconceptions presented in chapter 3, then applying those principles to independent research and staying up to date on global current events is key.

Before investing or trading in PM ETFs, ETNs, or trusts, you need to ask yourself a few questions: "*Do I want the ability to take physical redemptions?*" If so, PSLV is probably your only option. "*Do I want to be able to employ options strategies?*" This will limit your list as several do not have an options market. "*What is the underlying asset backing the ETF? Who has control? What level of entitlement do I have if the fund goes bankrupt? Am I comfortable with that arrangement?*" Finally, "*What is my timeframe and is the security appropriate?*"

As when entering any new market, a trader needs to do research beforehand and spend an adequate amount of time familiarizing themselves with the behavior of the security. Take small positions initially. Easing into and out of positions is a common method for managing risk. Never risk more than you are willing to lose. Finally, remember that trading is a skill set that takes time to develop, and even after it is developed, it still takes a lot of work/time to be successful.

Contrary to physical bullion, which we buy and then wait for significant moves due to premiums and shipping costs, most people will be more successful trading rather than investing when using ETFs and similar funds. Transactions are inexpensive, so one should not be afraid to step into and out of positions when the market is right.

Leveraged ETFs, for example, should only be traded and generally held for relatively short intervals, as underlying contract volatility can cause the price to decay. For experienced traders, they may be appropriate during a trending but choppy or volatile market when less leverage is desired than a futures contract. While other funds, such as PSLV and GLD, will not be subject to decay, they still have expense ratios/management fees, no options market, and do not pay interest, so having strategic entry and exit points is imperative.

One of my preferred trades with these securities is writing covered calls for leveraged gold or silver ETFs. I try to enter the stock after a 5 to 10% correction and write out of the money calls with a strike price several dollars above the current market price. As we saw looking at the historical gold charts in chapter 3, precious metals can have long periods of relatively flat trends and then high magnitude moves in a short time. This covered-call strategy works effectively with markets that are flat or have a gradual uptrend. If you are in a strong uptrend, it is usually better not to use covered calls but instead go long and add a trailing stop. Paying attention to macro-economic trends will help determine which strategy is likely to be more profitable and, if the former, where to best place your strike price.

Below is an incomplete list of precious metals ETFs, including some of the larger and more popular securities with good liquidity. Do your research as each is structured a little bit differently.

List 5-1: Some Common Precious Metals ETFs:

GLD- SPDR Gold Trust

SGOL- Aberdeen Physical Gold Shares ETF

BAR- GraniteShares Gold Shares

IAU- iShares Gold Trust

GLDM- SPDR Gold MiniShares Trust

SLV- iShares Silver Trust

SLVO- Credit Suisse X-links Silver Covered Call ETN

SIVR- Aberdeen Standard Physical Silver Shares ETF

SBUG- iPath Silver ETN

PSLV- Sprott Physical Silver Trust

UGL- ProShares Ultra Gold

AGQ- Proshares Ultra Silver

PALL- Aberdeen Standard Physical Palladium

PPLT- Aberdeen Standard Physical Platinum

PLTM- GraniteShares Platinum Trust

Mutual or Open-End Funds

These securities differ from the closed-end funds in several ways. First, mutual funds usually are actively managed, so the fund manager not only picks the investment but is responsible for timing entry and exit points. The fund manager is paid for this work, which translates to higher management fees than the passively managed ETFs where most of the work is performed by computers. Shares are purchased or redeemed at the NAV, which is calculated at the end of each day, at which time all "buy" and "sell" orders are processed. The mutual fund is its own company, meaning that shares are backed by the securities held in the fund. (STC, 2022)

PM mutual funds may trade metals or any companies related to them. As addressed in chapter 3, commodities have certain dynamics that require more from traders and fund managers in order to be profitable. The success of these funds is completely dependent on the capabilities of the fund manager(s), and good managers often do outperform the sector in times of volatility. It is important that you research the fund managers by name, however, because there are also several mediocre ones that will consistently underperform the sector. The Gabelli Gold Fund (GLDAX) is an example of a gold focused mutual fund. Mutual funds are generally less tax efficient than ETFs, chapter 9 about taxation, covers this topic in detail.

Sovereign Gold Bonds & Sukuk

In the past some countries have offered gold bonds to market participants, however this can be a loosing trade for the issuer if their currency is experiencing a high rate of inflation or if gold prices outperform. In 2025 there are currently no countries issuing gold bonds, and with gold approaching all time highs in both real and nominal terms it is understandable why.

India had the largest gold bond program, and it ran from 2015 to 2024. Part of its objective was to decrease gold imports. High interest rates, rising gold prices, and a limited impact on reducing gold imports caused India to discontinue the program in 2024, and no new issuances were made in 2025. Past issues continue to trade on secondary markets, however. (Prata, 2025)

Turkey also began a program in 2017, with a similar goal of India to reduce gold imports, but also as a way to integrate gold into their financial system. While Turkey has not officially ended their gold bond program, they have not offered any new issues since 2021. While these have been wonderful investments for those who got in pre and immediately post covid-19, do not expect any country to be offering a gold bond in the foreseeable future.

Countries like Malaysia and Indonesia have also entertained the idea of a gold bond, instead however they have issued gold backed sukuk. Sukuk are financial instruments that are structured to operate in accordance with Sharia law and are common in countries that have high Islamic populations. Restrictions to be sukuk include among other things, no burrowing or lending that causes either party to pay or receive interest, no involvement in business activities that include pornography, tobacco, alcohol and gambling. Sukuk must be backed by physical assets which can include real estate, commodities, businesses, equipment etc. Sukuk structures in comparison to traditional bonds puts the risk on both the issuer and the investor (Ross, 2025).

Sukuk are often securitized, though access in western economies is still limited because of differing securities laws. This is especially true in the US because as discussed above there are two regulating agencies, the SEC and CFTC, and many sukuk would fall under both jurisdictions. In the U.S. precious metals sukuk securities are not currently available, however SPSK is an ETF focused exclusively on sukuk for U.S. investors. AMAPX and WISEX are two mutual funds also on U.S. exchanges that hold sukuk. In general, these will perform similarly to fixed income securities but may offer less risk due to the sukuk structure. They fit in the international diversification of a portfolio, as such currency risk must be considered. Sukuk offer opportunities that fixed income investors will want to pay attention too, and while U.S. offerings are currently limited, that is changing. For those seeking individual issues, the Nasdaq Dubai offers the largest listing of sukuk securities. (Bennett, 2023)

Gold backed sukuk can be either issued by governments or corporations, usually banks, they are typically structured as trusts held by a special-purpose vehicle, and certificates are issued to the investors. While their function is similar to a bond, there is no interest earned or paid. A unique feature when compared to western ETFs is that they pay a dividend which is a combination of return of capital and money earned from leasing the underlying gold assets. Lessees of the gold are often large jewelry manufacturers seeking to stabilize their supply chain, bullion traders, or metal refineries. Storage expenses are paid by the issuer and are incorporated into their management fees. Currently Indonesia, Malysia, and Turkey have gold backed sukuk as well as several banks in the Persian Gulf region. It is not uncommon for issues only to be offered to institutions or accredited investors. (Tabarak, 2016; Muamalat Gold, 2025; Erkoyun, 2019)

In practical terms, gold backed sukuk can be a better investment than holding physical gold during periods of stagnant gold prices and helps mitigate losses in a decreasing gold environment due to the leasing and dividend features, but as a group sukuk are less responsive to inflation than direct investments in gold. (Simanjuntak et al., 2024)

Corporate Gold Bonds

Corporate gold bonds have not existed in the U.S. since the gold revaluation in 1934. Prior to that time gold was money, and some railroads and other issuers of corporate debt had gold redemption clauses written into the terms. Though sovereign, the Liberty Bonds issued during WWI were backed by the U.S. government and had provisions for gold redemption. Post 1934 U.S. based gold backed debt securities have not existed until recently, in 2020 Monetary Metals issued their first gold bond. They have since issued several funding businesses related to precious metals. They also offer gold lease and financing instruments. Their unique business model connects precious metal holders with industry related business offering a return for the metal owners while providing tax advantaged and non-dilutive financing options to industry. (Monetary Metals, 2025) It should be understood that these are private securities and regulations state that they may only solicit accredited and institutional investors (STC, 2022)

Summary

1- The primary advantage of ETFs or similar funds is that positions can be opened and closed both quickly and inexpensively.

2- Precious metal exchange traded securities are structured many different ways due to regulations and fund objectives. One should understand and be comfortable with the structure before trading/investing.

3- Several ETFs have options markets allowing for more sophisticated trading or risk management strategies.

4- Success with these securities requires understanding PM fundamentals (addressed in previous chapters) and then applying general trading skills which include charting and technical analysis.

5- Mutual funds are actively managed and generally more expensive. The capabilities of the fund manager determine if they under or outperform the sector. If investing in these funds research the managers by name.

6- Sukuk are common fixed income financial instruments in the Islamic world, precious metal backed versions exist and may soon be available to U.S. Investors.

7- In the U.S., Gold Backed Bonds existed prior to 1934 (when gold was money). The first domestic gold backed bond since then was issued in 2020 by Monetary Metals.

Disclosure:
I am an active trader of several of the funds listed and/or discussed in this chapter. I have not received compensation in any form from any of the listed funds/trusts in the preparation of this chapter. The ideas and opinions presented are my own and not on behalf of any fund or trust listed. This information is for educational use only and should not be understood or construed as a recommendation to buy or sell. All market participants are advised to do their own research.

Chapter 6: Precious Metal Securities: Part 2, Understanding Mining Stocks

Introduction

The other securities option, along with ETFs, is to trade mining stocks. As with ETFs, you can use limit orders, set stops, and use options strategies. As many of these companies are foreign what you may actually be trading is an American Depositary Receipt (ADR), which is a negotiable certificate issued by a U.S. depositary bank for a specified number (usually 1) of shares of a foreign company's stock. (TPB, 2020)

Mining companies offer a version of leveraged trading because they have reserves of unmined metal. An accounting of a publicly traded company's reserves is required to be available for investors. Often, these are in the 43-101 report for developing properties or in quarterly/semi-annual reports for larger and actively producing companies. As metal prices fluctuate, so does the value of their reserves. This fluctuation often exceeds the cost of mining the metal, which changes but generally stays in step with the true rate of inflation.

For example, company XYZ has a 5 million oz reserve of silver. The price of silver is $20, XYZ company has a breakeven point (cost of mining) that is $15/oz, the other five dollars is their profit. In this scenario, the reserves after mining expenses are subtracted represent $25 million in unrealized profits. Say the price of silver jumps to $30/oz. Now we have $75 million in unrealized profits. The valuation of the company is significantly more, and the share price may move significantly. This, of course, works in reverse also.

This fundamental, along with many of these companies being relatively small, has caused mining stocks to be one of the most volatile sectors in the share market. In my experience, only crypto surpasses. Volatility creates opportunity, which attracts a lot of traders hoping to make large gains. Generally speaking, to be successful in this space you will need to be a trader and not an investor. This requires effort, study, dedication, a stomach for volatility, and developing risk management skills. Accessing and trading mining companies is much more than just understanding the scenario above. It is an arena where some of the best traders participate, and you must understand once you step into it everyone is playing for keeps. The next section is to help you understand the dynamics of the mining industry, which will expedite your research efforts and help you develop trade ideas. For those already familiar with trading miners, this section is rather basic, but for novice to advanced traders new to this sector, you will find several useful definitions and clarifications.

Types of Miners

Within the industry, we generally refer to companies as being either majors or juniors. Majors, as you would expect, are the large companies. They often have several operating mines and employ hundreds to thousands of people. They are often multinational. Typically, their interest is mining/processing and most of their exploration activities are focused on expanding existing deposits already in or near production.

Juniors are small companies. Occasionally they may have a small operating mine or two, but for the most part these companies focus on exploration. They scour the earth looking for the next motherload. They tend to employ small teams of specialists and rely heavily on contractors and consultants. Their process usually involves evaluating dozens to hundreds of prospects. The most promising are advanced and receive more investment. Typically, these initial investments involve staking and land agreements, mapping, geochemical/geophysical studies, and drilling. The final product is data. If the team is successful, drilling will result in the discovery of mineralization.

At this point, the company will seek to again raise money for continued investment (more mapping, geochemical/geophysical surveys, metallurgical testing, and especially drilling). The goal is to find sufficient concentrations and volumes of metal along with developing a robust enough geologic model and mining/engineering/processing plan that the deposit can be built into an economically sustainable mine. Moving to the actual development phase usually requires the junior company to seek partnership with a major. Also, it is common for the junior to spin off a subsidiary company comprised only of the ready-to-be-developed asset (mineral deposit + data +

permits + mine plan) and sell it to a major. Often, such deals involve payment in both cash and stock and can make for good trade opportunities. To be successful, the junior company must be exceptional at both promotion and efficient use of capital for exploration. Even with simple permitting, deposits on average require 5 to 10 years of aggressive investment before becoming an operational mine.

The relationship between juniors and majors is symbiotic. Most majors no longer maintain large explorations teams; instead, they rely on juniors to consistently provide them with a selection of properties ready for development. This eliminates significant risk for the major as prospecting statistically is one of the least productive activities an individual or entity can engage in. It is quite comparable, in terms of both the capital and time required, to a pharmaceutical company developing a new drug.

To illustrate, I am often contracted by individuals or small companies to evaluate mining claims. This process usually involves a day or two of mapping, collecting samples for chemical analyses, observation of the mineralization, and a follow-up report detailing analytical results and recommendations. Literally only one in a million of these will ever become a mine. A thousand or so will reach various stages of exploration, often consuming several millions to tens of millions of dollars before the data demonstrate that it is not economic to mine. These properties are mothballed or sold, waiting for the time when commodity prices rise and/or technology improves enough to make them viable. Most major companies want no part of this. They specialize in mining. The successful junior is not only a good promoter but an expert in triage or, rather, knowing when to cut their losses and focus on the next deposit.

When trading, you need to know which companies are majors and which are juniors. Majors will be less volatile and are large enough you should never run into liquidity issues when trading. Many of these companies also pay dividends. Juniors, conversely, tend to be extremely volatile, often have poor liquidity (so when you want to sell it there may not be a buyer), and are prone to dilution as each time they raise money for exploration the company issues more shares. Some things juniors can do to make their stock more approachable to investors/traders include: hiring a market maker and providing them a large block of stock to trade with thus increasing liquidity, listing on a major exchange to gain access to more potential buyers, being prudent in their deployment of capital and timing of private placements to reduce dilution, keeping the number of shares outstanding within industry preferred norms, holding large reserves of stock to defend their share price and reduce risk of hostile take overs, having a committed group of key insiders and investors willing to buy at key levels maintaining a floor price, preparing regular press releases to keep investors engaged, and having a motivated investor relations manager. (Jones, 2025; Osterberg, 2025)

The sweet spot for many traders is finding companies that are somewhat between these two, maybe a junior with a couple of mines or a mine that has been spun off from a major. For these companies, volatility is tempered but not so much as to remove opportunity, and liquidity is adequate to ensure investors can trade in or out when desired.

Mine Logistics

In the first chapter we spent a lot of time discussing precious metal formation and distribution on earth. Hopefully, I succeeded in illustrating that metal deposits are quite variable; indeed, I would say each is unique both in chemistry, geometry, and (obviously) location. These variables dictate the logistics of exploring for and extracting ore. This all ultimately influences the cost of mining and contributes to how profitable a particular mine might be. Figures 6-1 and 6-2 illustrate geometrical differences of two mineral projects in the northern Nevada/southern Idaho region USA. The Marigold Mine near Valmy, Nevada is an extremely low-grade gold heap-leach operation. With relatively near-surface oxidized ore that is widely distributed, they use open pit methods, which involve moving huge amounts of material, literally mountains. (Figure 6-1) Open pit methods are usually only appropriate for near surface deposits and require large land packages for mine infrastructure, waste rock dumps, and heap leach pads. In general, open pit operations have large areas of disturbance. The equipment is huge, allowing these mine to move material more efficiently than any other hard rock mining method.

In contrast, the South Mountain project has an extremely narrow, steeply dipping, reduced ore rich in silver, zinc, gold, copper, and lead. (figure 6-2) Total metal concentrations are so high that they approach the stochiometric maximum for sulfide ores. In this case, they will need to use more expensive underground methods to extract their resource, however the higher ore grades (3 orders of magnitude greater than Marigold's) justify the expense. Underground mining is more expensive because more human labor, specialized equipment, and engineering is involved when mining and constructing tunnels. It also requires more effort and resources to be done safely. Conversely, some of the advantages of underground mining are significantly smaller surface disturbances and higher metal outputs with less milling infrastructure due in part to the high-grade nature of their ores. Underground operations can also develop significantly deeper targets, for example, Hecla's Lucky Friday mine sunk its deepest shaft to 9,587 ft, which for them is about 3000 ft. below sea level. (Els, 2016)

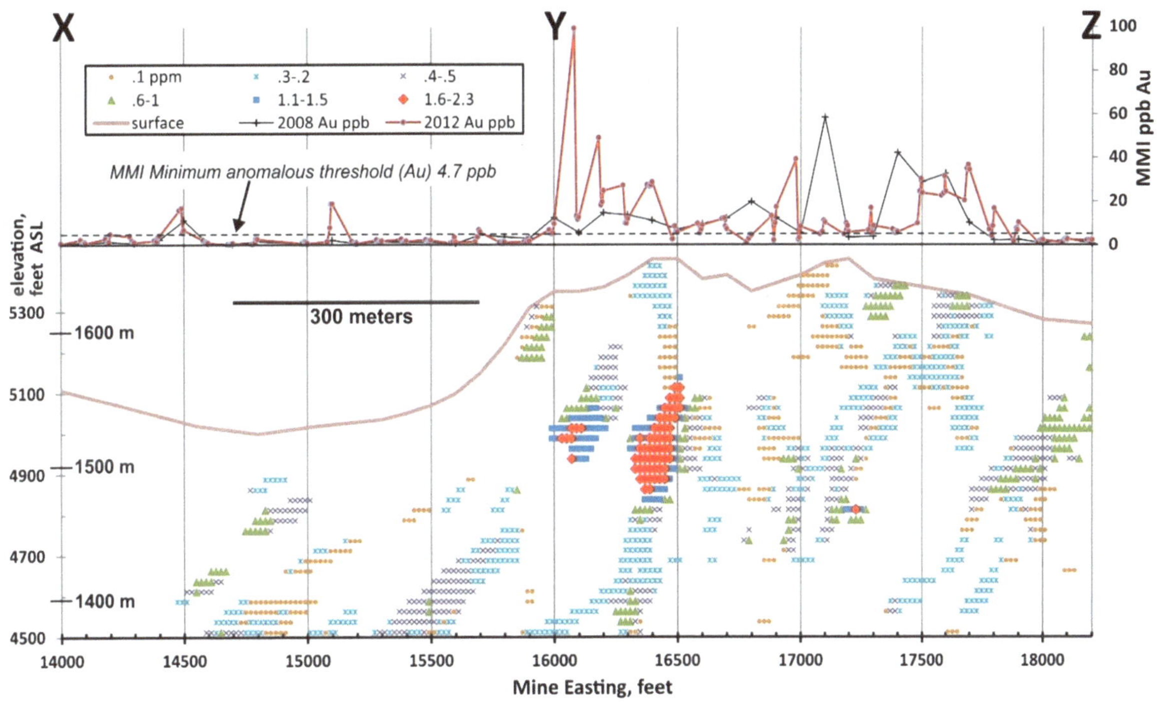

Figure 6-1: Marigold Mine (Valmy, NV) Block Model. *A section of the Marigold Mine's block model shows grade and distribution of ore in the subsurface. Brighter colors are higher grades, and blue colors are grades just above the break-even cost of mining. The solid gray line is the original surface topography. The line chart above the topography displays results from a geochemical survey used during the exploration phase of the project. This mine has oxidized (easy to process) ore, but it is low grade (0.2-0.003oz/t Au) and widely distributed. It is also relatively near surface. These attributes make it ideal for open-pit mining methods. Being located near Interstate-80 the logistics of building and operating the mine are relatively simple. (Forbush, 2016; SSR Mining, 2018)*

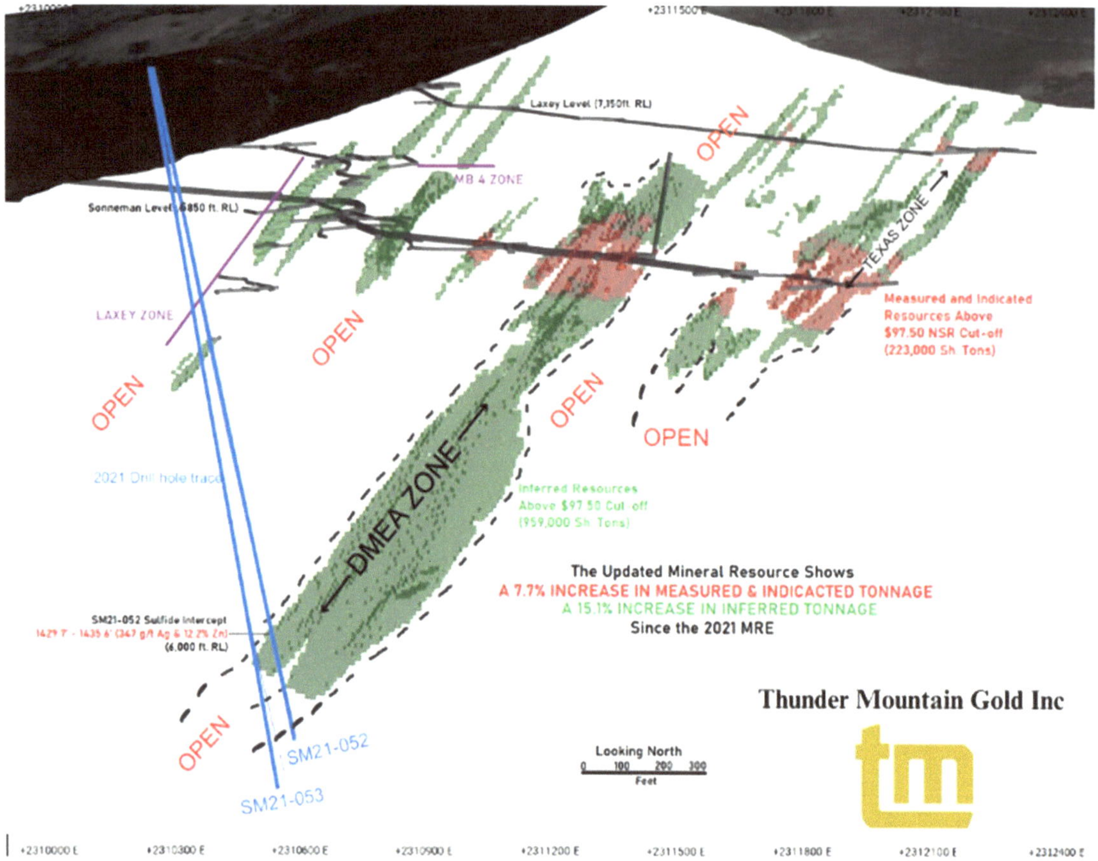

Figure 6-2: South Mountain Orebody, Idaho. *Green and red colors show tested and inferred ore grades. The wandering grayish brown horizontal lines are developed underground tunnels, and the blue/purple lines are the traces of two recent exploration drill holes. South Mountain is in a good mining jurisdiction, but its location is remote with extreme topography. It has a reduced (sulfide) high-grade (>14% Zn and 300g/ton Ag) silver, zinc, gold, copper, and lead ore. The orebodies themselves are narrow and steeply dipping. This deposit will need to be mined with underground methods (expensive), yet the high grade of the ore more than justifies the expense. (Jones, 2023)*

Not A Pure Metals Play

One will find difficulty trying to trade mining companies based strictly on movements in the prices of precious metals. You have to remember that these are companies that produce and explore for commodities, not commodities themselves.

Firstly, understand that many mines produce more than one metal. Remember back to the first chapter, Earth does a good job concentrating metal into an acidic fluid. The particular mix and what happens to that fluid ultimately determines the type of deposit. There are some circumstances that cause metals to come out sequentially and other reactions that cause them to come out together. Any of you who took an inorganic chemistry lab as part of your general curriculum in college have experienced this at a basic level. In the labs for such courses, we learn how to precipitate minerals out of a solution by adding different chemicals. Some chemicals will only allow one or two minerals to precipitate, while others will cause them all to drop out. The formation of a mineral deposit is usually just a messier, higher temperature, uncontrolled, and huge version of this. Additionally, complex geological structures often influence deposit formation and geometry. Often when the minerals precipitate, there is a certain degree of zonation within the deposit (more on this shortly).

Deposits that produce several minerals can be good from an economic position because they are diversified by nature. Precious metals and base metals (copper, lead, zinc, nickel, tin, aluminum) usually follow different economic cycles. For a multi-metallic mine, it is often easier to stay in business, because when base metals are down in price often precious metals are up. The flip side of this is that the more metals a mine has the more complicated (expensive) the milling and refining processes will be. In most cases, not all of the metals can be recovered economically.

Many major companies will intentionally add mines of different commodities to their portfolios simply for balance and diversification. In fact, unlike past decades, very few companies are strictly single commodity producers. Sometimes this is simply because the deposit(s) they are mining have a degree of zonation, so the mix of metals they are producing may change as their mine expands/matures. Often, there are company mergers or spin-offs that change the asset mix, in addition to mines these can include things like power plants, gas stations, trucking companies, and real estate; all assets that companies acquired as they attempted to vertically or horizontally integrate. (Chase, 2025) Consolidation in the mining industry has been like the trend observed in other sectors. The number of commodities and ratios both being produced and in reserves will influence valuations.

It is cumbersome to constantly keep track of all the changes within several companies. Regarding reserves and deposit aspects, it is often easier to focus on learning the different producing mines. Many of these will be in production for 20 to 100 years. Then, all you must do is keep track of who owns it, which may change every 5 to 10 years, and understand how it fits into a company's portfolio.

Shouldn't higher commodity prices result in higher profits?

In theory the answer to this question is yes, but the reality is that it depends. Again, remember these are companies that produce commodities and not the commodities themselves. The metals in most cases also must be physically mined out of the earth and then chemically extracted from the rock. The process takes time, and there are constraints depending on the local infrastructure and engineering. Also, the mine may have some flexibility in how it develops its resource thus, logistic, strategic, and timing variables are at play. For example, a company may in times of high metal prices choose to process lower grade ore. The higher prices make it economical to process this lower grade material now, although not very profitable. If prices fall, the mine now only processes the higher-grade ore, and with average prices they might blend the two together. This situation increases cash flow and extends the mine life but does not necessarily increase profits. It is good for both the company and environment, as extending the mine life means more resource is ultimately extracted from the site, meaning less disturbance elsewhere. It also provides the company with more time to get new/replacement mines online and provides more stability for the workforce and the local economy. As the permitting process seems to get longer, prudent companies try to expand existing mines until additional properties in the portfolio come online.

Conversely, if it works with the mine plan, companies may increase their production in times of rising commodities to capture higher prices. This better-than-expected return often provides the company with additional working capital. Being in tune with a company's production strategy can help traders predict which companies will respond the most or the least to significant movements in commodity prices.

Miner Specific Risks

There are some specific risks to keep in mind that will affect the success of miners. This is a very high input and high output industry with very little margin. Price changes of consumables can have large effects.

For example, in open-pit gold mining, depending on the specific methods used, the largest material expenses are mill media, fuel and oils, ammonium nitrate (blasting agent), rubber (tires), and cyanide (leaching agent). Interestingly, the latter three can make for good auxiliary trades as periods of increased mining may put significant pressure on the demand of these products both locally and regionally.

Labor: The workforce can be a risk, especially when either company or miner union expectations become unrealistic. This was recently demonstrated in the 2 ½ year long strike of union members at Hecla's Lucky Friday mine in north Idaho. (Edelen, 2020)

The technical professionals (geologists and engineers) in this sector are highly specialized, relatively few in number, and often direct multi-million-dollar budgets. "Busts" in the business cycle will cause many to change companies or even leave the industry. While some of these professionals return during the booms, the attrition rate makes it difficult for companies to expand when they need to the most, thus adding to late cycle inefficiency of capital that is often observed in the sector. The most extreme example of these professionals is the exploration geologist. A recent AI search suggests there are about 800 people in the U.S. out of a total population of 355 million capable of performing this job. Out of the 800 capable, AI estimates <500 are active in this role and only 3 or so U.S. universities offer comprehensive programs. The pool is limited by individuals needing to meet a plethora of criteria, including exceptional understanding of spatial relationships and pattern recognition, which usually requires a minimum IQ of 120, this needs to be coupled with an individual in excellent health with full use of all limbs and no color blindness. Training includes a B.S. in geology which is heavy in chemistry, physics, mathematics, and GIS and then a specialized master's level education including advance mineralogy, geology, and additional chemistry or physics. Most will be required to act as field managers of exploration programs, requiring management, budgeting, reporting and, advanced technical writing skills. In addition to all these many have several practical skills which could include intermediate level auto mechanics, carpentry, electrical, and welding capabilities, this self-sufficiency is a valuable asset when remote projects make vendor access impractical. Finally, a high degree of metal resiliency is required, as the lifestyle often includes months a year away from home living in remote areas. (Grok 3, 2025a) All this together one could describe them as astronauts who prefer to stay on Earth. While they don't get celebrity like astronauts, the reality is minerals exploration geologists have among the highest leverage potential of all occupations. Not many of these people are needed so not many are made, but ideas that lead to the discovery of new deposits and mines can ultimately be worth billions. Not surprisingly, companies that develop and retain talent (especially during the busts) are able to capitalize the most during the booms.

A final consideration is the integration of these companies with AI and how it will affect them. At the corporate level it will have similar trends to other office settings, at the business or development level, it is more complicated. As with many other industries, companies are scrambling to find ways to replace their employed intelligence with artificial ones. However, when asked, the AI themselves suggest that augmentation rather than replacement by AI is the best approach for many of these roles within the industry. Considering the exploration geologist again, Grok 3 provided one key reason they could not be replaced *"Human Intuition: Geology blends science and art. Experienced geologists "read" landscapes in ways AI can't replicate, like spotting a subtle vein exposure or intuiting structural controls from field cues."* (Grok 3, 2025b)

For investors, I would pay attention to how a company is using AI. If they are using it to augment professionals by increasing their ability to quickly acquire, plot, condition, search, store, or reference data these would be cost saving and efficiency improving methods that should be encouraged. Improving automation with AI in high-risk tasks, like many of those that exist in the mining & milling process, would also be encouraged. Companies trying to replace interpretive tasks in the data collection and review process will be putting themselves at risk of missing or misunderstanding data while also wasting money on expensive systems.

Remember while some deposits share certain characteristics, each ore body is unique. Contrast this to the medical field. There are two variations of the human body, male and female, and we have several billions of specimens to reference and at all stages of development. Conversely, 4 to 6 thousand major metallic deposits have been mined in human history, and they exhibit a high degree of variability. Thus, it is infinitely easier to build an AI that helps doctors vs miners. Those developing an AI for mining/exploration will spend a lot of money on development for a niche clientele with diverse needs. There are only about 125 majors and possibly up to 1000 mid-level companies globally that could be considered potential clients.

Jurisdiction and regulation: A significant risk that all deposits share to varying degrees. In the US, you must conform to federal and state environmental and health & safety regulations, no matter the type of land that is mined. Mining processes and methods used can require several permits before development can start. After that, an operator's level of regulation depends on the type of ground being developed. The eight most common jurisdiction scenarios are:

1: Private Land: You can pretty much do what you want, how you want, with general environmental restrictions.

2: Tribal Land: Basically, the tribe has the ultimate say. Some will run you off, while others welcome you with open arms. Often, they require a certain percentage of workers to be tribe members and are entitled to royalties, both of which help their local economies. This is not to say the inner financial and political workings of the tribe are not a risk. We are seeing this today with Kinross's Mahn Choh project in Central Alaska. (Parshley, 2023)

3: State Land: Mining on state lands is often complicated by political issues. Some states do not want mining within their borders; others see it as an opportunity to develop their economy. Instead of claim blocks of defined size, used for federal lands, state lands are usually secured for exploration and mining pursuits through lease agreements between the mining company and applicable state agency for the parcel of interest. State lands are entitled to royalties (5% is common), lease revenue and royalties are often used to fund education or state health initiatives. Some states are willing to sell or exchange parcels for land or other property if agreements can be made which benefit their objectives. Mines tend to create higher than average paying jobs, which many communities welcome. In some cases, communities try to protect jobs through local labor agreements. In theory, states could also protect jobs by requiring a percentage of mine employees to be residents, so long as the agreement does not violate interstate commerce laws.

4 & 5: Federally Controlled Land: Two agencies, the Bureau of Land Management (BLM) and the U.S. Forest Service (USFS) are the two primary entities encountered.

BLM:

Of these, the BLM is usually the easier to work with. The BLM requires operators to have and maintain mineral claims with assessments and costs that are collected annually. Lode claims (hard rock mining) are 1500-ft x 600-ft. A large mine may require several hundred to over a thousand claims, and at $225 per claim per year the costs can add up. (BLM.gov, 2022) The regulator, who must approve the development plan, may or may not approve certain areas, depending on the level of risk to wildlife or cultural resources. There is a bonding process to ensure reclamation is completed even if the company goes bankrupt. This adds expense to the company but protects the public.

USFS:

The USFS tends to be much more political than the BLM and is, therefore, more difficult to work with. The USFS often requires additional studies are conducted, some of which they perform themselves and others that operators will pay 3rd party vendors to execute.

Ultimately, minerals fall under jurisdiction of the BLM, so it becomes an interagency deal, where first the Forest Service authorizes and then the BLM manages claims, assessments, and receiving payments. (US Forrest Service, 2022) The same or similar bonding process is used on USFS lands.

6: Water Resource Agencies: Mines and exploration projects are obligated to work with federal and state water resource agencies to the extent their operations effect surface water ways and ground water. On federal grounds, this usually involves both the Army Corps of Engineers and the State's water resource agency.

7: Foreign jurisdictions: If operating outside of the United States, most western countries have requirements and processes like those of the U.S. and Canada regarding environmental protections, though regulation specifics, fees, and royalties can be quite different. Typically, third-world countries have minimal environmental and regulatory oversite. Projects usually can be developed quickly. The tradeoff is often stability. Mine lives can typically range between 20 and 100 years. Over that time frame risks can include increased taxation, political changes, nationalization of mines, and cartel activity cutting into profits. All are real and, if trading mining companies, you need to understand which are applicable.

8: Private Surface and Federal Minerals: in this scenario surface rights and minerals rights are separated. Those wanting minerals rights will need to establish an access agreement with the surface owner. While the surface owner has say in the agreement, they must ultimately agree to it, they cannot deny access to mineral rights holders. Once an agreement is in place, those seeking minerals rights have 30 days to stake claims. These are managed by the BLM and claim block sizes and fees are the same as on other federal lands. However, the number of claims that can be staked at once is limited to a portion of the parcel, which protects the surface owner. If more claims are desired, a waiting period must pass before more claims are filed and staked. Similar regulation and land disturbance rules apply. This can get complicated when large tracks of land is acquired with multiple surface rights holders as separate agreements will need to be in place with each one.

There are also different structures the government uses to collect fees on different commodities. In the U.S., most minerals fall under the claims system; however, some, such as phosphate, are managed under a lease system similar to what we see in the oil and gas industry.

Commonly, a large mine will have lands in two or more jurisdictions, each with its own degree of management and, therefore, risk. Depending on the location this can present difficulties. For example, a mine that is seeking to expand may have desired timetables, but the regulator timetables are often quite different than those of mine planners. Also, technical people in government will have significantly different experience from their counterparts in industry. Often the two are out of sync with practicalities relating to project logistics/advancement and steps required to navigate the agency's bureaucracy. Permit fees themselves are generally low, but the time spent by employees, consultants, and contractors adapting the permit to something that works for their project, while appeasing the regulators, is usually about 100 to 1000x the permit fee. It is not uncommon to have an exploration project in a jurisdiction without any operating mines. This results in an (unfortunately common) situation where the regulator is completely ignorant of the industry they are to regulate. The cost of the regulator's learning curve becomes the operator's expense. The best companies start working on permitting details years in advance to resolve issues before they become significant risks.

Recently, the U.S. Supreme Court overturned the *Chevron Doctrine*, which gave federal agencies power to interpret ambiguous laws within their jurisdiction. Doing so removes potential political and government bias by these agencies (an extension of the executive branch), which were effectively creating and modifying laws to which industry was forced to comply. The ruling removes this power from federal agencies and puts it back in the courts (judicial branch). (Howe, 2024) While this ruling will affect every industry in the U.S., with regards to the mining industry I anticipate a tumultuous few years for companies seeking federal permits as adjustments are made from the current system. In the long run, I expect this to streamline permitting, but in the short term it will require more involvement by the circuit courts, who will have to lean heavily on consulting expertise in regard to how science fits with local environmental needs and balance that with industry and economic concerns. This will cause delays. The outgoing system relied on experts within the federal agencies who in theory would be fair regulators. Unfortunately, this system in the U.S. became highly politicized, and the bureaucracy has grown enough to separate regulators from, in many cases, even basic understanding of the companies and processes they are to regulate. While hopefully this change will lead to better defined mining laws and more consistent regulation, the reality is most mining projects have several unique aspects, and many laws may need to be site specific.

Regulation aside, assuming a mine gets into production calculating and keeping track of what was mined in each block, in each jurisdiction, and determining the final grade, recovery, price realized, royalty agreements, and who get what cut of it can get quite involved on projects with complicated land packages. While the expense and complication involved with projects of complex jurisdiction can be hard to estimate, investors should at least have an idea of what the jurisdictions are, and the potential complications and risks involved. Sometimes it will feel like to much, and in those scenarios, it is ok to move to something else.

Management risk: While not unique to the minerals industry, it does present its own flavor. Finding the right leadership for mining companies is difficult. These entities need people who understand both the technical and business aspects of the industry. Most professionals working their way up the ranks will be scientists and engineers. Despite being exceptional technical people, they often are not great business people. They spent all their time in school attending math and science classes, and at work their career involved solving technical problems. Taxation and capex expenditure management are not necessarily their forte. However, strait finance people are usually worse and have historically made some horrific blunders, because they didn't understand the technical side enough. Again, margins in this space are much smaller than other sectors, and it is harder to make up for mistakes. Ideally, you will have a CEO and board of directors with broad and complimentary experience from within the sector. A C-suit that includes an engineer, geologist, legal professional, and business management/accounting/finance professional usually makes a good mix. Make sure you have a board that does something meaningful. Many companies have board members that collect hefty checks but work two days a year. They know how to "mine investors." There needs to be at least one geologist with significant exploration experience. Ultimately, they control the targets where capital is deployed. This needs to be a person with a good track record.

For operating companies, you want the company to run the mine(s) as a business, and not necessarily do what the market wants them to do. Corporate executives who do things that deviate from the business model and mine plan to boost share prices (and their compensation) usually set their company up for an unfavorable buyout in the next down cycle. (Desjardins, 2015) In contrast, junior companies without an income stream will have to make decisions and be flexible with their business plan based on market sentiment in order to raise money. This is ok if it is done ethically, and you as the investor/trader are aware of the companies goals and objectives.

Hedging Risk: Any company that produces a commodity as a product can potentially improve or hurt its business by trading futures. Selling contracts of product to be delivered at specified times at set prices can help stabilize the cash flow of a company. However, if commodity prices drastically outpace the futures contract, not only is the company realizing less profit, but it is required to use more of its capital to meet margin requirements. Ashanti Goldfields was an excellent example of how hedging can go horribly wrong. Be aware that companies with no hedging will probably experience more volatility as commodity prices fluctuate, this may also create trade opportunities. Fluctuating prices will force these companies to modify their business model to deal with the volatility, which is not necessarily a bad thing. Companies that exercise conservative hedging, i.e. limited amounts of leverage over their resource and contracts of usually no longer than a year, can experience greater profitability because of increased cash flow stability. Shorter-term contracts still allow profits to adjust with the markets but softens the move either up or down. This means the company will still need to adjust to current market conditions, but short-term swings are less impactful. If managed well, stability leads to profitability, which fosters growth and the opportunity to buy out weaker companies struggling with the cycle. (Brewster, 2017)

Deposit risk: Most prospects will never become a mine. Usually, this is because some aspect of the deposit makes its development uneconomic. Maybe it's the size or grade or that it requires more expensive mining/processing techniques. For example, I was consulting on a project some years ago. It was an oxide copper prospect with good grades in a good jurisdiction. The plan was to leach the copper out of the mined rock using a solution of sulfuric acid, which is a common practice for this kind of material. (Habbache et al., 2009) My investigations of the property, however, found some areas had an extreme abundance of the mineral fluorite. This presented a potential problem.

Leach pads are carefully designed. They need to be permeable but not so permeable that the solution just runs through. Engineers and metallurgists want to make sure the solution has adequate interaction with the mined material, which is usually crushed to a specific size to facilitate optimal leaching of the metal. Sulfuric acid is a liquid with the formula H_2SO_4, fluorite is a solid composed of CaF_2. When the two are combined the sulfuric acid dissolves the fluorite and precipitates a different mineral, gypsum ($CaSO_4$). The remaining solution is now hydrofluoric acid (HF). Even though HF sounds bad, it is the lesser of the two risks. The greater concern is that precipitating gypsum has the potential to plug the leach pad, similar to hard water deposits in pipes, which drastically reduces copper recovery. The HF could raise the acidity of the system enough to kill off natural bacteria living in the leach pad. This would also reduce recovery as these bacteria aid significantly in the leaching process. It is also probable that HF would interact with silicate minerals, creating a siliceous ooze exacerbating the blockage problem caused by the gypsum. Even ignoring blockage issues in the leach pad, all these extra reactions will increase consumption of sulfuric acid by 10x, raising the operating expense. (Forbush, 2024; Keane, 2015)

To the point, this deposit had a newly identified risk. Studies would need to be done to determine the level of risk and if there were mining and/or engineering controls that could remove the risk. In my example, the likelihood of finding engineering controls was highly probable, but it would require time and additional investment to determine. (Forbush, 2024) Every deposit will have its own degree of risk. Some are just milder than others.

Product Risk: The end product from a mine and the potential cost of further refinement is of concern. Mines produce a range of products from 1000 oz doré bars to floatation concentrates. Some mines even have multiple products. The closer the end product is to its retail or industrial form, the less the operation is dependent on further shipping or refining services. Typically, the refinery/smelter purchases the product directly from the mine, then sells the refined product to manufacturers. Depending on the purity plus or minus other metals, a refiner may apply credits/discounts to the purchased product. If there are few or no other smelters nearby for the refiner to compete with, this arrangement is usually more favorable for the refiner. Refining is its own science, and given the variability in concentrate products, most smelters can only process a set range of material. Because of this, and the relatively small number of smelters globally, it is not uncommon for a mine to ship its concentrate overseas. A refiner typically pays credits for gold and silver, but discounts are applied depending on the concentration of other metals. Payments received from the refiner are called the Net Smelter Return, and account for the credits and discounts. Usually this is about 85-95% of the gross metal value. (Blakely, 2021) It is a standard procedure for mines to perform additional analytical work on batches of concentrate shipped to the refiner. This helps mitigate the risk of the refiner "cheating", which has historically been a concern. Figure 6-3 is a map showing copper smelter distribution globally. A significant amount of gold and silver production is a byproduct of copper mining. Given the low number of copper smelters in North America, it is easy to imagine potential logistical and processing risks associated with ore concentrates. On a national level, even if a country has sufficient mining for its metal needs, that doesn't remove potential geopolitical and security risks if it does not have the infrastructure to process it. Even large countries like the U.S., Russia, and China have significant gaps of some of their most important mineral supply chains. China has been proactive in filling its gaps through their Belt and Road initiative focusing heavily on Africa. Russia generally has sufficient resources but lacks advanced refining and downstream techniques required for several of them to be integrated into domestic production. Their efforts are focused on partnerships to help develop these capabilities. Sadly, the U.S. is in a bit of an identity crisis. Some rare earth and critical minerals will require trade deals to acquire, but many could be mined and produced domestically. This would require fast tracking projects and easing regulations to allow these mines and refining facilities to operate domestically, which is in direct conflict politically for many. (Farooki, 2018; Roy, 2025; Holland, 2023) Understanding this does help the geopolitics make sense though.

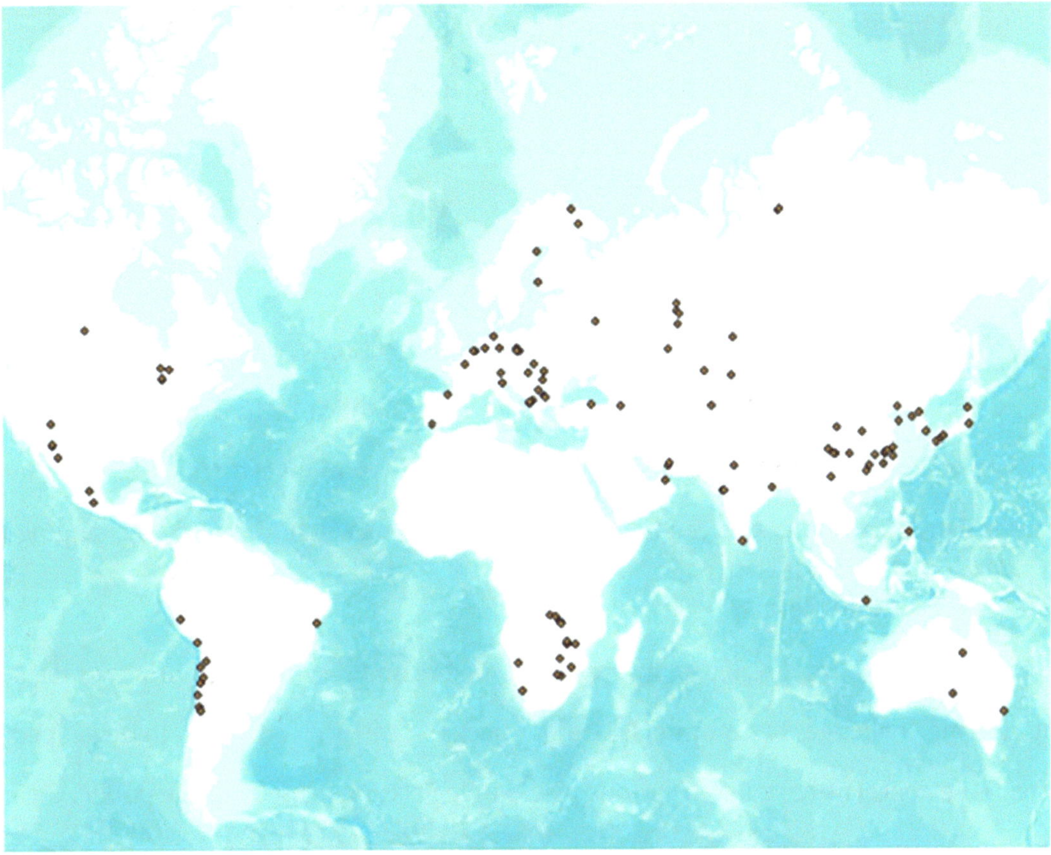

Figure 6-3: World Copper Smelters Location Map. *A significant amount of gold and silver production is a byproduct of copper mining. Refining copper ore concentrates has several risks for the mining companies: 1- they may need to ship overseas to a refiner with the ability to process their ore, 2- are at the mercy of the smelters contract, 3- may become subject to geopolitical risk if shipping concentrates out of country. Most smelters are located in Asia, with the majority under Chinese control. North America and western Europe have been decreasing their smelter capacity for decades over environmental concerns. The often-unmentioned trade off of this is the added geopolitical risk of being forced to process domestic mining production abroad. (Map: Torres, 2003)*

The Phoenix mine near Battle Mountain, NV is a good example of how a company can adapt to mitigate risk and increase revenue regarding ore processing. Phoenix has a mixed-commodity ore that contains gold, silver, copper, lead, plus some zinc, molybdenum, and other metals. The ore is also in two oxidation states, oxide (leachable) and sulfide (requires separation by floatation to create a concentrate). For many years they exclusively focused on the sulfide and shipped out a concentrate. The sulfide concentrate is where their precious metal production reports to. Instead of wasting the oxide ore, years later Phoenix installed a solvent extraction/ electrowinning (SX/EW) plant and leach pad to handle the copper oxide. With this system they electroplate >99% purity copper plates that they ship directly to manufacturers. (Coplan, 2013,

House, 2018) While they still ship out sulfide concentrate, they effectively removed product risk on a portion of their production by installing a process that allows them to produce a direct to market product.

As with all things there is a tradeoff, mills are designed and optimized for when production begins. Often market conditions and ore grade/content change over time which creates risk/opportunity as we see with Phoenix. Other times, production slows, or deposits are completely mined out. In these situations, companies seek to solicit or fund projects that will provide their milling facilities with sufficient ore to process. As an investor/trader, being familiar with a mine's products/processes can help you forecast how it will be affected by changing market conditions.

Legacy Risk: Legacy risk usually applies to majors and deals with environmental, safety, and engineering challenges of decommissioned projects. In the post WWII era in developed countries these concerns have led to various pieces of legislation protecting the public. Cleaning up messes is expensive. Even for large responsible companies, if they have too many legacy projects in their portfolio, required ongoing mitigation efforts can be a significant drag on profits.

Companies are required to have decommissioning/ reclamation plans in place in most developed jurisdictions before mine construction can begin. In the U.S., there is a bonding process for development on public ground. If a company goes bankrupt, the regulator will use surety bonds that the company purchased and continued to pay premiums on to fund reclamation activities. Estimating the scope and cost of reclamation and purchasing the bonds is a significant portion of the permitting process.

An example of this in action is the Black Pine Mine in southern Idaho. When Pegasus Gold Corp filed for bankruptcy in 1998, it was already planning on shutting down its Black Pine gold mine. Without the funds to either continue mining or reclaim, the U.S. Forest Service pulled the surety bonds and reclaimed the property. The property has since been restaked with claims by a new operator, and with today's significantly higher gold prices they have expanded the resource. Black pine is currently undergoing predevelopment and permitting work. (Rodney et al., 2023)

Sometimes, a company may invest in a historic property with significant legacy risk if there is a justifiable resource. Further development can generate the funds needed to later reclaim the property properly. Such instances can be considered a "win-win" for both the mining company and the public. The Stibnite Project, another Idaho property, is an example of this, where the mining company hopes to restore a fishery that was destroyed through antimony mining prior to WWII. (Zimmerman, 2021)

Debt and Financing Risk: This, again, is not exclusive to mining companies but can get a little more involved, depending on how the mine chose to finance its operations. The next topic regarding royalty and streaming companies will help readers understand how this can work. As with any company, you want to make sure the levels of debt are reasonable and serviceable before investing.

National Instrument 43-101 *Standards of Disclosure for Mineral Product*

"A gold mine is a hole in the ground with a liar at the top." *- Mark Twain*

"I want maps that make people greedy!" *-Undisclosed Mineral Development CEO*

The minerals industry traditionally has a reputation for being unscrupulous, funny enough, the second quote I heard just recently on a project call. The National Instrument 43-101 is a Canadian securities law that governs how companies disclose information regarding their properties. It was enacted in the wake of the industry rocking Bre-X Minerals scandal (1997) to prevent companies from defrauding investors. As its requirements are thorough, and a disproportionately large number of mining companies are Canadian, it has become a global standard. (Rawluk, 2023) The U.S. equivalent is SEC regulation S K 1300 which replaced the Industry Guide 7 (IG7) in 2021. These requirements include standardized technical reports prepared by "qualified person(s) (QP)" which disclose all material technical details related to a mineral property and its development. These reports are appended to a company's Form 10K which is filed annually. (Oommen, 2020) The QP must hold applicable technical, ethical, and regulatory certifications. They are responsible for making sure technical information is reported accurately and in a manner that won't mislead investors. Large projects will have several QPs with differing areas of expertise i.e. engineering, geology, environmental science etc. ensuring that projects are using industry best practices. You will see their names attached to these technical reports and press releases that disclose technical information.

As an investor/trader these technical reports will save a lot of time assessing risks related to the investment, as they detail results from feasibility studies conducted for a mine or mineral property. They can usually be found for download on a company's website.

Royalty & Streaming Companies

Royalty and streaming companies represent the final group of stocks. These are not mining companies, rather they are the financiers of mining companies. Most traditional banks do not have the expertise or desire to finance mines, thus cash rich groups with the expertise have moved into this niche. In both cases they provide upfront non-dilutive capital to advance projects.

A royalty company has an interesting business model. Instead of receiving interest on deployed capital, they are entitled to a percentage of revenue generated by the mine. This is accommodative to the mining company, as payments do not start until production starts. It can get pricy though, because depending on the agreement, the royalty company may get royalties for the life of the mine. If the mine expands, makes new discoveries, or if commodity prices rise, this can sweeten the deal for the royalty company. There is risk, however, that a mine could shut down for environmental or political reasons. Low commodity prices could minimize returns or make the mine uneconomic so that it is temporarily or permanently shut down. Given that each mine is unique in engineering and risk, contracts are heavily negotiated. In a very real sense, the royalty company is invested in their projects. The prudent investor will understand, at least at a basic level, the terms of contracts and use that as part of their risking calculus. (INN, 2021)

A streaming company operates similarly, but they take their payment in the form of a commodity. Often it is an agreement that gives the company an option to buy up to a certain percentage of a commodity produced at a significantly reduced rate, such as 70% below spot. The streaming company then sells this on the open market for their profit. For some mines, often those that have biproduct metals, this can be beneficial, as it provides a market for their biproducts. The way agreements are structured gives the streamer significant upside potential but limited downside risk. If they have an option to buy 25% of a mine's silver production at $5/oz and the spot price is $20, they are making money, but if spot prices jump to $30/oz they can still buy it for $5. If the price falls to $7 or even below $5, they have no obligation to buy. (INN, 2021)

Many royalty and streaming companies have low overhead, and their staff are small teams of engineers, geologists, and various financial professionals. These companies can offer good exposure to precious metals, but understand that some have diversified into other commodities, for instance oil and gas is common. They tend to be less volatile than miner's stocks and often pay dividends. Since most miners have projects financed through royalty companies, those agreements can influence share prices of both companies, as often significant portions of future reserves are optionable by the royalty company.

Mining Industry ETFs & ETNs

Several funds have been created targeting the mining sector. These funds are different from those discussed in the previous chapter which invest in precious metal commodities. These funds invest <u>in companies</u> whose businesses are tied to the exploration, production, refining, recycling, or selling of precious metals. Funds take two forms, Exchange Traded Funds (ETFs) and Exchange Traded Notes (ETNs) and while they trade similarly there are important structural differences. Both types focus on a number of subsectors; in some cases, the sponsoring firm creates an index of companies that fit their defined profile, other funds may use an already established index like the *NYSE Arca Gold Miners Index* or the *MSCI World Metals & Mining* Index. With ETFs, securities that comprise the index are purchased by the fund in proportional quantities as the fund attempts to track the performance of the index. An ETF is set up as its own entity separate from the issuing investment bank. The key is there are assets in the fund backing the share price which may or may not accurately track the index. Accurately tracking a niche index such as junior gold miners can be a difficult task for a fund. In contrast, the ETN is a contract based on the value of the index, meaning no tracking risk, but it also means there are no direct assets held as backing. In the case of liquidation, an ETF has assets that can be divided, while holders of an ETN are subject to the issuer's credit risk and must file claims against the issuer's general account. For short-term traders these risks are often not significant, but for long-term holders they could be. ETNs do have more favorable tax treatment, being contracts they receive capital gains rates. (Doak, 2023; McClay, 2023)

Targeted ETFs available for the precious metal sector offer limited diversification, an advantage is that the volatility is lower with less risk than single stock positions. As most of the companies held in such ETFs are foreign entities, foreign exchange risk applies. A rising U.S. dollar is hard on both equities and commodities, but when the equities are denominated in foreign currency that is also underperforming the U.S. dollar this can amplify headwinds. These securities are well suited for the investors trying to catch a general trend in the market. Those who don't want to spend as much time researching individual companies and who want to avoid concentrated exposure will gravitate to mining ETF/ETNs. Most of these securities will have associated option markets. Buying into ETFs in appropriate quantities that have option markets can be helpful, if you find yourself needing to play defensive. Those willing to do more research and who have sufficient capital will often forgo exchange traded products (ETPs) and build their own portfolio of 2 to 5 miners they think will do best, employing options strategies as a hedge.

Some ETPs are leveraged and can be either long or short biased. Funds that create these ETPs try to target 2x or 3x price movements. This leverage is achieved through a combination of futures and options contracts. These have some unique risks, one being that given a specific point in time, it may not move in accordance with the index it is meant to track. This movement is dependent on the specifics of the underlying contracts, which are not reported. Also, such funds are subject to "decay" or tend to lose value through time due to expense and leveraging inefficiencies. They are popular instruments for taking advantage of short-term price movements. They offer leverage, but not too the degree of directly traded options. With good timing, sellers of option contracts for these securities can also do well. Another strategy employed with these is to short them during flat or mildly declining market cycles, and profit as the decay of the underlying contracts pulls the share price down. In such instances a trader could also choose to hedge their position with a protective option contract. These are generally for experienced traders with shorter holding periods.

Bonds

Bonds are less common in the mineral sector than others due to the unique risks and valuation challenges mining projects possess, things which most banks have no appetite for. That said several of the well-established majors do have bonds that trade in the markets. When available a bond can be a good addition to an income generating portfolio. A company with several operating mines and a mix of precious and base metal products will be well prepared to handle an array of market cycles. Because of the difficulty lenders have in assigning risk to mines, the mining company often receives less favorable terms than other sectors simply because the lenders don't understand the business as well. This often results in higher-than-average coupon payments and creates opportunities for informed investors. As discussed before, most mining stocks need to be traded to make money. Conversely, good bond issues can be held, thus it is not uncommon for investors holding mining company bonds to experience better returns than long-term stockholders of the same companies.

When purchasing bonds pay attention to the yield to maturity (YTM) metric. This informs you of the total percentage return you will receive if you hold the bond until maturity expressed by year. For example, a bond may have 5 years left to maturity and an 8% coupon but a YTM of 6%. This means that the bond is trading at a premium to its issue rate, as a result your gain will be 6% a year instead of 8%. Bonds are interest rate sensitive, when interest rates go down bond prices go up as investors are willing to pay more for higher coupon rates. In turn, when interest rates go up bond prices will fall as they must compete with new issues that have higher coupon rates. Bonds may be callable, meaning the company can pay it off early, and are first in line, ahead of stockholders in the event of liquidation. (STC, 2022)

Personally, I like to find bonds with YTM rates that meet my objective with shorter maturities, say 2-7 years and trying to purchase longer maturities at interest rate highs. The reason is I do not want to sell before maturity, as a change in interest rates could negatively impact the return in this scenario. If the bond reaches maturity, I have received the return I was planning on. A retiree who buys a 30-year bond will most likely need to liquidate the bond before its maturity exposing themselves to interest rate risk. Maybe laddered 2 to 5-year bonds would be more appropriate, with additional purchases influenced by the capital needs of the individual and overall portfolio performance. For me, bonds are part of an income portfolio strategy.

Insurance companies usually hold their bonds to maturity also using laddering strategies to eliminate interest rate and claims risk. These companies often have longer time horizons than individuals and can safely purchase longer maturity products. It is not riskless for them; however, a series of high claim experience years could force them to liquidate their bonds early and they would be at the mercy of the current market conditions.

Traders may take a different approach, trading the bonds based on what they expect interest rates to do, and profiting from the price changes. This can work well as the higher coupon rates of these companies often translate to larger than average spreads in the bond prices.

Preferred Stocks

Preferred stocks are a type of hybrid security with features similar to both common stock and bonds. They are a common but often overlooked security by retail investors. In essence, they are debt instruments, and their features can make them good financing options for established miners with cashflow who may need to raise money for operation expansion or improvements.

While the preferred stock does represent ownership in a company, it lacks voting rights; however, it comes with a higher claim on dividends. Dividends must be paid on preferred stock before the common stock. Dividends on a preferred stock will usually be 5 to 10%. If a company does not have the money to pay dividends on the preferred stock, missed dividends will accrue until the company has the money in the case of <u>cumulative</u> preferreds, but dividends will not accrue on those that are non-cumulative. Knowing if a preferred stock is cumulative is one of the first questions to answer when researching this particular type of security. Also, understand that these securities are callable, meaning the issuing company can buy them back (paying off their debt) to save the dividend payments. This risk is usually higher during periods of falling interest rates and lower in times of rising rates. (TPB, 2020; Ganti, 2024)

In the event a company goes bankrupt, and liquidation takes place, priority for recovering funds goes first to bondholders, then preferred stockholders, and finally to common shareholders, if any assets are left. However, as most mining companies do not use bonds, but rather go through royalty and streaming companies to finance them, often such agreements tie the security of the royalty to a particular asset. Meaning a preferred stockholder could have a higher priority or even be first in line. (Ganti, 2024; Norton-Rose-Fulbright, 2017)

Preferred stocks sometimes come with conversion rights, allowing them to be exchanged for common shares under agreed conditions. Preferred shares have their own ticker. They are issued at a set price/dividend rate but then trade on the secondary market at either a premium or discount, depending on market sentiment. Because the amount of dividend dollars paid per share is fixed at issue, if the share price falls, the dividend percentage received by new buyers will be larger. This works the opposite way when shares trade at a premium.

While valuations of common and preferred shares will have a relationship for valuation, usually the preferred shares will be more stable, similar to a bond, in that you expect to make money by receiving dividends, not necessarily price appreciation. That said, well-timed purchases of preferred shares can give you both. They can make particularly good additions to income-producing portfolios, especially if there is a mix of preferred stocks from different sectors. This helps balance the overall portfolio as it progresses through different market cycles.

Hopefully by now it is understood that many more variables than simply the price of gold are at play when trading a mining stock. While complex at times, the reality is that it is just a matter of being aware of all the potential risk factors and then determining which are applicable to the security you are trading.

Summary

1- Mining companies are usually divided between "Majors" and "Juniors," both play different rolls in the development of projects and have different risk profiles.

2- Mining companies should not be expected to move directly with commodity prices. A company's asset/production mix, hedging, mining plan, and business model will affect how closely it follows metal price movements.

3- When researching mining companies, pay special attention to identify and weigh the following risks: labor, jurisdiction, regulation and permitting, management, hedging, deposit, product, legacy and reclamation, foreign exchange, and financing which includes agreements with royalty and streaming companies.

4- As mines are often bought and sold frequently, it is often easier to learn the business model of a particular mine. That knowledge is then applied to the risk analysis of whichever company may be holding it at the time.

5- Royalty and streaming companies have a unique business model that is usually a win/win for both them and the mining companies. Understanding this business model and their specific contracts will help identify opportunities and risks with both companies involved.

6- Opportunities may exist with companies/products related to the mining process. Some common ones are energy, rubber, ammonium nitrate, and producers of specialty mining equipment.

7- The Nation Instrument (NI 43-101) is the industry's standardized disclosure of all technical aspects related to a mineral deposit/mine. It should be the first resource when researching a mining company's assets.

8- Bonds are less common in the mining industry but can present better than average opportunities when found. Shorter term and laddered strategies are recommended for income strategies.

9- Several types of securities can be found, including common stocks, preferred stocks, ETFs, and leveraged ETFs. Understanding the attributes of each along with industry specific risks, opportunities, and business cycle will help you know how to use them appropriately in various types of portfolios.

List 6-1: Mining, Royalty Company, and Related Industry Stocks & ETFs

This is an incomplete list for U.S. exchanges. This is not a recommendation to buy or sell.

Mining Companies:

Barrick Gold- GOLD

Newmont- NEM

AngloGold Ashanti- AU

Kinross Gold- KGC

Gold Fields- GFI

Rio Tinto- RIO

BHP Billiton- BHP

Freeport-McMoRan- FCX

Agnico Eagle- AEM

First Majestic Silver- AG

Pan American Silver- PAAS

Hecla Mining- HL, HL/PRB (preferred)

Coeur Mining- CDE

Impala Platinum- IMPUY

Sumitomo Corp-SSUMF

SSR Mining Inc.- SSRM

Thunder Mountain Gold- THMG

I-80 Gold Corp.- IAUX

Precious Metals Recycling & Jewelry

Envela Corp- ELA

Brilliant Earth- BRLT

Signet Jewelers- SIG

Pandora A/S- PNDRY (ADR)

Royalty Companies:

Wheaton Precious Metals- WPM

Franco-Nevada Corp- FNV

Royal Gold- RGLD

Sandstorm Gold- SAND

Metalla Royalty & Streaming- MTA

Osisko Gold Royalties Ltd- OR

Mining ETFs:

iShares MSCI Global Metals & Mining Producers- PICK

SPDR S&P Metals & Mining- XME

Global X Silver Miners- SIL

VanEck Vectors Gold Miners- GDX

Sprott Gold Miners- SGDM

Sprott Junior Gold Miners-SGDJ

Global X Gold Explorers- GOEX

U.S. Global GO Gold & Precious Metal Miners- GOAU

Leveraged Miner ETFs:

Direxion Daily Gold Miners Index Bull 2x- NUGT

Direxion Daily Junior Gold Miners Index Bull 2x- JNUG

MicroSectors Gold Miners 3x Leveraged ETN- GDXU

Direxion Daily Gold Miners Index Bear 2x- DUST

Direxion Daily Junior Gold Miners Bear 2x- JDST

MicroSectors Gold Minors 3x Inverse Leveraged ETN- GDXD

Ammonium Nitrate Producers

LSB Industries Inc.- LXU

Rubber & Tire Suppliers

Titan International- TWI

Goodyear Tire & Rubber Company- GT

Michelin Compagnie- MGDDY (OTC ADR)

Related Industrial

Steel Partners Holdings- SPLP, SPLP/PRA (preferred)

Howmet Aerospace Inc-, HWM, HWM/PR (preferred)

Materion- MTRN

List 6-2: Sample of Mining Company Bond Issues

Company	S&P Rating	Coupon	Maturity	CUSIP#
Barrick Gold	BBB+	6.375%	3/1/2033	725906AH4
BHP Group	A-	4.875%	2/27/2026	055451AY4
BHP Group	A-	5.25%	9/8/2026	055451BB3
BHP Group	A-	5.3%	2/21/2035	055451BL1
Freeport	BBB-	5.25%	9/1/2029	35671DCP5
Rio Tinto	A	4.875%	3/14/2030	76720AAS5
Rio Tinto	A	5.25%	3/14/2035	76720AAN0
Kinross Gold	BBB-	4.5%	7/15/2027	496902AQ0
Newmont	BBB+	5.875%	4/1/2035	651639AW6

Disclosure:

I have not received compensation from any of the companies or funds mentioned in this chapter regarding the preparation of this book. I have worked as either an employee, contractor, or consultant on properties held by several of the companies listed. I currently hold a long position in THMG and PICK, and I am a frequent trader of mining related securities. This information is for educational purposes only and should not be understood or construed as a recommendation to buy or sell. Trading securities involves risk. It is highly recommended that readers do their own research before entering or exiting any trade positions.

Notes

Chapter 7: Precious Metal Derivatives; Futures, Options, and Warrants

Introduction

This chapter focuses on tradeable contracts. Collectively, these are referred to as derivatives, and traditionally concerned futures contracts for physical delivery of commodities, such as grain. Today, they have evolved to include not just futures of commodities but also: indexes, interest rates on treasuries, crypto currency, warrants, and options on securities.

Contracts differ from stocks, which represent partial ownership of a company and confer voting rights. Common stock shares signify ownership of assets and the right to benefit from future earnings of those assets. Futures are legally binding contracts for the future delivery of a set amount of the underlying commodity or security. Options are contracts providing an option to buy or sell the underlying assets.

Futures and options trade on exchanges like stocks, but these exchanges are separate organizations from the exchanges that deal in stock. This is sometimes unnoticed by traders today, as both securities and derivatives primarily trade electronically and many major brokers offer trading on both types of exchanges. A key difference in the U.S. is that derivatives are regulated by the Commodity Futures Trading Commission (CFTC), while securities are regulated by the Securities and Exchange Commission (SEC). Both agencies have significant overlap in their purpose and jurisdiction, making for a complex and often contradictory regulatory environment.

Futures

Concerning metal, futures are binding contracts for the future delivery of a specific amount of metal at a specific time. Upon expiration, the owner of a contract is expected to take delivery of the contracted quantity and pay the contract value, while the seller of the contract is expected to deliver the specified amount of metal in exchange for the contract value. There are primarily three kinds of entities who engage in trading futures contracts, these are:

Producers:

Often a mining company or metals refiner. They sell contracts to lock in a guaranteed price of their commodities, which when done well adds stability to their business.

Manufacturers:

These are companies that use metal to produce their goods for sale. These could be private mints, electronics/solar panel manufacturers, jewelry manufacturing companies, and specialty components manufactures, such as those serving aerospace or military clients. Their goal is to lock in a future purchase price of the raw materials needed to make their goods. Likewise, when done well this adds stability to their business.

Speculators:

Most readers will fall into this category. These are those who seek to profit from price movements of the underlying commodity. As with any form of trading, the goal is to buy low and sell high.

Contract sizes are for standardized amounts that traditionally have been workable amounts for both producers and manufacturers, but these quantities will seem large to most retail investors. The standard size contract for the following precious metals are:

Silver: 5000-oz

Gold: 100-oz

Platinum: 50-oz

Palladium: 100-oz

Catering to the retail market, futures contracts for smaller volumes have been created. Gold, for example, now has three contract sizes that can be traded:
Standard: 100-oz, Mini: 50-oz, and Micro: 10-oz.

Be aware that not all brokers will deal in all contract sizes. Trading fees and commissions are the same amount per contract regardless of the contract size, meaning your commissions will eat into your gains more when trading smaller sized contracts. Also, you are not expected to pay the full price of the contract when you trade, rather you put up what is called the **Initial Margin Requirement**, this is usually 3 to 12% of the notional value of the contract. If silver is trading at $25/oz, a micro silver contract (1000 oz) will have a notional value of $25,000.00 ($25 x 1000). If the initial margin requirement is 10%, you would be required to put up $2,500.00 to get into the trade. In this case each tick (trade price increment) of $0.01 is equal to $10.

Margin works differently with futures compared to stocks. With stocks, you borrow against positions and capital. With futures you set aside your initial margin requirement as a good faith deposit and are then expected to keep a **maintenance margin,** which is somewhat less than the initial margin requirement. If your position moves far enough against you so that you have less than the required maintenance margin your broker will issue a margin call, which will require you to add more funds to your account to stay in the trade. Futures carry a high degree of leverage, with the above example being 10x.

Futures tickers will also vary between platforms but denote specifics about the contract. For the micro silver contract above one platform may list it as:

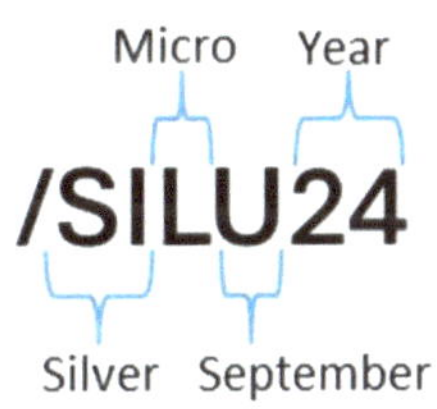

Futures carry some advantages over the other instruments discussed thus far:

1- You don't have to bother with physically trading the commodity which has transport, security, storage expenses, and requires more time.
2- A future derives its value directly from the value of the underlying commodity. One of the challenges of trading mining stocks is that you are trading a company as a proxy for metal, but as discussed this opens an entire new realm of risk analysis.

3- Leverage, which many investors try to achieve through trading leveraged EFTs or funds which derive their value from underlying futures contracts and options. Usually the specific details of contracts they are invested in are not visible, and depending on the funds purchase price, expiration dates, rolling, and fees, the fund may not track price movements as closely as expected. Trading a futures contract directly puts you in control of managing the position.
4- Liquidity is better because you are dealing in the primary market.
5- Metals futures trade overnight, giving you access to more opportunities.
6- Like stocks, positions can be opened and closed almost instantaneously.
7- Futures (currently) have more accommodating tax rules. Instead of 100% short term capital gains on positions held less than a year, gains are split 60% long-term/ 40% short-term with your tax rate applied. See the chapter on taxation for more detail.

All that said, futures also have their own risks, which include:

1- Contract size: Traders often like to ease into and out of large positions. This becomes more difficult with large contract sizes.
2- Leverage: It is bad enough to be wrong, but 5 to 10x wrong can become dangerous if positions are not well managed. You must remember that leverage works both ways. Even with proper risk management, it can get expensive if you have to close several positions in a row that have moved against you.
3- Contract expiration: If you let a contract expire, are you prepared to physically deliver or receive and pay for the contracted amount of metal? Some brokers will automatically close your position before this happens, and others do not. If you choose to stay in the trade, you will need to roll your position into a later dated contract, which typically will involve the standard trading fees.

Strategies for using futures

An investor in physical metal may expect a temporary decline in metals prices. As an example, let's say they own 2,000 oz of silver. As discussed previously, trading physical metal is cumbersome, takes time, and is expensive. It is usually only appropriate before and after large moves in price. While the investor is still bullish on silver in the long term, they are also confident prices will decrease in the short term. They could choose to hedge their physical silver position by shorting two silver micro futures contracts (1000 oz each). If the expected decline in prices materializes, they can close their futures position. Profits made from the futures trade should mostly offset the decrease in value of the physical position.

Another example is a speculator who has watched gold spike during a particular geopolitical event. After watching the price peak, they could short (sell) a contract as the price begins moving back to realistic levels, which would be expected as the tension of the event winds down. They may also set a protective stop near their entry price in the event the price reverses and continues up. If gold prices come down, they can then buy to cover the position at a profit.

A third scenario: In March of 2020, silver prices dropped from $18/oz to almost $12/oz. Sellers of physical silver, anticipating a fast recovery, refused to sell at that price by tacking on hefty premiums, so the end cost to the buyer was still $16+/oz. Buyers could have gotten around the supply crunch by buying a futures contract instead and waiting for the contract value to match the "street" value.

Also understand that many institutional, and now even retail, traders will day or swing trade metals futures because of the amount of leverage they offer. This additional activity can often add significant energy to the metals markets and cause prices to move quickly. These traders, are looking for shorter-term price movements and tend to rely heavily on technical analysis and charting techniques for entry and exit points. Those planning on short term trading of futures contracts should be well versed in technical analysis and the various chart patterns which tend to indicate future movements. Remesh (2024) provides a good introduction to recognizing and understanding several of the most common patterns. Typically, a trader will use the chart pattern in combination with several other technical indicators while still being aware of recent news and fundamental drivers behind the broader price movements. The importance of waiting for the right setup and having both an exit and risk management plan before entering the trade cannot be stressed enough.

Futures usually work best for the speculator when there is a significant move in price (up or down) that is expected or in process. Conversely, highly volatile consolidation patterns with unpredictable oscillations are usually avoided by experienced traders until a pattern has developed sufficiently to indicate the direction of the next significant move.

While the above examples are primarily for speculators, producers and manufactures also have some considerations. Manufacturers, arguably, have the most flexibility regarding price moves. Their primary concern should be maintaining their supply chain as the cost of disruptions to factory operations will usually far exceed whatever damage could be caused by a price move. They are, in part, protected from inflation because they control the prices of the products they sell. Raw material prices are just one, and usually not the largest, of many areas of their business where costs need to be controlled to remain competitive. Generally speaking, they will want contract lengths that match their production needs, but ideally these should be 1-3 months and in almost all circumstances less than a year. Prices on futures contracts factor in storage costs, and arguably some time-value. The holder of a long contract pays this cost. An exception to this advice is when metal prices experience a fluke low. In such cases, a manufacturer could buy several months of supply or contracts with laddered expirations and potentially improve their bottom line.

Miner's and Hedging

Producers (i.e. miners) are usually in a more difficult position than manufacturers. For one, they do not set the price of their product; the market does. Second, they are at the mercy of their deposit's cut-off grade as to whether or not they make money, and that cut-off grade can change with the other input costs to mining. These are also the two primary reasons mining companies will sell futures contracts, so as to lock in profitable prices for their product. There are risks to this, however, and not so distant history provides us with a few spectacular disasters that companies have created for themselves, Ashanti Goldfields being the most notable.

In Ashanti's case, on advice from Goldman Sachs, they hedged their reserves by selling futures during the cycle low in gold. According to end-of-year (2000) reporting, they achieved a 44% hedge at an average strike of $273/oz, which was slightly above spot. Their total gold production cost was about $200/oz. They were the 3rd largest gold producer in the world at the time (~1.7 million oz/year). By 2002, spot gold was $350/oz and continued to climb, eventually peaking at $1800/oz in 2012. As the price climbed, the hedge book deteriorated, and margin calls pulled cash from a company that was realizing only a fraction of the returns from their production. The hedge book was not unwound until 2010, after a takeover bid by AngloGold was completed in 2004. (Brewster, 2017)

The lessons to be learned from Ashanti and other epic fails include:

1- Producers should not engage in long-term (>1yr) futures contracts, as major price swings to the upside will create margin calls, pulling much needed cash from the operation.
2- Producers should not hedge reserves but rather near-term production.
3- Hedges should not be 100% of production but rather a smaller percentage, say ~25%. This protects against underproduction. If you are 100% hedged and you have a significant production delay due to a wall failure or a metallurgical issue, you still have to deliver on the contracts you sold, which means buying on the spot market to fulfill your contracts. (Keane, 2015; NCS-Import, 2003)
4- Do not let the executive time the hedges (they are the dumb money, or at least the busy/distracted/biased money); use a professional. (Saville, 2015) Unfortunately for Ashanti, Goldman Sachs, supposedly the experts, didn't prove any better. (Brewster, 2017)

Industry hedging in mass can exacerbate weak prices by flooding the market with metal. In addition to this, investors typically don't like it when miners hedge aggressively. The reason an investor typically buys a mining stock is to gain metals exposure, which hedging negates. Furthermore, a hedge book in a rapidly rising gold environment may not only exclude a company profiting from high metal prices, but margin calls will pull capital from them when they need it most, as often higher production costs come with higher spot prices. (Fowler, 2023)

Finally, a mining company should not expect their trading unit to make up for a flawed business model or poor management, the goal, rather, is to smooth out some of the volatility. A company still needs to adjust and adapt to market conditions. Many mining companies have successfully operated for decades without hedging, and if they have a low production cost, they arguably are better off without using hedges. This is one of the overlaps between stocks and futures, but understanding a mining company's hedge book is one of the first questions that should be answered when performing your risk analysis.

Options

Whereas futures are relatively simple, options are less so. With futures, we are generally dealing with contracts for commodities. Even with futures for currency or indexes, it is probably better to think of them as commodities, at least in the sense that the contracts are for set quantities of these assets, they are deliverable, have a degree of utility, and the underlying asset doesn't represent a share of something or come with voting rights. Options primarily are for stocks, which represent ownership in a company. That being said, you can now also buy/sell options on some futures contracts, thus trading a derivative of a derivative, which can add some complication. Gold futures, for example, have a healthy options market.

Options are still contracts; however, you are not buying/selling a contract for guaranteed delivery like a future, rather a contract for the option to buy or sell if certain price and time conditions are met. Options contracts are usually for 100 shares of whatever security is being traded, and they are in force for a set period of time before they expire. This is usually on a monthly or quarterly schedule for most securities related to precious metals, though for some high liquidity and heavily traded securities you will observe an options market with weekly expiration dates.

You can buy/sell "call" option contracts which are the option to buy shares at a given "strike" price, or you can buy/sell "put" option contracts, which are the option to sell shares at an agreed upon strike price. The price paid when buying contracts is called the "premium," and if you are a seller of contracts, then you receive this premium from the buyer with the obligation to deliver (if you sold a call option) or buy (if you sold a put option) the agreed upon number of shares. Because the premium paid per share is significantly less than the share price, options contracts allow the buyer to potentially control a significant number of shares for a fraction of the price. This is how options can offer a significant amount of leverage.

Options have a "time value," meaning the more distant the expiration date the more valuable the contract, because the chances that the security will move beyond the strike price is greater. All other things equal, the value of a contract will decay as it approaches the expiration date. Contracts that do not reach the strike price by the expiration date expire worthless. Contracts where the security price has moved beyond the strike price are considered "in the money" and for American style options can be exercised at any time. If they expire in the money, the contracts are automatically exercised upon expiration. Remember that European style options cannot be exercised until the expiration date.

A good way to view options is to think of them as insurance, and one of the primary uses of them by investors and traders is to use them as a hedge. For example:

1- Covered Call

An investor may own 200 shares in a mining stock currently valued at $10/share that is approaching a cycle high. The investor could sell two call options contracts (each contract is worth 100 shares) at a strike price of $12, a price the investor feels is at or near the peak of the cycle. The buyer of the option pays the investor a premium, for this example $0.20/share or $40 total for the two contracts. If the stock price has exceeded the strike price by expiration, the contracts will be executed, and the investor's shares will be "called away." The buyer is required to pay you the strike price ($12/per share) for the shares, and you also keep the $40.

In this case, the investor is happy to sell the shares at $12, because it is near their projected target price, and the extra $40 adds to the gains. If the price closed at $13/share, they would still only receive the $12 per share and retain the premium. The buyer would probably immediately sell the shares. The buyer's profit would be $160 (=(($13-$12)x$200)-$40(premium paid)). The farther into the money the option expires the greater the buyer's gains will be. But let us say the price closed at $11.75. In this scenario the contracts expire worthless. The investor still keeps the premium, but the buyer is out $40. (Downey, 2024)

2- Protective Put

Let us say an investor owns the same 200 shares as above. They are concerned the upcoming earnings report may negatively affect the share price but do not want to liquidate their position in case the opposite unfolds. They could buy two put option contracts that give them the option to sell shares at the strike price. The investor chooses a strike of $9/share and pays $.25/share or $50 to the put option seller. After earnings, the share price drops to $7.25. The investor exercises the option, and the seller must now pay the investor $9/share. The put seller keeps the $50 premium the investor paid but is forced to overpay for the shares and now has an unrealized loss; the investor has thus minimized their losses by putting the risk on the put seller. But let's say the shares only fell to $9.25 in value. The contracts would expire worthless. The put seller keeps the premium, and ultimately the investor paid for insurance that they didn't end up using.

3- Finally, you could act as the insurer by selling put options. Your risk in this scenario is overpaying for a particular security yet many use the selling of put options as part of their entrance strategy.

Again, viewing options as insurance, statistically, most option contracts expire worthless, similar to most insurance policies. Understanding this, you will realize that in most scenarios for an investor or trader, it is better to be a seller of contracts than a buyer. But also, like selling insurance, there are times that sellers of contracts will be required to pay out, and this is where properly managing contracts becomes important.

Example 2 and even example 1 to a degree are defensive ways to use options. Two other defensive examples include the "Married Put" and the "Protective Collar." There are several spread strategies that can be designed to work in different market conditions. Overall, the majority of spread strategies are offensive, though their structure is still designed to mitigate risk. The objective is not to protect money but to make it. Typically, for advanced traders, the various spreads are popular because they help define risk vs reward and increase the overall number of market conditions in which a trader can make money. The following is a list of option strategies and the ideal scenario in which to employ them. For those who are unfamiliar or need a refresher with a particular strategy, please see the associated reference.

Covered Call- Best for flat and mildly bullish markets. (Downey, 2024)

Married Put- Strictly insurance, usually purchased at the same time the initial position is taken. A protective put is similar but is not necessarily purchased when the position is entered. (Downey, 2024)

Protective Collar- Best after a significant rise in the share price. Provides downside protection with some room to grow. (Downey, 2024)

Vertical Spreads- There are both **Bull Spreads** and **Bear Put Spreads**. The Bull Spread is used with the expectation of rising share prices and the Bear Put Spread with falling share prices. (Downey, 2024)

Straddle- Profits from a high volatility move in either direction. (Chen, 2024b)

Strangle- Function is similar to the straddle but is structured differently. It also profits from a significant move in either direction. Appropriate

	for situations where you expect a strong reaction but are not certain in which direction it will be. Could include key earnings reports, permitting announcements, and mergers, among other things. (Hayes, 2024)
Butterfly Spreads-	These can be structured in different ways but usually are a market neutral, low volatility strategy that profits the most if the price doesn't move before expiration. (Mitchell, 2024a)
Christmas Tree-	Is a combination of 3 vertical spreads. Can be built with either calls or puts. Generally best suited for moderately bullish markets. (Hayes, 2022)
Condor/Iron Condor-	Generally, a market natural strategy that can be built with either a slightly bullish or bearish bias. The Condor will only use either puts or calls whereas, the Iron Condor uses a combination of both. Both maximum profit and loss are defined by the spread design. (Mitchell, 2024b; Ganti, 2022)

Generally, options strategies will be used with stocks or similar securities that have a large options market with several expiration dates and strike prices. This gives traders the maximum flexibility to design or customize the strategy to their needs and offers more confidence that they will be able to fill and close their trades when desired.

Market neutral strategies rely to a significant degree on the time decay dynamics of the contract values, along with other factors describing the contract's price in relation to the underlying asset. As a group, these factors are often referred to as "Greeks" and the major ones consist of: delta, gamma, vega, theta, and rho. Understanding how these all work together is an important part of options trading.

Briefly:

- Delta measures how much the price of an option is expected to change per $1 change in the underlying asset's price.
- Gamma indicates how much of the delta of an option is expected to change per $1 change in the underlying asset's price.
- Theta provides the rate at which an option's value declines as time passes, reflecting the option's time decay.
- Vega shows how much the price of an option is expected to change with a 1% change in the underlying asset's volatility.
- Rho measures the expected change in an option's price for a 1% change in the risk-free interest rate.

Combined, these help a trader understand the risk, reward, and probability of trades, and help them monitor the position as the trade evolves. Many of the advanced trading platforms now have software that helps a trader chart and follow the Greeks as their trade progresses. A trader should not expect themselves to know everything before getting started, but they should at least know the basics and apply it to their strategies. (Thompson, 2024)

All these concepts and strategies can also be applied to options on futures when available. However, on most platforms, gold is the only precious metal future that has a large enough retail options market to support spread strategies.

Even if an investor or trader decides not to use option contracts, they should be aware of how they are used, the overall size of the option market associated with the security they are trading, and key contract expiration dates. Expiration dates with high volumes often cause significant price swings in a stock, likewise those just days ahead of earnings reports, when options activity amplifies already high trading volumes. This increase of energy in a particular market can either cause high volatility or provide the momentum to break through key support or resistance levels.

Psychology

Investing and especially especially trading, involves a unique kind of stress that becomes more acute when dealing with leveraged instruments. Successful traders develop what I will call "tempered confidence." They must be confident enough in themselves, their trade ideas, and their risk management abilities to enter a trade but not become overconfident or greedy, which usually results in losing money. They must be patient yet decisive, focused, and know when to take gains and cut losses. They must also be determined, resilient, and honest with themselves when they make mistakes. I have yet to meet a trader who feels they have mastered themselves, but I think some have come close.

There are often misunderstandings around options strategies. Many of these strategies have been developed and are used regularly by traders because they know themselves and that they do not get it right all the time. They understand the risks and are willing to sacrifice a portion of their potential gains for a higher probability of some gains and reduced and defined maximum losses. It is hard for many traders to get used to losing money on their hedges, for example, and for this reason many tend to not place hedges. You should never feel bad about losing money on a hedge if the trade works out as planned. It did what it was supposed to do. You bought insurance and, thankfully, you didn't need it.

Warrants

Warrants are another class of derivatives. Like options, these are contracts that give the owner the right, but not the obligation, to buy shares in the case of call warrants or to sell shares in the case of put warrants. Unlike options, which are written by market participants, warrants are issued directly by the company. Because of this, they are regulated by the SEC and not the CFTC as are options and futures. After issuance, they can trade on the secondary market like stocks and bonds. Warrants also have similar functionality and terminology to options. They have a strike price, expiration date, and similarly are termed "in" or "out of the money," depending on the relation of the underlying share price to that of the strike price. They also come in American and European style, with the European variant requiring the holder to wait until expiration for exercising. Warrants, however, are longer-dated contracts. The longest option contracts are usually around a year, whereas warrants typically start at 3-year contracts but could be as long as 10-year contracts. (Baldridge, 2022; TPB, 2020)

Warrants trade on the exchange with their own ticker symbol and usually include the expiration date in their name. This is different from viewing an options chain, which is a chart showing the strike price of call and put option quotes. With warrants, the trader is responsible for knowing the strike or exercise price, which they will have to look up. One of the places this information is found is on the required filings with the exchange. It was pleasantly surprising to see the 43-101 attached to a Form 8-K filing for U.S. GoldMining Inc. The filing lists the tickers USGO (the common stock) and USGOW (the warrant) and shows the exercise price (strike) price of $13 of one warrant for one share of the common stock. (SEC, 2024) The industry has come a long way since the Bre-X scandal of 1997 that inspired the live action film "Gold," as the highest level of technical disclosure, the 43-101, is now being linked directly to the securities themselves.

Warrants are a popular money-raising vehicle for junior mining companies, as these companies require a lot of capital for exploration and are not making any money, so bonds or other debt instruments are not feasible. If exploration efforts are unfruitful and the share price falls, the warrants will expire worthless, but if they succeed, issuing shares is a small price to pay. Warrants are popular for start-up oil companies for the same reasons. Companies often use them as sweeteners to agreements, adding them to preferred stock deals or as part of compensation plans for key company personnel. A recent example of this is Thunder Mountain Gold Inc., a junior company, which issued warrants as part of its private placement to raise funds for exploration. In the deal, investors who buy common shares at $0.05 per share will also receive 1 warrant per share purchased. Each warrant carries a strike price of $0.10 and an expiration of 36 months. (Jones, 2024)

When warrants are exercised, the company typically issues new shares. This is a dilutive process to holders of common shares, so another fundamental to understand when trading mining companies is if they have issued any warrants, and if so, how many, the strike price, and the expiration date. (Baldridge, 2022)

Once one understands warrants, trading and strategies are straightforward. As this relates to the mining industry Wilson, 2023 provides a few important considerations for American holders trading Canadian warrants:

1- Most mining companies are Canadian and, therefore, trade on the Canadian exchanges. While some warrants will be duel listed on American and Canadian exchanges, this is not usually the case. If you want access to all the options, use a broker that provides access to the Toronto Stock Exchange (TSX).
2- While a warrant may be listed on multiple exchanges, it is unlikely to have the same ticker on each. Use the CUSIP numbers (the unique security identifier for all North American Securities) to avoid confusion.
3- American holders of warrants issued from Canadian companies cannot exercise warrants, unless they are dually registered with the SEC. They may only sell them due to current securities laws and agreements between the U.S. and Canada. This can limit the trader's options, because while they can still sell the warrant if it moves "into the money," they would not be able to exercise for common shares and continue to hold for appreciation.
4- Unlike "in the money" options that execute automatically if warrants are "in the money", you must initiate the process to exercise with your broker or the issuing company.

It is also worth noting that the total number of warrants issued may not make for a deep market. This is another item to check into, making sure the security has an acceptable amount of liquidity.

For investors and traders, warrants can provide a better mid-term holding option than options. Because they have time value, they tend to hold up better when price of the common stock falls. Price decay over time still happens, usually becoming most extreme in the last six months. Many of the mining companies that issue warrants trade on the OTC. These are often penny stocks and typically do not have an options market. Warrants, therefore, provide the only leveraged option for these companies. Like futures and options contracts, the warrant's activity will have an effect on the share price, and market participants should be aware if a company has warrants and the contract details before making trade choices. Two examples of currently trading U.S. exploration company warrants are:

Dakota Gold: DC/WS

U.S. Gold Mining Inc: USGOW

Warrants provide leverage, which is one of the aspects that make them popular. Since this entire chapter has been devoted to leveraged contracts, it is worth saying that the most leveraged investment that can be made in the metals market is to drill an exploration hole. This is what the good juniors do with the money they raise, and it is extremely high risk.

Understanding the horribly low probability of deposits becoming mines and the junior companies that try to develop them, especially if adding a time constraint, my initial inclination as a trader is to sell or "short" the warrants. However, as an exploration geologist, I have been on the other side of this.

I was working night shift as a geologist doing drill support on a small and remote core program. We had drilled through several hundred feet of dead rock, and I was instructed by management to "kill" or end the drill hole. Before giving the order, I looked at the last box of core and saw a 1 cm-long crystal of ilvaite, a rare mineral we had observed to occur adjacent to mineralized rocks. Since it was the middle of the night and no one was there to argue with me, I made the decision to continue drilling. By morning, the drill had recovered several tens of feet of massive sulfide, or ore. That hole plus the immediate follow up drilling added about 300,000 tons to the deposit model with a gross value of about $360 million at the time. The company capital I risked by extending the drill hole was about $10,000.00. (Wilton, 2020)

Sometimes companies just get lucky like we did, and sometimes it can cause a drastic increase in share value. If you are short and end up being on the wrong side of luck, and leveraged, when one of these companies wins the lottery, it can be a bad place. It reminds me of something the late Charles Munger said about another high-risk investment at the time when asked:

"My thoughts are two: I would never buy it (Tesla), and I would never sell it short."

-Charles Munger

(Reinicke, 2020)

Summary

1- Futures, options, and warrants are contracts that derive their value from underlying assets.
2- All three offer a high degree of leverage that can be deployed with defensive and offensive strategies.
3- For speculators, futures usually work best when there is a strong trend in play either up or down.
4- Most investors and traders benefit from defensive options strategies.
5- Mining companies can benefit from hedging a portion of their <u>short-term</u> production. Adjusting mining and business models for long-term changes in commodity prices historically is better than long-term hedging.
6- If the goal is to trade metal, it is usually better to trade a futures contract than using a mining company as a proxy, because the miner's hedging activity and business model will likely cause their share price to behave differently than metal prices.
7- Options strategies are most applicable to stocks and similar securities.

8- More advanced options strategies are used to create trading opportunities, achieve leverage, and define risk.

9- "Greeks" are several measurements that define an options relationship through time with its underlying security. Understanding how these work is a key part of options trading.

10- Those who choose not trade options or futures should still understand how they work and be aware of how those markets affect the instruments they are invested in.

11- Warrants are a popular instrument for junior mining companies to raise money. As these companies often have a thin or non-existent options market, warrants may be the only leveraged trading tool available.

12- Developing a healthy psychology around investing/trading behavior is inarguably the most important part of success.

Notes

Chapter 8: Precious Metal Collectables

The final area of precious metal investing is the collectables market. While to many the most interesting, it is by far the most difficult. It demands the most research and is most certainly the least liquid of all classes we have touched on. Pricing is also the most subjective. It is a true blend of commodities and collectables. Understanding the types of items available will help buyers understand if they are more on the commodity or collectable end of the spectrum. For these reasons, I recommend that only those who have a genuine interest in the space from a hobby or historical perspective participate. My take on my personal collection is that it is simply a hobby that is going to be worth something in the end.

Coins, Rounds, Medals, and Tokens

When talking about collectables, we will be considering coins, rounds, and medals/tokens. Figurines also exist, but that tends to be a highly specialized and ever-evolving area with few publications. Recently, some mints have started producing figurines of specific weights. For example, instead of buying a 20 oz silver bar, you could buy a 20 oz silver bust of Donald Trump (MAGA hat not included). For you to know this space exists is enough for our discussion.

Coins:

Coins are usually circular, flat pieces of metal with images on both sides. They can be single or multi-metallic. The key point is they are produced or contracted to be produced by a national mint. Coins are stamped with a denomination that may be more or less than the actual value of their metal content. In many cases, coins were intended to be actual money such as 1964 and earlier U.S. silver quarters and dimes, while others are produced strictly for collectors. Since the creation of fiat currency, no countries are currently producing coins intended for circulation that are composed of precious metals. However, most developed countries have a national mint and, in addition to their circulating coinage, will produce coins intended to be collectables out of silver, gold, platinum and/or palladium, with silver being the most common. Usually, the stamped denomination on the collectable bullion products will be significantly less than the bullion value. In the US, it is perfectly legal to melt down the gold and silver eagles, as they are not considered money, but rather "numismatic products." (Public Law 99-185, 1985)

Smaller nations may contract private mints to produce these "national coins" for them. Two of the largest private mints are the Sunshine Mint and the Scottsdale mint, both are U.S. based companies. Collectable coins are produced by countries to generate revenue, meaning they are often sold with high premiums.

Figure 8-1: Collectable Silver Coins. *Coins in the top row from left to right, France 1873, France 1851, USA 1878, USA 1921, Panama 1934, and Bermuda (Sovereign UK state)1956. All pictured coins on the top row were minted to be used as money and consist of "coin silver" usually 85% Ag for European mints and 90% for the U.S. The other coins are examples of products produced by modern mints and are intended as collectable numismatics. Barbados (middle row left), Canada (2nd row right), Malta (bottom left), Australia (bottom right), U.S. Territories Silver Quarters (red 6-piece set). These typically are 99.9 to 99.99% pure Ag depending on the mint and issue and are sold through revenue-generating programs for the affiliated government. (Image courtesy of GeoTech LLC)*

Chapter 8: Precious Metal Collectables

Rounds:

Rounds are no different than coins in their shape, ranges of metal content, or designs. The key difference is they are not produced by or for a national mint. They were never intended to be money and do not have a denomination stamped on them. Often, they were intended to be bullion. Instead of a denomination, rounds will often have a grade and weight stamped on them. Some, especially silver, have been minted for possible trade and may be stamped "trade unit" or similar, which is 1 troy oz silver. Usually, all these tend to trade closer to the bullion/commodity market. The exception is when a particular piece has become more desirable for whatever reason and collectors are willing to pay a higher price. Figure 4-2 shows several common examples of these available in the U.S.

Medals:

Medals are similar to rounds but are often produced to commemorate a specific event, like a fair or trade show, or maybe the opening of a park or memorial. In some cases, this can be an actual award, for example an Olympic or war medal. They were not intended to be money or bullion, rather a recognition or memento. Often, they are made out of precious metals. These can have high values depending on the particular award, recipient, and verifiable chain of custody. Olympic medals, for example, have an interesting history. It was the U.S. who in 1904 set the precedent of awarding a gold, silver, and bronze medal. The 1904 St. Louis Games and the 1908 London games were the only games to award gold medals made out of predominantly gold. All subsequent gold medals have been made out of gilt silver, basically silver gilded with gold. The actual composition is usually around 92.5% silver, 6% gold, and the balance zinc and/or copper. Copper improves hardness and zinc enhances luster when combined with copper.

It is interesting how even the Olympic medals show the effects of inflation and the transition of gold from money to a commodity during this period of two world wars. Also interesting is that the 2002 Salt Lake winter games had the heaviest (20-oz) medals in Olympic history (Maybe, they felt obligated due to their proximity to the Bingham Canyon mine.), and the recent Paris 2024 games had one of the lowest uses of precious metal, but they did incorporate pieces of iron from the original Eiffel Tower. (Olympics.com, 2024)

Figure 8-2: Paris 2024 Olympic Medals. *Olympic gold medals were only made predominantly of gold in 1904 and 1908. Subsequent games have used silver gilded with gold and even other materials including polycarbonate in the Sochi 2014 games. The Paris 2024 games included pieces of iron crafted from original components of the Eiffel Tower that had been replaced for structural reasons. Medals remain a popular category in the collectables market. (Ford, 2024)*

Tokens:

Tokens, like coins, are intended to be used as a means of exchange; however, they differ because they are not produced by a recognized governmental authority. Think of a local arcade, Chuck E. Cheese, or mass transit tokens as a kid. These were definitely used as a means of exchange but are pretty much worthless outside of the arcade or when not riding the bus. These are marketing tokens, which include casino tokens and exist as their own sub class. However, during the U.S. Civil War, many private groups minted tokens, as there was not enough actual coinage circulating to meet the needs of the people, and the tokens were literally used along with quarters, nickels, and dollars to facilitate transactions. These were made illegal for use after the war but are now highly sought-after collectables. Figure 3-5 shows several examples of U.S. Civil War era tokens.

Many people are surprised how many different tokens are out there. Historically, they mark times of economic distress where actual money supplies did not meet the needs of the people, local governments and even individuals minted them, as people would prefer to have some means of exchange instead of allowing the economy to degrade back to strictly barter transactions. (Armstrong, 2021)

Medieval Europe is an extreme example of a multiple centuries long period of economic distress. The surviving numismatics tell a story of regionalized and fragmented trade and commerce. What little coin and token to be had was usually horded, and transactions consisted of whatever mix of coin could be scraped together, often each struck by a different issuer, not to mention bartered goods. Transactors also had the challenge of determining the provenance of each coin or token and determining a total value based on a combination of the metals value and monetary value, all of which would vary depending on the issuer. Anyone willing to devote 30 minutes of research into how economies worked during this period will come away with a deep appreciation for the role money has played in society, and how the average life today is significantly more comfortable than even the nobles at the time because of it. From this period there are several examples of tokens, struck in gold, silver, and copper. Issuers included city states, regional bankers, local lords, and occasionally private gold and silver smiths. Tokens were supplemental coinage to what was supplied by the few large regional authorities. Their existence documents the struggle and subsequent attempts to mitigate challenges caused by a continent-wide shortage in the money supply. (Feliu & Gorné, 2018)

Medieval tokens generally have a less geographically constrained collectors' market than modern coins, such as U.S. or Canadian coins that realize their best sales prices in the domestic market. Figure 8-3 represents a variety of tokens that can be found from the medieval period.

Figure 8-3: Assorted Medieval Coins & Tokens. *Medieval Europe was a period marked by severely restricted trade and commerce that lasted several centuries. Part of the problem was a limited money supply. To supplement the limited coinage produced by the few larger authorities; cities, lords, money lenders, and even private gold/silver smiths would issue their own tokens. Imagine the challenge in trying to make change if you had to trade in a combination of dollars, pesos, euros, bus tokens, and possibly a few eggs! The everyday life for a person living in this period would not have been a terribly different scenario. (Feliu & Gorné, 2018; image: Eveland, 2023)*

When collecting tokens as an investment individuals need to gain expertise on the token type of interests. The number of available educational resources can vary widely depending on the token type. It is recommended the collector focus on specimens that are of interest to the collector but also have a well-established market. That said, it is interesting to see how many modern tokens can quickly develop a collector's market. If you by chance have any of those old Chuck E. Cheese tokens lying around, check them out on eBay. You may be surprised that some have held their value better than the quarters they were bought with.

Intrinsic Value vs Collector Value

Two key concepts to keep straight while operating in the collectables market are **intrinsic value** and **Collector value**. In simplest terms, intrinsic value is the actual metal or melt value of the item. Anything made of metal, and even some other materials, has an intrinsic value. For metal objects, it is equivalent to the melt value. When buying collectables, you should view the intrinsic value as your floor. The piece should never become worth less than the intrinsic value. The intrinsic value will fluctuate with metal spot prices, but as long as the metal has some value so will the piece. Most common people tend to be ignorant of intrinsic value, either drastically undervaluing or overvaluing the piece. Auction house and pawn dealers often take advantage of this on both sides to realize profits.

Collector value is the price above the intrinsic value that a collector is willing to pay. This is rather subjective and may depend on several factors, like grade, design, rarity, etc. But it still boils down to supply and demand. How many potential buyers want your coin, and how many other sellers have one like it?

Collectable coins are a combination of both intrinsic value and collector value. The space varies somewhat from other collectable markets. Fine art, for example, has very little intrinsic value. It is not like you are going to reuse the canvas. An even more drastic example is collectable currency, where the paper itself is essentially worthless. In both of these markets, most of the value is collector value. A collectable automobile would be different though, because it could be scrapped, and the salvaged metal could be recycled. If it is drivable, it will be worth yet more, simply because of the utility. In essence, you can always sell that old 57 chevy on the back lot to the scrap dealer, and he will give you a fair price on the metal, but would you want to?

Coins and automobiles will have both intrinsic and collector value. Part of being successful in this market is accurately estimating what proportion of the value of your item is allocated to each, because it truly is a broad spectrum. Keeping track of both will help to identify opportunities.

Liquidity

Probably the most important concept to understand with these types of investments is liquidity. Collectable coins that are common have an abundance of buyers and sellers, in an established market with an expected price range. In contrast, a rare and highly desirable ancient coin that may only have a few specimens, will be difficult to price. Valuation is estimated from previous auction sales and sales of similar pieces.

Generally speaking, the more common the type, the higher its liquidity will be and the rarer it is, the lower its liquidity. Both will be less liquid than bullion, for which there is always a market. There is a give and take, because the rarest pieces often appreciate the best, but they may take several years to buy or sell. Prices for more common pieces will be less, because there are more available. This causes sellers to compete for buyers, hence lower prices. Appreciation is less because of this, but the coin dealer will still give an offer, because he knows he can resell it to another collector.

Price will also affect liquidity. Something in the $50.00 range simply has more potential buyers than an item in the $50,000.00 range. Be mindful of the liquidity of the pieces you buy and make sure you are comfortable with the timeline. This is the primary reason I recommend collectibles to only those with a genuine interest, because you might have it a very long time, so you will want to enjoy it.

Considerations Concerning Collector Value

Age:

This is a misconception. Age in and of itself adds no value. Some ancient coins are valuable because very few of them have survived the centuries, and this rarity has added to their value, but there are also several ancient coins for which tens of thousands are still in existence, and these trade inexpensively. Age simply does not matter in terms of valuation, but in my opinion it does increase coolness!

Rarity:

How many exist? If there are more specimens than there are buyers, then it may not be a valuable piece; conversely, if there are few, say not enough to go around, the collectors who really want them will pay a premium, and this creates a competitive marketplace. Several things affect rarity, but the most common is the initial production volume. As many collectors want a complete set of a coin type, if one of the series has significantly lower production, it will have a higher price as collectors bid it up.

Historical Significance:

If a coin bears some kind of historical significance, this can greatly increase its collector value. Historical significance can mean several things. It could be as simple as a commemorative struck to remember a certain event; it could be a coin recovered from a shipwreck; be a coin made from the remains of something else historical such as a structure or weapon; or it could be a coin used or previously owned by a famous person. Interestingly, some collectables have become even more so because of the prestige of their prior owners. Depending on the significance, it can greatly affect the expected premium. Figure 8-4 is an example of one such coin recovered from the wreck of the SS Central America.

Figure 8-4: 1854-S Liberty Double Eagle Variety-11A, Broken A, AU-55 Certified by PCGS & CAC. *This coin is an example of how, rarity, grade, and historical significance can combine to add significant collector value to a specimen. This coin is a rare gold coin in its own right. Its grade, AU-55, is commonly given to newly minted coins that have just entered circulation. This coin was recovered from the wreck of the SS Central America. It last sold March 21st, 2016, at the Baltimore Convention Center for $25,850. Gold at the time had a spot price of $1,300/oz. (Stack's Bowers, 2016)*

Grade:

This is the quality of the coin. Things like strike, wear, scratches etc. are taken into consideration when a coin is graded. Think of grading as the first step in appraisal for coins. It is where the overall quality is assessed relative to all others of its kind. Similar to how "cut" is considered to have the greatest effect on gemstone quality, so does grade for coins. This ties into rarity, as in most circumstances there will be fewer high-grade coins than lower-grade coins. Grading can be an involved process and is inherently subjective. The hobby has worked over the years to improve this, and today with the high population varieties, it is a quasi-science. The Sheldon coin grading scale is that most commonly used today and the following version of it with descriptions is provided by the American Numismatic Association:

List 8-1: The Sheldon Coin Grading Scale

The Sheldon scale is the most common coin grading scale and is the scale used by grading services. It contains grades from 0 to 70, with 70 being the best and 0 the worst. One or two letters in front of the number denote general grade: P = poor, F/FR = fair, AG = almost good, G = good, VG = very good, F = fine, VF = very fine, EF = extremely fine, AU = almost uncirculated, MS = mint state, while the number attributes a more specific grade.

P-00 (No Grade): This "grade" is used for coins in which the coin, date, and/or mintmark cannot be identified. This grade is used only for coins in very bad condition. This grade is not used by the popular grading services, like PCGS and NGC.
P-01: This is used when the date, type, and mintmark can be identified, but the other details cannot. The rims are worn, the high details are gone, and the coin is in poor condition.
FR-02: The coin is in poor condition, the rims are barely visible, and few details are visible.
AG-03: Most letters and details on the the coin are visible and/or readable.
G-04: Letters are mostly full, but rims are worn.
G-06: Letters and many details are full and the rim is less worn.
VG-08: The entire coin is worn and letters, while full, are soft.
VG-10: The entire coin is worn and the letters, while full, are soft, but sharper than VG-08.
F-12: Letters are sharp, but parts of the coin are still worn.
F-15: Letters are sharp, but parts of the coin are slightly worn.
VF-20: Details are not sharp, but all shown to some extent.
VF-25: Almost complete details, but many design areas are soft.
VF-30: Almost complete details, and the design areas are sharper than VF-25.
VF-35: While wear is clear, all details are shown clearly.
EF-40: Also known as XF-40, minor wear is on the high details.
EF-45: Also known as XF-45, minor wear is on some of the high details.
AU-50: Slight wear is obvious, especially on the high points.
AU-53: Slight wear can be seen, but mostly on the high points.
AU-55: Slight wear can be seen, but only on the high points.
AU-58: Slight wear can be seen only on the highest points of the coin.

60-70 is reserved for uncirculated and proof coinage that is uncirculated. Uncirculated coins that were meant for circulation or had a circulating finish will get an MS, or mint state grade, while proof coins that were meant for collectors with a special proof finish and careful handling will get a PR, or proof grade. PR can also be stated as PF. The lower grades in these categories are reserved for coins with several marks and imperfections, while the higher grades are reserved for coins with no marks or incredibly minimal marks and exceptional eye appeal.

The grading scale is especially helpful for those new to coin collecting, unaware of coin grades, or are trying to decipher the alpha numeric coding on graded coin slabs. A warning to those new to collecting:

There is nothing good at all about a coin with a "good" grade.

-unknown

What the common person would consider good, is probably extremely fine to almost uncirculated, and what are considered "perfect" coins, most non collectors will have never seen. When trading coins, establishing the grade is key. Often a coin dealer and a potential buyer each grade a piece the buyer is considering. As much as collectors have tried to turn grading into a science, the matter is still quite subjective. The dealer and buyer will haggle over grade and ultimately price. Now, it is common to have coins that have been graded by a professional service. The service was paid to grade and encapsulate the coin, acting as an "unbiased" third party. With the grade established, the discussion centers solely on price. Recognized grading services commonly encountered will include:

Professional Coin Grading Service (PCGS)

Numismatic Guarantee Company (NGC)

American Numismatic Association Certification Service (ANACS)

Independent Coin Graders (IGC)

Certified Acceptance Corporation (CAC)

PCGS and NCG are currently the most commonly used, and CAC is a relative newcomer that in the last few years has become more common. Also of note is that the parent companies of both PCGS and NGC were taken private in 2021, as large investors wanted to capitalize on the post Covid-19 collecting trend. (Blackstone, 2021; Pendleton & Javier, 2021)

Each grading service has its own proprietary welded plastic encapsulation case. Many collectors stick with one grading service because they prefer their case style over the competing services. In some instances, this leads to potentially higher or lower premiums, depending on how many coins each service has graded for a particular coin type and the current preference/demand from collectors.

In the world of internet listings and auctions, grading services have brought serious value to the marketplace, allowing collectors to understand what they are buying even if they can't be there physically to exam the piece. Today, several of these companies offer professional photography that sellers can use when listing the coins and buyers can subsequently use later when selling. Coins are also assigned a number and entered into the grading company's database. While no names are attached, once the coin has sold, it allows populations of coins with specific grades to be determined, as well as recent auction prices for a coin type and grade to be listed. This enhances the collector's ability to be a prudent and informed consumer. Grading is not perfect. "Gradeflation," a term used for when owners resubmit coins in attempts to get higher grades, does exist. But, overall, grading services have taken some of the risk and guess work out of the trading process. While I wouldn't recommend buying any ungraded collectable coins on eBay (or bullion products either), I have comfortably and confidently bought several graded coins from reputable sellers on the platform. Figures 8-5 & 8-6 illustrate the utility a grading service can provide when shopping for a coin.

In this example, I went shopping on eBay for a collectable coin, specifically a 2003 Britania. The Britania is a popular silver bullion coin produced by the Royal Mint. It has a subseries that changes designs every year. I prefer the 1-oz silver size, which in this case has a stamped value of £2. The 2003 mintage has an aesthetic design, and valuations seem to appreciate well compared to similar coins.

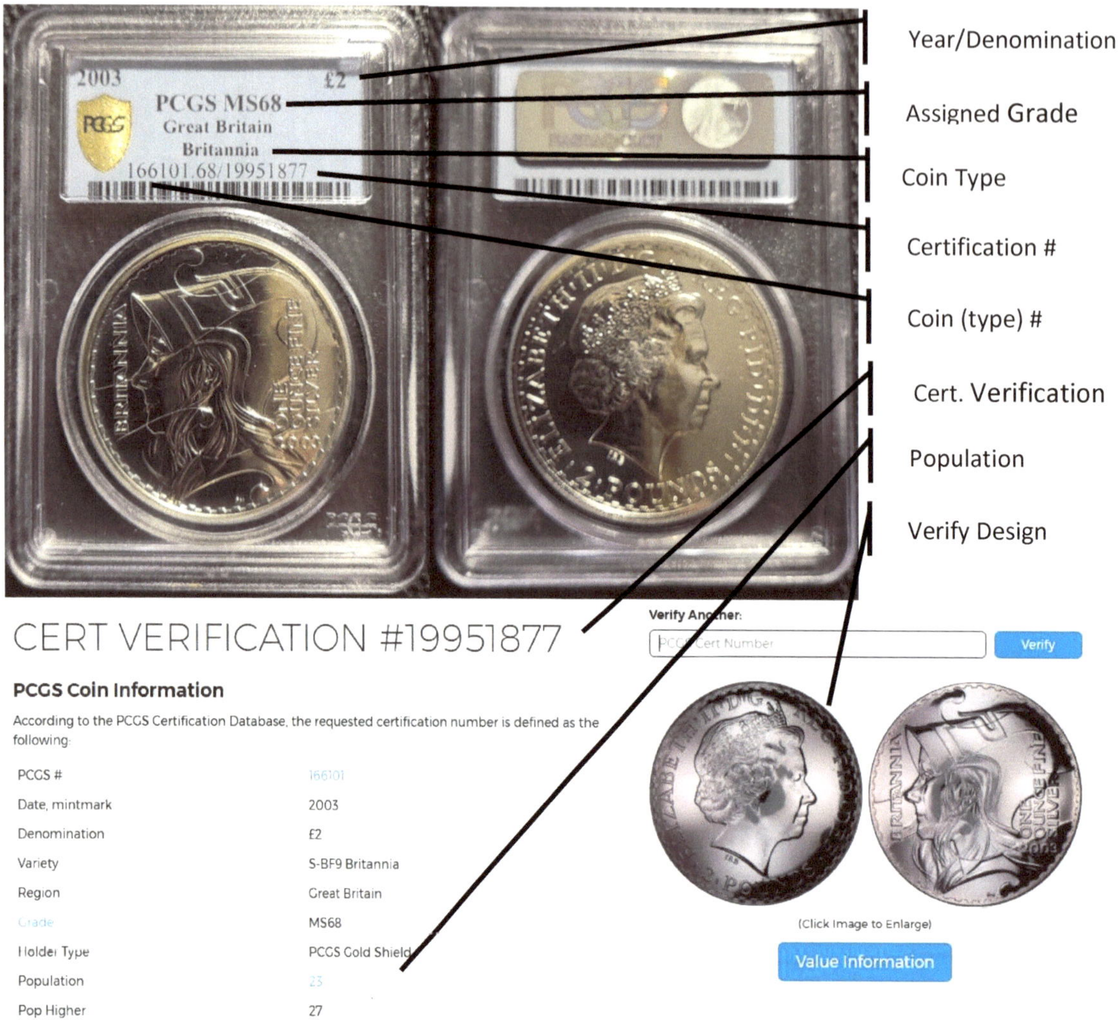

***Figure 8-5: Coin Verification of Grading Services**. Each case or "slab" will have several pieces of important information for the collector. First will be the year and denomination of the coin followed by the issuer and coin type. The number ahead of the slash is the Coin #. It is a code given to the type or design. All coins of a specific population will have this number. The number after the slash is the Certification #. This number is unique and specific to the coin. When shopping for a coin, a collector can go to the grading service's website and enter the certification #. If the coin is genuine, the number will link to the certificate, which will include the information on the slab but also current population data that can help the collector understand the coins rarity and how its grade compares to other existing specimens. Another link is often provided to report recent auction sales of the coin type, further helping a collector estimate a coin's value. (Image: modified PCGS, 2024a)*

I found a listing from a reputable seller, in this case a small coin shop that has an eBay store. I take the certification number off of the photo in the listing and enter it into the grading service's website for verification, and it links me to the coin's certificate. If you do not see a certificate, double-check the certification number. If a certificate does not exist, it is a red flag that the specimen may be fraudulent, and I would pass on the coin. This is not common but does occasionally happen.

Clicking on the "value information" link provides more detailed population data (Figure 8-6), which illustrates that there is a relatively small number of specimens. Understand, this is only the population for this particular grading service. By investigating the websites of the other grading services, one can get an accurate estimate of how many graded specimens exist. I usually want an MS70 grade, but it appears none exist. Given only 27 coins are registered with an MS69 grade, I may be forced to settle for the MS68, unless I want to risk waiting and hunting a long time. It also lists the sale price, date, grade, and auction house for the last sale of the coin type. In this case, the auction record was back in 2019, an MS69 that sold for $299. The expanded auction data shows all reported sales back to 2015, along with the grading service. Given the range of prices, grade, and appreciation of silver, any price between $100 to 175 at the end of 2024 would seem reasonable for an MS68 grade coin. Using the auction data and being willing to accept sweeteners, like free insured shipping, when negotiating with the seller are usually helpful. Note that, valuation becomes increasingly more subjective as specimen population and sale frequency decreases.

Having a coin professionally graded and encapsulated, colloquially referred to as "slabbing," usually costs $14 to 25, but increases with coin rarity and value. Many collectors believe the coin should be worth at least as much as the cost of grading before you go to the effort of having the coin slabbed. The floor price for a slabbed coin trading retail will usually be its original sales price, which incorporates intrinsic value, and manufacturing cost plus the cost of grading. The coin used as the example currently has an intrinsic value of around $30, about $5 manufacturing/premium cost, and the grading/slabbing cost of about $20 and the floor would be about $55. If the seller was willing to take $125 for the coin, $70 or the difference between the combined inputs and the purchase price would be considered the collectible value.

PCGS #	MINTAGE	METAL CONTENT
166101	100,000	SILVER

AUCTION RECORD

$299 · NGC MS69 · 4-5-2019 · EBAY

View a PCGS Set Registry set that requires this coin

Show eBay

Go To Grade

	65	66	67	68	69
Price Guide					
PCGS Population	19	15	24	23	27
Auctions - PCGS Graded					

PCGS #	DATE	PRICE	GRADE	SVC.	FIRM	SALE	TYPE	LOT #	NOTES
166101	Oct-2023	$58	MS68	NGC	eBay	eBay Sales 10/01/2023 - 10/07/2023	Auction	225787731922	
166101	Aug-2023	$51	MS67	PCGS	eBay	eBay Sales 08/13/2023 - 08/19/2023	Auction	115885943116	
166101	Mar-2023	$185	MS69	NGC	eBay	eBay Sales 03/12/2023 - 03/18/2023	Best Offer	334659481517	
166101	Dec-2022	$50	MS67	PCGS	eBay	eBay Sales 12/04/2022 - 12/10/2022	Auction	404018222170	
166101	Nov-2022	$46	MS67	NGC	eBay	eBay Sales 11/27/2022 - 12/03/2022	Auction	165783721793	
166101	Feb-2022	$72	MS68	NGC	eBay	eBay Sales 02/20/2022 - 02/26/2022	Auction	165334360704	
166101	Jul-2021	$96	MS68	NGC	eBay	eBay Sales 07/25/2021 - 07/31/2021	Auction	294288192514	
166101	Apr-2021	$120	MS68	NGC	eBay	eBay Sales 04/18/2021 - 04/24/2021	Best Offer	174730202207	
166101	Oct-2020	$31	NGC Genuine	NGC	eBay	eBay Sales 10/11/2020 - 10/17/2020	Auction	392971424714	
166101	Aug-2020	$150	MS68	NGC	eBay	eBay Sales 08/09/2020 - 08/15/2020	Auction	283969877171	
166101	Sep-2019	$44	MS68	NGC	eBay	eBay Sales 09/22/2019 - 09/28/2019	Auction	372772963062	
166101	Jul-2019	$59	MS68	NGC	eBay	eBay Sales 07/07/2019 - 07/13/2019	Auction	233283230157	
166101	May-2019	$99	MS68	NGC	eBay	eBay Sales 05/05/2019 - 05/11/2019	Buy It Now	333116803792	
166101	May-2019	$41	MS65	NGC	eBay	eBay Sales 05/05/2019 - 05/11/2019	Auction	333177763307	
166101	Apr-2019	$65	MS67	NGC	eBay	eBay Sales 03/31/2019 - 04/06/2019	Best Offer	283425806474	
166101	Apr-2019	$299	MS69	NGC	eBay	eBay Sales 03/31/2019 - 04/06/2019	Buy It Now	332880611942	
166101	Mar-2019	$32	MS67	NGC	eBay	eBay Sales 03/17/2019 - 03/23/2019	Auction	293002871190	
166101	Feb-2019	$99	MS68	NGC	eBay	eBay Sales 02/17/2019 - 02/23/2019	Buy It Now	332943510703	
166101	Feb-2019	$188	MS69	NGC	eBay	eBay Sales 02/17/2019 - 02/23/2019	Auction	372598827169	
166101	Jan-2017	$46	MS67	PCGS	eBay	eBay World Coin Sales in January, 2017	Auction	1602	
166101	Jul-2015	$23	Genuine	PCGS	eBay	eBay World Coin Sales in July, 2015	Auction	1693	Unc. Details
166101	Mar-2015	$41	MS65	PCGS	eBay	eBay World Coin Sales in March, 2015	Auction	2091	

Figure 8-6: Auction Data for 2003 S-BF9 Type Britania. *Coin grading services help collectors estimate the value of collections and specimens under consideration for purchase by providing auction data for these coins. Using the above data, a collector can get an idea of the coins rarity, frequency it may come up for auction, spread between grade values, spread between grading service values, and a general feel for the rate of appreciation or depreciation. Such data is often helpful when negotiating with buyers and sellers. Chart data (PCGS, 2024a)*

Identifying Future Collectables

No matter the type, be it coins, jewelry, whisk(e)y, trading cards, musical instruments, or cars, all collectables share a few common attributes. Understanding these will help you identify future collectables. The section above focused on precious metal collectables. But more generally collectable items tend to be:

1- Well-known. In order for there to be future demand an item must have many potential buyers.

2- Good quality. For a coin this would be a high grade, for a whisk(e)y this would be an exceptionally high rating by a judge or professional critic. An instrument may have a unique manufacturer and sound. It must be desirable to have many potential buyers.

3- Aesthetically pleasing. Beauty is in the eye of the beholder, but the better something looks to the masses the more potential buyers there will be.

4- Rare. It must be limited in number, so several potential buyers have to bid against each other to own one.

5- Easy identification and published information. Items with information on them that denote their uniqueness and authenticity, can help investors identify which will become collectable. These can include limited release or anniversary designations, mint or issue dates, a stamped brand, serial number, mint mark, or artist signature. Items with detailed information on how it was manufactured and the number issued and documents providing authenticity and provenance tend to become more collectable than those that don't because it de-risks the product. Typically, the more unique features and information the more difficult it is to produce a convincing counterfeit, this increases the confidence of potential buyers, which usually translates to more competitive bidding and a higher realized price.

6- Historical significance. As discussed earlier being tied to history can increase the collectability of an item, but in this case instead of looking back in history the collector is observing current events and trying to acquire items tied to those events that they think will be deemed as the most historically significant.

Goldbacks a future collectable?

Considering the above observations, one precious metal product that may become a valuable collectible are gold foil notes. Produced by Goldback Inc., these notes use an innovative gold vapor deposition on polymer technology that create artful bills of polymer encapsulating a gold core. They are flexible, fractional, and fungible with the smallest denomination containing 1/1000th troy oz of 0.999 or 24k gold. They carry about a 100% premium over spot. (Goldback, 2025)

While it is doubtful that they will achieve their intended purpose of displacing currency, there is an existing network of dealers and businesses that will accept these bills in exchange for goods and services. Being made of gold they have intrinsic value, but the company publishes an exchange rate each day. Per the discussion in chapter 3, it is obvious that many still are confused about whether gold is money or a commodity. Currently gold is a commodity. Goldback Inc. on their website claims their exchange rate is pegged to the market value of a 1-oz gold eagle. Today a 1-ounce gold eagle is trading at $3000 if pegged a single gold back (1/1000-oz gold) should be equal to $3. Yet, their published exchange rate is $5.80. In essence their "peg" has already broken. Their exchange rate reflects their cost of manufacturing and distribution. A Goldback contains much smaller amounts of gold than a 1 oz gold eagle, it is presumably much more expensive to produce a thousand 1/1000-oz Goldbacks than to mint a 1-oz gold eagle. The cost of manufacturing is in dollars (not gold), so per unit gold the company will continually need to charge higher premiums (and publish a higher exchange rate) to stay in business as the spread between the production cost of a gold eagle and their production cost of Goldbacks increases. Because gold is an imperfect hedge against inflation, also discussed in chapter 3, the value of gold will not keep up with the increased production cost. In essence, Goldbacks will continue to inflate relative to gold eagles so long as inflation in the U.S. dollar continues because the manufacturing cost is in dollars, and this inflation is only partly mitigated by gold performance against the dollar. The manufacturer offers owners of Goldbacks the ability to exchange their notes for gold eagles at a rate of 1000 for 1, but this currently would result in a 48.2% loss for the owner. Ironically, despite being made of gold, the notes will continue to experience a form of debasement caused by increasing manufacturing and distribution costs. Their use in trade is essentially barter and not barter for gold but for a product with gold in it, similar maybe to the premiums paid over metal value for jewelry. The bartering process is streamlined however by the fractional and fungible nature of the notes. On a material science and artistic level, they are beautiful products, only possible due to gold's unique physical properties.

Their popularity is a modern manifestation of the deteriorating confidence in government and government issued fiat currency by a portion of the population. If this deterioration in confidence became generally adopted, we could expect such notes to be our modern-day equivalent of the token monies used during the Middle Ages. In such a scenario imagine shopping with a combination of gold notes, pre 1965 quarters and dimes, silver and copper rounds, old sticks of computer RAM, jewelry, and who knows what else. Assuming we elect competent leaders, who prevent us falling into anarchy. These notes will likely have a strong collector's market in the next 20-50 years. Some of the features that make them good as collectables include issuances of 5 to 8 denominations in each series, and their plan is to have a series for each state. Each issue has its own aesthetic design, serial number, and issues date. They also have some intrinsic value, and production and advertising has been adequate to distribute over 8 million to date. Manufacture is constrained by material and labor costs and production, which will limit total production. My advice to the producers is to continue to add new series and designs catering to the collector's market, this way when the Goldbacks as currency plan ultimately fails there will still be a demand for the products, similar to the coins and rounds produced by the governments and private mints each year.

A final interesting fact about Goldbacks is they are produced in Utah, the source of another popular collectable made 170 years ago, Mormon Gold, or coins minted by members of the Church of Jesus Christ of Latter-day Saints. Soon after arriving in the Salt Lake Valley the isolated and fledgling economy was facing a severe shortage of money.

James Marshal, the discoverer of the gold deposit at Sutter's Mill, CA in 1848 that initiated the 1849 gold rush, was also a member of the church. He and several others are said to have brought gold to Utah for the minting of coin. These coins were the first minted from 1849 gold rush extractions. The provenance of gold used in these coins is from deposits along the American

River, near Mormon Island, CA. Coins were minted from 1849 to 1860, by which point the San Francisco Mint was producing enough coin to meet local demand. (Sensible Collector, 2025)

Figure 8-7: Goldback currency. *First introduced in 2019, these are privately issued notes made of polymer encapsulated gold through an innovative gold vapor deposition process. They are fractional, from smallest to largest they contain 1/1000, 1/200, 1/100, 1/40, 1/20-oz of 24K or 0.999 gold. While they will likely never achieve their intended purpose of displacing the dollar in part to the manufacturing limitations and economic principles discussed in chapter 3, they have many attributes that make them collectable. Aside from their intrinsic value this includes their quality, unique manufacturing process, serries issue, aesthetic designs, and widespread distribution network. (Image: Money Metals, 2025)*

Figure 8-8: Mormon Gold coins. *Four of a total of six designs are pictured. Denominations were 2.5, 5, 10 and 20 dollars. These coins represent the efforts of the early Mormon pioneers to stabilize their isolated economy. They are the first coins to be minted from 1849 gold rush gold, taken from deposits along the American R., CA. They were produced from 1849 to 1860. Most of the coins that made their way east were melted down. Today some types have less than 500 specimens. Present day values of uncirculated specimens range from $95,000 to $975,000. (Sensible Collector, 2025; APMEX, 2022; Image courtesy Reid Moon)*

Risks of buying Collectables

Liquidity:

As discussed earlier, depending on the piece and investment timeframe, liquidity can be a significant risk. Price points and the number of potential buyers will affect liquidity, auction data can help determine market interest and sale frequency. Make sure you are comfortable with the timeline.

Geographical Market:

Coins typically experience their best prices in their domestic market. This is because there are fewer interested buyers for foreign coin types than domestic ones. For example, both U.S. and Canadian coins trade at a discount if outside of the country. I paid $0.25-0.50 apiece for several early 1900's UK pennies I found at a local coin shop. The same coins in similar conditions would bring a price 6-10x that in London. The price spread in this trend is becoming less as internet sales have increased, both expanding market access and interest to collectors outside a dealers domestic market. A notable exception to foreign coin type discounts are ancient coins. Roman coins have an international market, and prices are relatively similar no matter where in the world you trade them. (Armstrong, 2017) Medieval coins seem to be developing a similar trend, where Asian collectors are willing to buy them to hold a piece of world history.

Trend Change:

Some coins simply fall out of popularity, resulting in fewer potential buyers. It can be some are just less interesting than others that have come into the market or a generational shift in interest. For example, many popular collectable coins now feature comic book characters, but I doubt similar coins would have been as popular with my father's generation. And will they be popular with future generations who will grow up with their own set of superheroes? Auction data can help determine if a trend change affects coins you own or are interested in. It should influence purchase and sale decisions.

Someone Finds a Hoard:

Hoards are where someone hides a lot of something of value, such as coins or gold, because they fear a loss; then, something happens to them before they can recover the hoard, and it becomes lost to time. While some may think this is an old age phenomenon; it is not. Hoarding has been around as long as people themselves, and there is no reason to expect that to change. Historically, hoarding is more common during times of turmoil or political unrest. The hoarders may be trying to protect assets from an invading army or an authoritarian government hunting for taxes. (Armstrong, 2023a)

A modern example is when a family contacted me in 2010 wanting to price different geophysical methods. Their father, in his mid-sixties, had buried about $100,000.00 (over $400k today) worth of gold somewhere on his 800-acre ranch with his backhoe. He died suddenly from a heart attack before he let anyone know where it was. Thinking of American history, this would have been the most significant period of economic turmoil in this man's adult life, which undoubtedly contributed to his motivation. Geophysical surveys, while significantly cheaper than direct testing methods like drilling, are often expensive to conduct. The family decided to pass and try other methods. Chances are that this modern hoard will be found. Someday.

Interestingly, hoards of Roman coins are found surprisingly often. Maybe, most famous is the Roman Hoxne Hoard found in England in 1992. Often a hoard will have well preserved coins that are higher grade than those already in the marketplace, the higher-grade coins will sell at a premium when they enter the market. Even with similar grades they often carry a premium (historical significance). In both cases they increase the population of coins with similar designs and grades, this increase in supply places downward price pressure on the rest of the population. The discovery of the Saddle Ridge Hoard (California) in 2013 is an American example, where $10 million worth of 1847 to 1896 US gold coins were found. (Haughton, 2016; Rogers, 2014)

Unfortunately, there is little you can do to protect yourself from someone finding a hoard, other than potentially liquidating early in the event you are lucky enough to learn about the discovery before they reach the market.

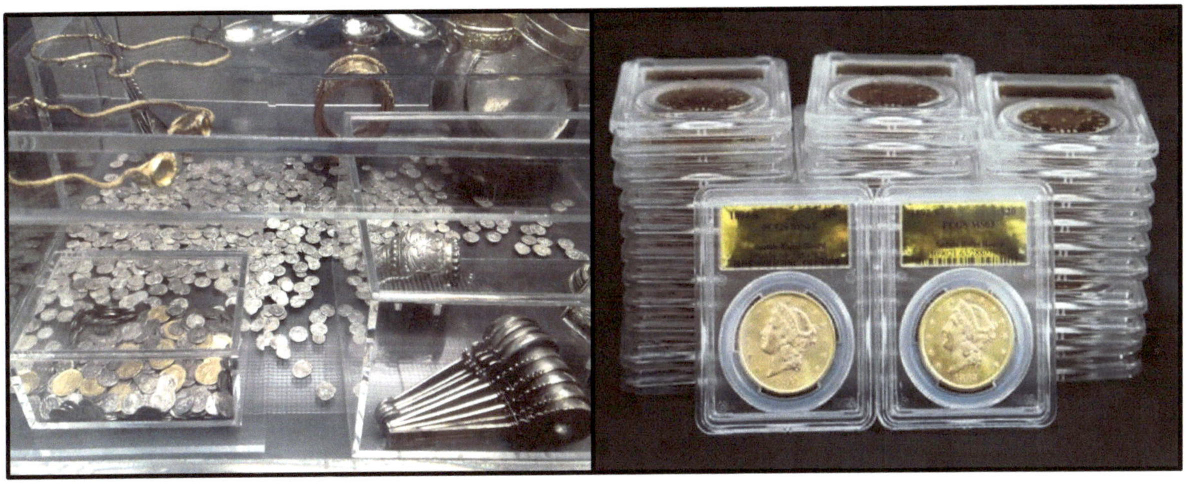

Figure 8-9: Two Significant Hoards Discovered in Recent History. *The Roman Hoxne Hoard (left) found in Suffolk, England 1992 and the Saddle Ridge Hoard (right) unearthed in California, USA 2013 are two examples of valuable hoards recently recovered. Most hoards can be dated using coins or other contents found in them and tend to mark periods of economic turmoil. Hoards are thus extremely important for understanding history. When high grade coins from hoards enter the collectibles market they tend to carry a high premium due to their historical significance, however they also increase the total population of specimens. This tends to apply downward price pressure on other coins of the same population. (Armstrong, 2023a) image modified from: (Houghton, 2016; Rogers, 2014)*

Fakes/Counterfeits:

Fakes and counterfeits are one of the main reasons coin grading services started. Initially, fraudsters would alter dates or mint marks of common coins to mimic those of less common coins. With advances in technology, sophisticated counterfeits exist that often even fool dealers. Most of these currently come from Asia; the time and resources involved to make passable counterfeits is usually not cost effective in most western economies. Still, there are plenty of them out there, even fake graded coins that the ignorant “think” they are getting a deal on. Sometimes a legitimate graded coin will be taken out of its case and a similar lower value put in its case and sold. Coin grading services have worked on improving the weld on the cases, but this is yet another reason to use reputable dealers.

This risk can be mitigated by:

1. Doing research. Comparison of the piece to high resolution photos of known genuine coins is a good start.
2. Chain of custody records
3. Buying from reputable dealers
4. Using grading services

Naturally the time spent on due diligence increases with price. Many collectors choose only to use an existing network of reputable dealers. They know they may pay higher premiums, but they will also have significantly more confidence that the piece is genuine.

Loss/Damage/theft:

How is it stored? Hopefully, not in a basement that is prone to flooding. Like bullion or firearms, collectible coins are not covered by typical homeowner insurance policies, unless you purchase a rider, and those often have small limits of <$2,000.00.

As we talked about with storage, there are expenses and risks that must be considered. The good news is that Americans in general like to collect stuff, so this is a concern for many folks, and there are now several specialty insurance and security options that can help with mitigation. Recognize that one of the reasons collectables go up in value is because over time, a certain number get lost or destroyed.

This aspect becomes particularly relevant when collecting consumables like wine or whiskey, because at some point it is expected that all specimens of a particular bottling will be consumed. In theory at least, the last bottle left will command the highest price.

Buying and selling process and costs:

Depending on the item, setting the price can be somewhat subjective. If it is a rare and high value item, you will probably buy or sell at auction, in which case the auction house fees will also apply. These typically range from 5 to 25%, depending on the auction house, though fees for items $3 million+ are often negotiable. Fees at major auction houses are usually paid by the seller, but the buyer pays premiums to the auction house as well, so they generate revenue on both sides. Online auctions, like eBay, are usually less, but you are doing more leg work. (Cleary, 2023)

Regarding the collectible coin market I would recommend that buyers/sellers wanting to get away from eBay check out GreatCollections.com which is the preferred auctioneer of the American Numismatic Association. They will only deal with professionally graded coins. USA Coin Book is another option that has lower fees and is particularly well suited for the <$300 market.

Outside of auction houses, there are seller's agents who will find a buyer for a fee, and this may prove more cost effective. For more common/liquid collectibles there are collection/coin dealers.

Most modern collectible coins have an established market. Before buying or selling, one can check out online auctions and establish what a particular grade of a piece seems to be going for. So armed, they can negotiate a price with a local coin dealer. Remember, coin dealers are going to have some overhead costs, so they will give a buy price below retail and a sell price usually at full retail. Not much different from a bullion dealer. Transactions can usually be made then and there. In this case, the spread is the cost for convenience.

If a private buyer/seller can be found, these will usually be the best transactions as the costs of all other parties are cut out entirely. There is usually plenty of wiggle room on both sides to still make the transaction a win-win. This, of course, will not always be possible, and you will want to be familiar with and use the other options, depending on your timeframe, level of desired convenience, and acceptable price point.

You can mitigate much of the buying and selling risks by doing research, only using trusted venders, collecting graded coins, and keeping a good catalog. The catalog cannot be stressed enough, as it keeps the collector informed of what they have, where they have it, and what they paid for it. Free online catalogs exist, such as that offered by USA Coin Book, or you can also purchase several custom-made programs with varying cost and utility. A spread sheet is also an option. My collection has enough unique specimens that I went with one of the inexpensive database options. Numismatist's Notebook II, is one such program that is inexpensive and has the basic required utility. Nothing is wrong with keeping the catalog in a special notebook. Just make sure you keep one.

Taxes:

We will talk about this in chapter 9.

You:

Yes, you potentially are your greatest risk. If you are prone to poorly thought-out impulse buys, this is not the investment space for you. Also, if you are not the type to keep good records of purchase prices and take the time for care, organization, and proper storage, this will be a money-losing endeavor.

Finally, there is a saying in the industry: "You are either a collector or a dealer but never both." While there are a few rare exceptions, the statement is getting at the psychological difference observed in the sector. Dealers are in essence traders. They enjoy valuing, buying, and selling aspects. Collectors, generally, are more sentimental, enjoy looking at or displaying their collections, and tend to get attached to their coins. The two psychologies, while dependent on each other for an effective marketplace, are usually incompatible in the same person, though some have switched from one camp to the other. Good traders probably make more money over time than good collectors, primarily because their capital has a higher velocity or turnaround. In all fairness, their effort is probably also higher and not dissimilar to comparing securities traders to investors who employ “buy and hold” strategies. This does not mean however that securities traders who own collectible coins will by default be coin traders. Many securities traders fall in the collector’s camp. It is a form of recreation for them where they can still employ their valuation skills.

Both trading and collecting methodologies can be successful. Identifying early if you are a dealer or collector and then operating within those expectations is an important lesson to learn.

Why buy collectables?

Inflation Hedge:

As established earlier: precious metals are not a hedge against inflation, rather, the hedge against government. Conversely, the right collectables will keep up with and may even significantly outpace inflation, while bullion prices express the inputs to produce metal, ultimately, more is still produced, whereas, the true number of a particular collectable can only go down. Speaking of coins, “the right collectables” will be high grade, rare, and have aesthetic designs. (Armstrong, 2017)

Collectable coins made of precious metals tend to hold up better when commodity prices decline, as the “collector’s value” insulates falling prices. Certain collectables experience their best performance during or immediately after periods of war. This happens for a few reasons:

First, collectors are motivated to purchase these items while they are still available in order to preserve them. Collectors are specialized historians and true protectors of history. Potentially losing that history is terribly motivating for them. During WWII, many collections and museums were motivated to purchase European art, as the Nazis where quickly confiscating or destroying it. Even I was motivated to buy several rare silver coins from dealer I have used in Kiev, simply to get the pieces out amidst the ongoing Ukraine war. Time will tell how this investment works out, but history is on my side.

Second, during natural disasters and wars collections can be lost forever. If you have one of only two known coins in the world and the other gets destroyed because a museum or another collector's house has a fire, then the value of your coin just went up significantly.

Prior to COVID-19, collectable coins had been in a slightly bearish to flat market. The abrupt crisis caused an initial crash in collectable valuations, similar to what was seen in both the equities and precious metal commodities markets; however, by 2021 we saw coin valuations make a significant correction to the upside and appear to start a new bull market. The fundamentals driving this rise were a combination of free money and deteriorating confidence in government, which left many people asking themselves what can I buy that will still be worth something later? This stands as the most recent period of crisis-driven activity in the collectables market.

A key part of having a collection be a good investment is collecting the right kinds of collectables. Studying Figure 8-10 and Table 8-1 make this clear. The 20th Century Coin Index is a composite of most modern collectable coins. It has a similar pattern to that of the inflation adjusted gold chart we looked at in chapter 3 earlier. The major difference is that the inflation adjusted gold chart peaks near the beginning of the USSR/Afghanistan conflict and the 20th Century Coin Index peaks at the end of it. Many of these coins are made of gold and silver, so a relationship between the two charts is not surprising. Its performance since the 1989 high has been mediocre at best and is only recently looking to enter a new bull market.

The 1893-S Morgan Dollar historical data (Table 8-1), however, tells a completely different story with valuations of high-grade specimens deep into six figure territory. The 1893-S is not just a one off. Figure 8-11 is the Key Date and Rarities Index. Whereas, I described the performance of the 20th Century Index as mediocre, the Rarities Index has been in a broad uptrend and is currently making all-time highs. While not immune to the 12-year bear market that started in 2008, it held up much better. The lesson to be learned is to seek the rarest and highest-grade specimens and identify them early. The game is not necessarily all that different from a securities trader or real estate investor performing fundamental analysis and market research on several investments searching for a winner and trying to get in first.

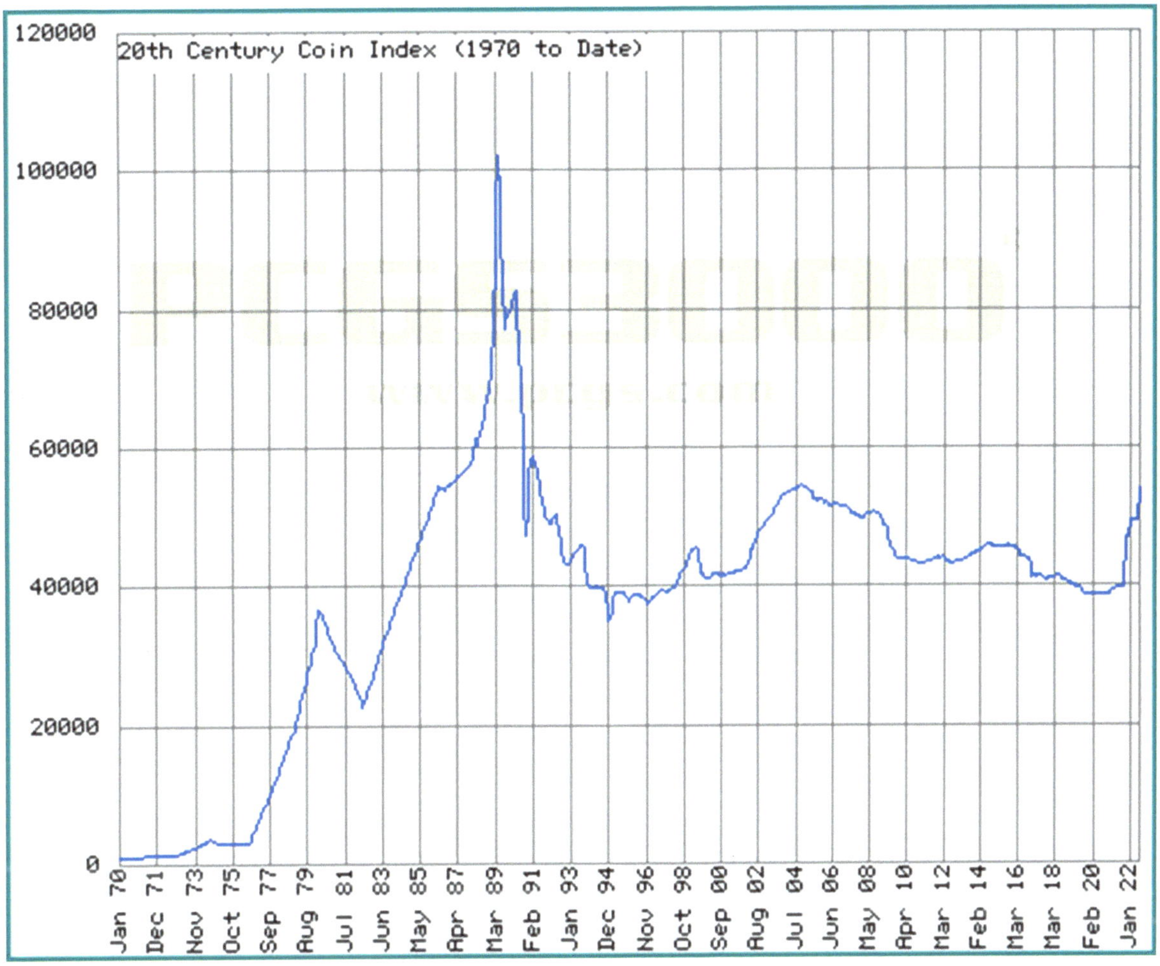

***Figure 8-10, Twentieth Century Coin Index expressed in $US**. It is interesting how this chart mimics the inflation adjusted gold chart. It is also interesting how this chart peaks at the end of the USSR/Afghanistan conflict whereas the inflation adjusted gold chart peaked near the beginning of it, about a month after the initial invasion. Several of the coins in this index are made of gold and silver, so the chart ultimately is an expression of both intrinsic and collector value. Chart data (PCGS, 2024b)*

Table 8-1: 1893-S Morgan Dollar Historical Values ($) by Grade.

The 1893-S is a key date in the Morgan series due to its low mintage. The table illustrates that collectors have been willing to pay significant premiums for specimens, especially those with high grades. Lower grades were initially worth their melt value. In the case of the 1893-S rarity within an otherwise prolific and popular series combined with the additional rarity of the high-grade specimens caused these coins to appreciate exponentially. The type has an auction record of $735,000.00. The current melt value is about $27.50. Compiled from historical spot silver prices and auction data. (PCGS, 2024c; uscoinbook.com (image))

1893-S Morgan Dollar Historical Values ($) By Grade									
Grade→ Year↓	**FR2**	**AG3**	**G4**	**VG8**	**F12**	**VF20**	**EF40**	**MS60**	**MS65+**
1945	1	1	1	1	1	1	10	50	75
1958	1	1	1	1	1	35	78	385	
1965	2	2	2	2	2	90	165	1700	2400
1980	20	20	20	20	20	875	2300	19750	
1986	5	5	5	5	5	1550	3200	19750	58750
2000	4	604	661	891	990	1840	3500	25750	299000
2015	1416	1234	1821	2585	3290	3760	9400	100000	635000
2020	1505	1930	2040	2520	3480	3960	9000	150000	635000
2025	1945	2331	3623	4450	6064	6475	11767	224012	702483
PCGS Pop.	**41**	**223**	**1340**	**1574**	**1264**	**1790**	**1449**	**105**	**18**

I have read the negative opinions of many investors and traders regarding collectables, and some are quite strong. My conclusion, however, is simply that those folks either do not understand or do not have the patience for them, because the data are clear. As an investor if you are good at identifying winners and are OK managing the real and unique risks associated with this asset class, there are very few buy and hold investments that can compete with collectables.

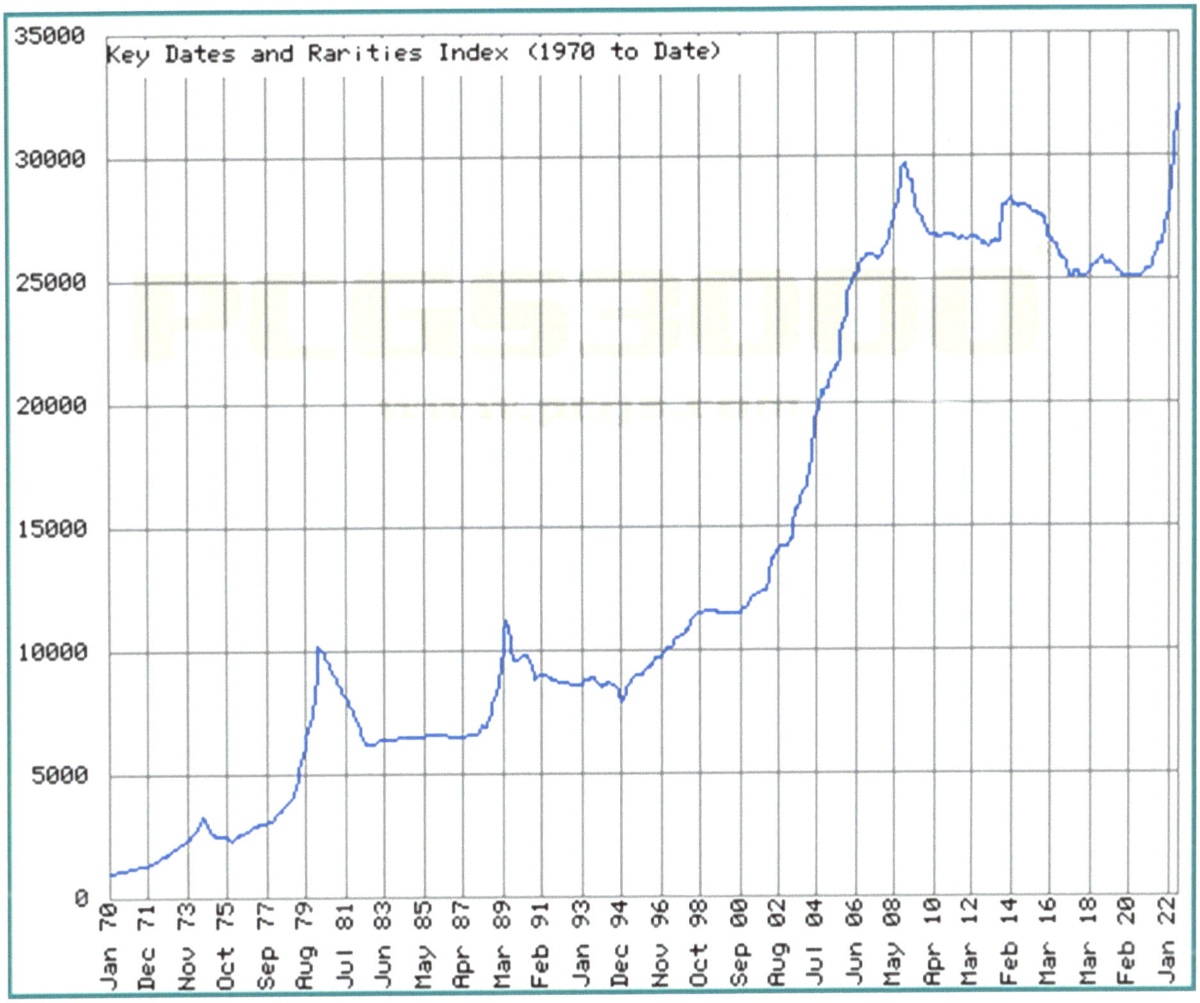

Figure 8-11: Key Dates and Rarities Index. *A composite of rare and key date collectable coins. In stark contrast to the 20th Century Rarities Index, key dates and rarities have enjoyed a more robust market being in a long term upward trend. It is currently making new all-time highs. The lesson to be learned, is that as a whole, key date and rare specimens will make better investments than their more generic collectable counterparts. (PCGS, 2024d)*

Arguably, there is some psychology around these higher value specimens that helps their price. A collector is likely not going to sell a piece for less than they bought it for, including auction house fees and expenses. Likewise, most buyers in this situation, while they want a good price, understand that the collector can choose to sit on it if they want to. Lastly, the view of many collectors with these rare specimens is that it is an opportunity to own history and thus become a part of it. To other investors, this idea may seem romanticized, yet as we know, the price of anything is what someone is willing to pay for it.

Real estate has historically been another good hedge against inflation. As with any investment, it has its own set of risks that need to be managed. For comparison, Figure 8-12 illustrates the nominal and real value of the U.S. House Index. Notice, that long-term performance of nominal home values is about 250% since 1970, compared to the Key Date coin index which is a little above 300%. A key difference in the charts is that Key Date collectible coins did not start to decline until further into the 2007-2008 financial crisis, and the fall was less. Arguably this reflects that as a group owners and buyers of Key Date coins were more financially secure than the average homeowner during this period. The bear market did last longer however not starting to recover until 2020. While not a complete analysis, this lag at least partially represents two factors. First, assuming Key Date coin owners and potential buyers are predominantly high net worth households, this group was deploying significant amounts of capital into real estate and equities during this period to take advantage of depressed prices and other opportunities. Second, this group would have faced higher tax rates than the previous decade moving into 2018. Both factors would have reduced the capital these households would be willing to spend on collectables.

While both real estate and collectables have their advantages when trying to hedge against inflation there are some differences. Comparing the two, investors may not be able or want to deploy the amount of capital required for a property but can find a collectable at a more amenable price point. Unlike real estate, the collectable is private, portable, and has no annual tax, and no maintenance costs howbeit the collectable will have storage expenses. Depending on the type of real estate, it could be rented or leased to generate income, whereas collectables, unless charging viewing fees, are not expected to generate any income. Both assets will have an involved purchase/sales process with appraisals, commissions, and fees.

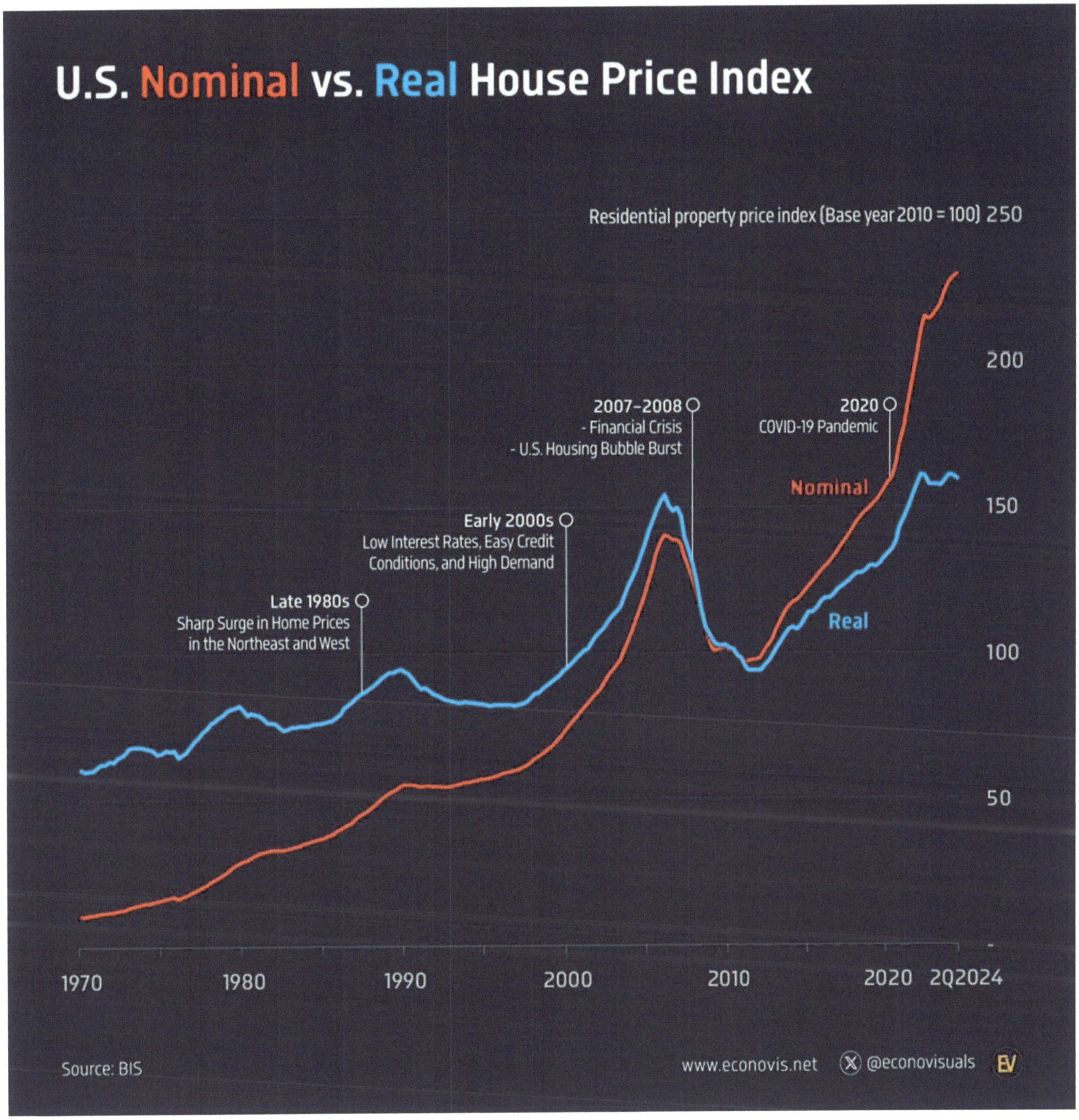

***Figure 8-12: U.S. Nominal vs Real House Price Index**. Real estate has long been viewed as a hedge against inflation. For the average investor, this will mean their personal residence and potentially additional investment property, often a rental or vacation home. Compared to the Key Date and Rarities Index (figure 8-11) both peaked about the same time with the 07-08 financial crisis and didn't make new highs until the Covid-19 period, with the Rarities index lagging a few years. An additional inference is that people usually buy a house before the expensive things that go in it. From these charts, it would appear the argument of rare collectibles as an inflation hedge is sound, even outperforming the U.S. House Price Index over a 50-year period. Chart (Soltani, 2024)*

Collectables Tell Stories:

As an undergraduate geology major, my professors with enthusiasm always told us that "rocks tell stories," and they were absolutely right; they do, and I have a whole pile of rocks with cool stories. I have noticed, however, that the stories told by my coins are received with far more interest than my rocks, at least by the general population.

One such story to illustrate the point. Figure 8-13 presents photographs of a 1941 and a 1942 six pence from Fiji. At the time, Fiji was a British territory. Notice that the 1942 also has an "S" mint mark, while the 1941 does not. "S" is the mint mark for the U.S. mint in San Francisco. So why does it appear on a British coin? Turns out that the 1942 six pence was minted in San Francisco by the U.S. Mint under contract for the British government. As confirmation, 1942 has the 90% Ag composition used in all American coins of the time; whereas, the 1941 has the 85% Ag composition of all British coin silver.

Figure 8-13: 1941 & 1942 Fiji 6 pence (reverse) magnification 10x. *These coins, while they look nearly identical are actually quite different. Fiji, during this period, was a British territory. The 1941 coin was struck by the Royal Mint and has a composition of 85% Ag as all other British coin silver for the period. The 1942 has the "S" mint mark (under the 42) of the U.S. San Francisco mint in California. It has a composition of 90% Ag, the same as all other U.S. coin silver for the period. Facing wartime challenges of maintaining the money supply for the empire, a situation aggravated by the sinking of the SS Gairsoppa in February 1941, the British government contracted the U.S. mint to produce and supply coins to Fiji. (Numista, 2024)*

Chapter 8: Precious Metal Collectables

While many people understand the importance of maintaining a stable money supply, few will ever appreciate the logistical challenges. With WWII raging and Germany on England's doorstep, the British were facing significant challenges to maintain a stable money supply and turned to their American allies for help. One of those war pressures was the sinking of the SS Gairsoppa, a merchant vessel, torpedoed by German submarine U-101 on February 17, 1941. The Gairsoppa was in transit from Bombay, India to London caring a cargo of 7 million ounces of silver. Much was to be used by the empire for coinage. It was sunk 300 miles off the coast of Ireland at a depth of 4700 meters with complete loss of cargo and all but one of her crew. It stands as the largest precious metal loss to shipwreck in history. The wreck was partially salvaged in 2012 to 2013 recovering over 1.8 million ounces of silver and setting records in terms of both value and water depth. Per contract, the salvage company received 80% of the salvage and the British government the balance. Both parties struck commemorative coins in 2014 from the recovered bullion. (Milligan, 2011) Money touches everything, and the Fiji 6 pence coins and the commemorative S.S. Gairsoppa products are modern examples of how history is recorded in money.

As a group, coin collectors have a significantly higher understanding of history and how events shaped the world we live in now. Several individuals have become and stay collectors because they like how the hobby forces them to learn history in order to put their collections in context. In many cases, studying collections is better than reading history books, because the collectibles, essentially being artifacts, are the historical facts. They are what they are and cannot be changed, whereas the history books are simply the interpretations, which are subject to bias.

***Figure 8-14: Bullion Products Produced from Silver Salvaged from the SS Gairsoppa Wreck**. The SS Gairsoppa was a British merchant vessel torpedoed by German U-boat U-101 in February 1941. Onboard were 7 million ounces of silver. This loss compounded problems of maintaining a wartime money supply to the territories and helped motivate the decision to contract the U.S. Mint to produce 6 pence coins for Fiji (figure) 8-9. From 2012 to 2013 1.8 million ounces were recovered from the wreck, setting records for both the amount recovered and water depth (4700m). Per the salvage agreement, the British government was entitled to 20% of the recovery and Odyssey, the Florida based savage company received 80%. The above commemorative products were produced from the recovery and made available to the public. They are the 2013 fifty pence (¼- oz Ag) Britania, produced by the Royal Mint (top left), the 1-oz round (lower left) and the 10-oz bar (right). The round and bar were manufacture by the Sunshine Mint under contract with Odyssey from their awarded portion of the recovered silver. (Milligan, 2011; Blanchard™, 2024)*

A Hobby with Value:

Finally, many collectors buy simply because they enjoy the pieces. What they have effectively done is found a way to deploy their hobby dollars in a manner that not only provides recreation but, when done properly, is also an investment. Considering that in 2024 the average American spent $3,458.00/year on their hobby activities, the value of a collection could quickly grow. (Sola, 2024) This is especially true if seeking out potential future rarities and capturing the appreciation. Most collectors will say they have also developed a stronger understanding and appreciation for history in the process. What one does with that knowledge is up to them, but it often leads to better investment choices and additional gains.

I recently purchased two high grade silver coins from a collector online. He had almost a hundred unique items listed. I complemented him on the quality and completeness of his collection which was impressive. He thanked me and replied:

"I'm in my mid-sixties and retiring. I have enjoyed these over the years, to me they are true works of art. But it is time for some of them to go, and someone else to be their watchkeeper."

My final word on the subject is that to be successful in this sector you must enjoy it and most do, because, after all, they are protectors of history.

Summary:

1- Common collectables made out of precious metals include coins, rounds, medals, and tokens.
2- Investors should understand the difference between intrinsic (metal) value and collector value; and learn to access how much of a particular collectable's value is attributable to each.
3- Things that affect collector value include rarity, grade, and historical significance.
4- Risk factors a collector should consider before buying a specimen include liquidity, geographical market, trend changes, frauds/counterfeits, and the potential for loss, theft, or damage.
5- Keeping an up-to-date catalog makes liquidating a collection easier and helps prevent loss.
6- Coin grading services help reduce fraud and simplify the buying/selling process.
7- Key dates and rare coins in high grades historically have enjoyed significantly better performance than their more common counterparts.
8- People buy collectables as an inflation hedge and/or a hobby that builds value.
9- One should not invest in collectables unless they have a genuine interest. Success on the investment side is often dependent on becoming an expert through independent research on your own and similar collections.

Notes

Chapter 9: Precious Metals Taxation & Privacy

The type of precious metal investment and the vehicle in which it is located will dictate how it is to be taxed. I would advise you to talk with your tax professional before making a significant sale of any of these types of investments.

We are going to cover the basics. Understanding these details should affect overall strategy by helping to calculate the true cost of a purchase or sale. More advanced traders using futures or options straddle techniques will want to do additional homework, but I will give enough to get started. My goal is not to turn you into a tax professional (I do not have the licensing as such.); rather, my aim is a solid working foundation of applicable tax rules, and their implications related to your investments. This will, hopefully, eliminate surprises and help you identify planning opportunities.

Sales Tax

In the US, sales tax is a very different experience, depending on where you are located. It applies to the physical form of the metal. Some states view precious metals strictly as an investment, not charging a sales tax; while, on the opposite side of the spectrum, we see up to a 7% tax. Others fall in-between and/or with limits or modifications by type and quantity.

Noble Gold produced the following summary of state sale tax rules. This is an excellent start for U.S. investors. Please double check with your local tax professional. Be aware, many states are proposing changes. For collectible coins of precious metal, sales tax is usually at the bullion rates listed.

LIST 9-1: BULLION SALES TAX RULES STATE BY STATE

In the list below, any figures shown are for the state-wide rate and are the minimum you can expect to pay. These do not include any county-specific tax rates. (Noble Gold Investments, 2022)

- Alabama: No sales tax on bullion
- Alaska: No sales tax at a state level
- Arizona: No sales tax on bullion
- Arkansas: 6.5% on all precious metal sales
- California: 7.5% on transactions below $1,500
- Colorado: No sales tax on most precious metals
- Connecticut: 6% on purchase values below $1,000
- Delaware: No sales tax
- Florida: 6% on values below $500, with an exemption for legal tender
- Georgia: No sales tax
- Hawaii: 4% general excise tax paid by the seller, often added to the purchase price
- Idaho: No sales tax
- Illinois: 6.25% on South African Krugerrands only; all other bullion is exempt
- Indiana: No tax on high-purity bullion, 7% on other types of precious metal
- Iowa: No sales tax
- Kansas: No sales tax
- Kentucky: 6% on all orders
- Louisiana: No tax on precious metals
- Maine: 5% flat rate
- Maryland: 6% on order values below $1,000
- Massachusetts: 6.25% on transactions below $1,000
- Michigan: No sales tax on high-purity bullion
- Minnesota: 6.88%
- Mississippi: 7%
- Missouri: No sales tax on high-purity bullion
- Montana: No sales tax
- Nebraska: No sales tax
- Nevada: 6.85% with some exemptions
- New Hampshire: No sales tax
- New Jersey: 7%
- New Mexico: 5% paid by the seller
- New York: 4% on transactions below $1,000
- North Carolina: No sales tax
- North Dakota: 5%, but with high-purity bullion exempt
- Ohio: Basic sales tax of 5.75% applies to silver and gold bezels; high-purity bullion is exempt
- Oklahoma: No sales tax on precious metals
- Oregon: No sales tax on any precious metals purchase

- Pennsylvania: 6% on silver and gold coins which are not legal tender, bullion is exempt
- Rhode Island: 7% tax applies only to bullion that has not been refined or smelted
- South Carolina: Most precious metals are exempt, but some coins and processed items attract 6%
- South Dakota: No sales tax on investment-grade bullion or legal tender
- Tennessee: No sales tax on gold or silver bullion
- Texas: No sales tax on gold or silver bullion
- Utah: A 4.75% tax applies to bullion with purity below 50%
- Vermont: 6% on all precious metal transactions
- Virginia: 5.3% levied on all precious metals with no exemptions
- Washington: No tax on any non-collectible precious metals
- West Virginia: Investment-grade bullion and coins are tax-exempt
- Wisconsin: A 5% tax on all precious metal purchases
- Wyoming: A basic 4% rate on all precious metal purchases

I have seen at least one of the less common internet dealers to get this wrong charging sales tax on bullion products for customers in states that do not require it. This was over confusion of the 2018 internet sales rule change. Basically, the Supreme Court in the 2018 case S. Dakota v. Wayfair, increased the ability of states to require online sellers to charge sales tax by eliminating something known as the “physical presence” rule. However, this should not apply to bullion products for the states that have an exemption for precious metals. The takeaway is to learn your local tax requirements and always double check before pulling the trigger on a purchase to make sure you are not paying more than you are required to. (U.S. Supreme Court, 2018)

Capital Gains Tax

U.S. Investors have 4 different classifications of capital gains tax with different rates associated.

Short-term Capital Gains/loss- *This is the marginal tax rate. It applies to investments held less than 1 year.*

<u>0%/15%/20% Long-term Capital Gains/loss</u>- *The net gain or loss on investments held for more than a year.*

Long term capital gains tax rates (2025) are:

Single	Married
0% for <$48,350	<$96,400
15% for >$48,350 but <$533,400	>$96,400 but <$600,050
20% for >$533,400	>$600,050

Updated tax brackets (Royal, 2025)

<u>25% Unrecaptured Capital Gain</u>- Applies to depreciable assets, like real estate. If you have depreciated the asset and received tax savings but later sell the asset above the depreciated price this is the tax rate you pay on the depreciated portion. (Reams, 2017)

Example: You Purchased a rental condo 10 years ago for $100,000.00, and over that time you depreciated it $20,000.00 for tax savings. Then today you sold it for $150,000.

Calculations:

$100,000.00(purchase price) - $20,000.00 (total depreciation) = $80,000.00 (depreciated value)

$150,000.00 (sale price) - $100,000.00 (purchase price) = $50,000.00 (capital gains taxed at the 0%/15%/20% rate)

$100,000.00 (purchase price) - $80,000.00 (depreciated value) = $20,000.00 (unrecaptured capital gain taxed at a maximum of 25%. This could be less, depending on how sale payments are structured; Bird, 2022)

<u>28% Collectables Capital Gains</u>- This higher rate applies to collectibles and some other assets, like small business stock, all of which were generally considered a "rich person's" investment in 1997, when lawmakers enacted the Taxpayer Relief Act. Rates were kept at this level for collectables as a tax on the rich, while rates for most other investments were lowered to the 0%/15%/20% long-term capital gains rates discussed above.

Collectibles can include just about any tangible item, but major defined categories include:

-Works of Art
-Musical Instruments
-Rugs
-Historical objects
-Antiques
-Alcoholic drinks held over 1yr.
-Medals
-Metal bullion
-Gems
-Coins
-Stamps
-Any other tangible personal property specified by the Treasury.

Some argue that ETFs and tradable Trust securities, because they are backed by precious metals, are also subject to this higher rate. This interpretation was presented in a 2008 IRS memo. While this interpretation is not law, some tax and legal professionals do follow its guidance. (Lewis et al., 2019; IRS, 2023a; Hyde, 2008)

Capital Losses and Netting

If you are a trader, you will at some point experience losses. Understanding the rules will help when employing strategies to mitigate the damage.

Losses, like gains, fall into both long-term and short-term categories and can be used to offset gains for tax purposes. Short-term losses must be applied to short-term gains before they can be applied to long-term gains. You want to do this anyway, as the short-term gains tax rate is usually higher.

Losses can be carried over from year to year. Limits are currently $1500 for individual filers and $3000 for joint filers. (IRS, 2023a; Perez, 2023)

An example of how to apply this:

If you are a joint filer, and in year 1 lose $10,000.00, you can deduct $3,000.00 from your taxable income. The remaining $7,000.00 loss is carried into year 2.

In year 2 you then experience a $5,000.00 gain before applying the carried-over loss of $7,000.00. Therefore, $5,000.00 - $7,000.00 = -$2,000.00. You can then deduct $2,000.00 from your taxable income, as it is still under the $3000.00 max limit. You no longer have any taxable loss to carry forward.

When it comes to collectibles and precious metals, there are a few additional considerations. For instance, have you classified it as an investment or as personal property? You must pay capital gains on personal property, but you cannot deduct losses. Whereas, with investments, you can deduct losses. (IRS, 2023a)

Think of it this way:

Ex.1- You bought a painting, and display the painting in your house for enjoyment. Over time, it experiences some photo degradation and has a reduced value when you sell it years later. Most would view this as personal property, and you would not be able to write off the loss. Conversely, if covered or stored in a dark, climate controlled space, this would be an investment, and you could even subtract applicable storage costs from the gains upon sale.

Ex.2- You initially buy a bottle of 80-year-old Madeira wine for $500 as an investment. Five years later you decide to drink it with your significant other during a special occasion. I wouldn't try to claim a $500 loss, even though the asset is undeniably gone.

Ex.3- You have a dozen graded bullion coins from different mints. You have kept purchase records. Though you may pull them out from time to time to enjoy them, you store them appropriately to preserve their condition. Five years later, you sell them. Some have appreciated; others have lost value. After subtracting applicable expenses (e.g. safety deposit box fees, collectible insurance premiums, or storage materials) you experience a $1,000.00 loss. This would be considered a legitimately deductible capital loss.

You should treat all metals and collectibles as investments to preserve your opportunity to deduct losses if that scenario becomes relevant. Keeping records of purchase prices and related expenses is part of that process. I have a database program I purchased inexpensively for my coin collection to track purchase costs and save copies of receipts for the storage materials in a folder. Remember, paper trails are your friend when it comes to counting and deducting losses.

Also, when you are netting (the process of applying losses to gains), you can and should apply losses to the most expensive category first. For example, you may have gains in the 28% category that you will want to offset before those in the 0%/15%/20% category. This will help you reap the maximum benefit for your losses. (Lewis et al., 2019)

Finaly, a reminder for traders. Short-term gains are taxed at your ordinary income rate. Yes, losses can be used to offset gains; however, you must pay attention to ***Wash Sales*** rules, which limit you from repurchasing the same or substantially the same security within 30 days of the sale. If you do so, any losses will be considered disallowed losses and cannot be used to offset gains (IRS, 2023b). This is one of many reasons why position trading is usually more profitable than day trading.

Taxation of ETFs vs Mutual Funds

In terms of rules and rates for taxes on capital gains and dividends ETFs and Mutual funds are treated exactly the same. The big difference is in the number of taxable events which is almost always more with a mutual fund and makes them a little more costly to hold. In a mutual fund the investor purchases fund shares that trade at the Net Asset Value (NAV) of the fund which is calculated at the end of each trading day. Once the NAV has been calculated all of the buy and sell orders are processed. The fund shares are actually redeemed and issued by the fund, not traded. This creates a taxable event, and if "sell" orders significantly outweigh "buy" orders the fund manager may need to sell securities and rebalance the fund, also a taxable event, and in both cases capital gains are distributed to the remaining shareholders. (TurboTax, 2025; Maverick, 2025)

ETF shares trade on the exchanges throughout the day and the price may be above or below the NAV. The ETF structure allows fund managers to trade directly in shares, meaning when someone sells, they may then directly use those share to fill "buy" orders circumventing the redemption/new issue problem. An ETF also does not need to rebalance in the same way, when a large batch of orders come in the ETF manager can redeem or issue "creation units" which are baskets of the underlying securities. This usually shields the rest of the ETF holders from capital gains. (TurboTax, 2025; Maverick 2025; Johnson, 2019)

Other aspects to understand are that mutual funds are actively managed, whereas ETFs are usually passively managed. This typically translates to higher turnover (more taxable events), and higher fees for mutual funds, while ETFs being passive, will have lower fees. Also, mutual funds being actively managed may have significant turn over, especially in volatile years, as managers cycle into and out of large positions. This can create exceptionally large capital gains distributions for shareholders. This is one reason many high-net-worth investors choose not to use mutual funds as these distribution "surprises" can often make tax planning difficult. (Johnson, 2029) Still others prefer actively managed funds because in a volatile market often a good fund manager can outperform a passively managed fund. In this case, retirement accounts make a good option as the capital gains distributions are exempt, instead the investor is subject to tax rules applicable to the retirement account type. (Maverick, 2025)

Capital Gains Regarding Options and Futures

A few things to understand about options and futures. (IRS, 2023c; Kowalski, 2023)

1- Wash sale rules apply to options but not to futures.
2- Options are usually considered essentially the same security as the stocks they are options for. So, the 30-day loss rule for wash sales applies if you sold the stock at a loss but then buy an option contract for the same stock.

3- Retained premiums from sold option contracts are considered short term gains. Unless it was a contract for over a year. I typically recommend contracts of 2-weeks to 2-months length as lower risk and more lucrative, so all these get classified as short-term.

4- Futures have their own tax structure. 60% Gains taxes as long term, and 40% as short term. So, taxation on $5,000.00 of net capital gain on a futures contract would look like:

$5,000.00 x 0.6 = $3,000.00 (subject to your long-term capital gains rate)

and

$5,000.00 x 0.4 = $2,000.00 (subject to your short-term or marginal tax rate)

5- Gains/losses for futures contracts are "marked to market" or, in other words, calculated based off the fair-market value for the last trading day of the year, even if contracts are still open and gains/losses are unrealized.

6- Some commodities focused ETFs are structured as a limited partnership and issue shareholders a K-1 form. When these funds exclusively purchase futures and options contracts, capital gains from these funds can be taxed using the 60/40 rule. (Doak, 2023b)

Taxation for Professional Traders

Special rules apply if you trade in securities and are in the business of buying and selling securities for your own account. To be engaged in business as a trader in securities, you must meet all the following conditions:

- *You must seek to profit from daily market movements in the prices of securities and not from dividends, interest, or capital appreciation.*

- *Your activity must be substantial.*
- *You must carry on the activity with continuity and regularity.*

The following facts and circumstances should be considered in determining if your activity is a securities trading business:

- *The typical holding periods for securities bought and sold.*
- *The frequency and dollar amount of your trades during the year.*
- *The extent to which you pursue the activity to produce income for a livelihood.*
- *The amount of time you devote to the activity.*

If your trading activities do not meet the above definition of a business, you are considered an investor and not a trader. It does not matter whether you call yourself a trader or a "day trader." (IRS, 2023a)

If you meet the above criteria, you could choose to take the "mark-to-market election," which must be claimed for the current year when you file taxes from the previous year. Mark-to-market means you treat a trading position as closed at year end and account for any gains or losses based on the market value. When the position is later sold or covered, the cost is adjusted to the marked value. (IRS, 2023a)

To obtain this tax classification, traders are required to file Form 3115 (Application for Change in Accounting Method). IRS Publication 550 describes the procedures in making this election with the IRS. Therefore, to take the election in 2025, you would have had to file a statement to that effect with your 2024 income tax return. (IRS, 2023b)

For tax reporting purposes, full-time traders have no open positions come December 31. The mark-to-market price is used against your cost basis to determine if you have a profit or loss on those positions. (IRS, 2023a)

There are some pros and cons to selecting this election. On the pros side, you are effectively a business. As such, all related and justifiable business expenses are write-offs. This can include software, computers, and fees related to education and research, to name a few. You are also no longer subject to the wash sales rule, and your deductible losses are no longer limited to $1500 (single)/$3000 (married); however, your gains are now considered personal income and taxed at your marginal rate. For active traders, this may not be a big deal, as most of their gains are short-term and taxed at this rate anyway. (IRS, 2023a; Charles Schwab, 2023)

Many professional traders will have an account designated "marked to market" for their trading activities and a separate account for investing subject to the capital gains rules discussed at the beginning of the chapter.

Precious Metals in an IRA

Individuals can set up what are called self-directed IRAs. These can be structured as either a traditional IRA or Roth IRA. A Business owner could also do the same with either a traditional 401(k) or Roth 401(k). This type of retirement account lets owners invest in some types of metals; certain types of real estate, promissory notes, and other non-traditional investments not found at a brokerage house. These are governed by the same section of code as the IRA's you are already familiar with. They follow the same rules, in that assets must be in a designated account. Owners are subject to the same taxation rules and early withdrawal penalties. (IRS, 2023d; Hoff, 2016)

The main difference comes down to the custodian's licensing. Brokerage firms or broker/dealers are SEC regulated (because they market securities) and due to those regulations and related expense/ complexity/ conflicts of interest they either cannot or choose to not engage in these additional lines of business. Remember that securities, brokers/dealers of those securities, investments advisors giving advice on securities, and representatives of these firms must register with either the SEC or at the state level. (STC, 2022)

Most of the custodians for self-directed IRAs specialize in financial instruments that are not required to register with either the SEC or state regulators. As long as they only deal in these instruments they too are not required to register, nor are they subject to related regulation beyond general fraud and money laundering provisions.

Regarding precious metal investments, the custodian's job is more that of a bookkeeper. You set up an account with the custodian and choose a bullion dealer. They will help you understand which metal products qualify (basically high purity bullion and US produced gold and silver eagles), and you choose a repository. The custodian then makes sure your funds are used to purchase the desired types and quantities and that they end up in the repository but physically separated from other account holder's products in the repository. They handle subsequent transactions, storage fees paid using cash in the account, and statements. (IRS, 2023d)

The repository I toured was in a non-descript concrete building. Bullion was segregated using 6 x 12 x 4-in locking metal boxes sealed with numbered wire locking clips. These were stacked on very heavy-duty shelves inside a UL Class III vault that I have no doubt could survive a nuclear blast.

Precious Metals Purchases and Privacy

Reporting of transactions to the U.S. Government for the declared purpose of anti-money laundering (AML) began in 1970 with the Bank Secrecy Act and has continued since. These laws affect essentially every financial industry from securities to life insurance, private and corporate business, to cash transactions. (FinCEN, 2023)

In addition to the Bank Secrecy Act, these laws include:

-Money Laundering Control Act (1986)

-Anti-Drug Abuse Act (1988)

-Annunzio-Wylie Anti-Money Laundering Act (1992)

-Money Laundering Suppression Act (1994)

-Money Laundering and Financial Crimes Strategy Act (1998)

-Uniting and Strengthening America by Providing Appropriate Tools Required to Intercept and Obstruct Terrorism Act (USA PATRIOT Act, 2001)

-Intelligence Reform & Terrorism Prevention Act (2004)

Regarding precious metals, most metal dealers will refrain from reporting transactions unless both of the following circumstances apply:

1 – The transaction (or sum of related transactions) is larger than $10,000

and

2 – Payment is made using actual cash (i.e. Federal Reserve notes and/or U.S. coins, like gold coins pre-1933) or cash instruments (defined as money orders, cashier's checks, or traveler's checks) which, when totaled together, equal more than $10,000.

Reporting involves form 8300 and applies to all U.S. cash transactions, not just precious metals. Checks, wire transfers, and debit/credit cards are not considered cash transactions and, therefore, do not trigger the reporting requirement. Of course, these are all traceable transactions, thus eliminating the need for reporting. (Singer, 2016; IRS, 2023e)

Traveling is becoming increasingly more complicated, but this isn't specific to precious metals. Anything with a value of ≥$10,000.00 that you are bringing into or taking out of the U.S. needs to be declared. (FinCen, 2017)

Dense metals show up extremely well on scanning equipment, so do not try to "sneak" anything when flying. It is best to request private screenings with TSA agents. Be prepared to answer a lot of questions: who, what, when, where, why, how much? Have documentation that supports your story. To be on the safe side contact the TSA office at your departure airport 24 hours in advance and inform them of the items you will be traveling with. Ask them for any specific instructions. This type of upfront disclosure removes suspicion, and you may even find it puts them into customer service mode.

There is nothing illegal about traveling with large amounts of money or high value items domestically. The challenge is that TSA agents are trained to identify suspicious activity in order to counter drug trade and money laundering activities. If you look and act suspicious, be aware they will contact the airport police who may confiscate your property and then you must go through a lengthy process in court to try and get it back. If you have a criminal record, you may want to consider other options of transport to avoid any potential hassle.

Shipping

Instead of the stress of traveling with coins or bars, you may opt for shipping. Domestically, the USPS is the best for values up to $50,000.00. If you have been a customer of an online dealer, I would contact them for values above that. Online dealers ship every day as part of their business. They know the best current options for the different needs and price points and will be happy to help, especially if you are a customer. This, of course, adds expense that should be subtracted from capital gains and, depending on the situation, may be worth it. (Anderson, 2018)

Privacy and the Hedge against Government

"Gold is the hedge against government."

-Martin Armstong

Chapter 9: Precious Metals Taxation & Privacy

Previously, when talking about owning physical metals, we explored reasons why investors gravitate to these investments. Many dealt with the uncertainty around government, usually on the fiscal mismanagement side. Another reason is when you have a government going through an authoritative cycle. In the U.S. and Canada, we are already well past the beginning stages of one of these. These cycles tend to be marked by censorship and tracking of citizens. Usually, the goals include extracting additional tax revenue and suppressing opposing views to the party in power. Actions are typically precursors to greater economic and political calamities. (Armstrong, 2018)

We recently witnessed the debanking of several hundred Canadian protesters during the 2022 "Freedom Convoy." This included freezing financial assets and disclosure of bitcoin wallet addresses. (Elamroussi et al., 2022).

This, coupled with the development of Central Bank Digital Currencies (CBDCs), creates unique risks. For example, even with electronic banking as it now is, if you receive or send a transaction, the record stops there. With crypto or blockchain currencies, you see the entire record of everyone that has ever owned that coin. Leaders are already discussing the programmability of CBDCs so they can restrict transactions they don't approve of, and one can only imagine the surveillance capabilities such money will afford governments. (Sociable, 2023)

If you find yourself on the wrong side of the government, like the Canadian truckers, you could be left with no way to even execute transactions with the money you have, not to mention risk of confiscation. Never before in the history of mankind have governments had so much control and surveillance capability over their general population. For any trader or investor accustomed to performing a risk analysis, I'd say the privacy argument for owning physical precious metal is as strong as it has ever been in my lifetime.

Precious Metals & Medicaid

So, we are back to those five gold rings mentioned earlier. Most precious metal assets we have discussed would be countable assets in regard to Medicaid spend-down rules. This would include bullion products, as well as any of the market-traded instruments. The exemption to this would be some jewelry and possibly some collectables that could be considered personal items. (Lamkin, 2021)

There are not a lot of specifics in the law regarding this. Heirloom jewelry, however, is considered a personal item. Obviously, if the jewelry were part of a large collection worth several tens of thousands of dollars, regulators would want to consider it qualifying. Likewise, a few collectable coins is probably not worth bothering about, and maybe the plan is to bequeath them to a grandchild anyway. A large valuable collection would be considered qualifying. Bear in mind, Medicaid is a partnership between state and federal governments, so limits, procedures, and interpretations will vary. On the Idaho Medicaid application, Appendix B is three pages dealing with assets. While it asks for a list of assets, including bank, investment, retirement accounts, life insurance, burial funds, real properties, trusts, bonds, stocks, mutual funds, vehicles and even cash on hand, nowhere does it specify anything about bullion, jewelry, or collectables. (IDHW, 2022)

Privacy again comes into play regarding physical assets. Unless you purchase these things with a credit card, there is really no way for the government to know you have the assets, unless you self-report them. While regulators are likely to happily count any listed asset, regulations are vague enough, especially for jewelry, that there is plenty of room for interpretation either way. If concerned, check the application and rules of your local jurisdiction as they vary.

Certain types of non-revocable trusts and state partnership qualifying long-term care insurance are ways of protecting reportable assets from Medicaid spend down and liens. More on this in the financial planning chapter. (Idaho Legal Aid Services,2020)

Discussion

As with most of the U.S. tax code, there is what is written and then there is the application or common interpretation by tax professionals and the IRS. In my experience, most tax professionals treat capital gains/losses generated from precious metal ETF's/trusts like other securities subject to either your short-term rate or the long-term 0%/15%/20% rule instead of trying to apply the 28% rule. The brokerage does not distinguish between them in their reporting and breaking them out for separate taxation would be cumbersome. A lot also depends on the funds structure, as discussed earlier. Is it an ETF, ETN, some form of a mutual or unit investment trust, or a limited partnership. Each its own applicable taxes on the fund side, and the limited partnerships will issue a K-1 to owners with reportable gains and losses to file with their taxes. Most other financial professionals and traders agree that the collectable rate should not be applied to these instruments. They are securities, so tax them as securities. The system is complicated enough already.

With physical metals, many preparers either use the 28% rate or your marginal tax rate, whichever is less. This fits better with the original intention of the law and aligns better with our incremental tax system. (Allied Financial Services, 2024) However, grouping bullion with collectibles has never made much sense. As discussed in an earlier chapter, 40% of mined gold becomes bullion, and almost all of that is purchased for investment purposes. For this reason, many argue the short-term/long-term 0%/15%/20% rates would be best, as it simplifies and aligns again with the incremental tax system. Still others accurately argue that precious metals are commodities with significant amounts being consumed by industrial processes. Their argument is they should be taxed as other commodities following the 60%/40% capital gains rule applied to futures. This also would be a simplification.

Bear in mind that transactions under $10,000.00 would be self-reported. Given the off-the-grid nature of the instrument, the government would be wise to set gains taxes on metals at equal standing (or better) than traditional investments (definitely not worse) if they want to realize more tax revenue.

There are mixed opinions about the self-directed IRA for physical metals. I personally am not a fan. Yes, you can realize some tax savings; however, one of the unique aspects of physical metals is their off-the-grid nature. This is completely negated once you put them into an IRA. As talked about earlier, there are inefficiencies when buying or selling physical metal. With the IRA structure, you are adding custodial fees and risk. Being required to store the metal at a repository is a turn-off for many.

Most buyers who like physical metals do so, because metals are hands-on, off-grid, moveable, and they are in total control. They don't mind paying the extra premiums, because they get these benefits. In an IRA, you lose those benefits and have higher costs. So, in a way it is the worst of both worlds.

I still like self-directed IRAs for real estate and other outside investment opportunities like promissory notes, but for metal, to me, it is a classic example of just because you can do something it doesn't mean that you should. I trade gold/silver ETFs in my brokerage IRAs, and that has been a good strategy for me.

If you feel overwhelmed at this point, don't. There are a lot of resources, many of them free, available to you. Your coin and bullion dealer can be a great resource for most questions. If you catch them on a slow day, many will be content to shoot the breeze for hours while you are drinking from their well of knowledge. Remember, it is beneficial to their business for you to succeed, so it is in their interest to help. If they won't, you can always take your business to one that does.

Finally, use professional tax services. For most people with a well-balanced financial plan, precious metals or related investments are only going to comprise 2-10% of their total assets. Most mid-career individuals will have a combination of real estate, business interests, insurances, and other investments. As each of these areas has specific tax requirements keeping it all strait is cumbersome at best. Leave tax preparation to a professional with the appropriate software and experience. That said, you should have a working knowledge of applicable tax laws for each of your investments. This will help you communicate with your tax person and help you develop proactive tax plans with them. You should feel comfortable asking them questions, and they should be willing to answer them in detail. All this will help determine if they are preparing your taxes in the way you want. It is ok if you decide to change. Most people will use two or three preparers before they find the best fit. I would encourage the use of small firms with the same preparer from year to year. This fosters more proactive vs reactive tax planning.

Keep all documents and finances well organized. Invest in accounting software to track your income and expenses. Not only will this save time, but when you give your CPA a well-organized file of your forms/statements and accompanying electronic file of your books that they can load directly into their software, you have saved them a lot of time. Now their entire energy is focused on doing the complicated stuff that you cannot do. They spend less time creating a better return. You save the maximum on both their preparations fees and your taxes.

In the U.S., we have arguably the most complicated tax system in the world. Yet, consider that we also have the highest concentration of millionaires and billionaires who still choose to live here. That tells us that despite the complexity, it is still one of the most efficient tax systems in the world - if you can navigate it.

Disclaimer:

This chapter has been reviewed by Allied Financial Services PLLC, a certified public accountant & business consultant, to verify all statements. This review was conducted in August 2024. All statements are accurate as presented at time of review. Laws and regulations change frequently. This chapter is for education purposes only; individuals should seek professional tax advice within their jurisdiction of residence for the most timely and accurate information.

Notes

Chapter 10: Recognizing Conflicts of Interest

Introduction

The financial industry is riddled with conflicts of interest (COI), so much so that it would take a book several times larger than this to document. The goal of this chapter is to identify for the retail investor/trader of precious metals some of the key COI and help them learn to identify others. COI will always exist in the financial industry and, depending on who you are dealing with, may or may not be a concern. You need to be aware of where COI exist and, if at all possible, avoid or eliminate them.

In the U.S., securities licensed individuals are required to disclose existing COI with current or potential clients. If COI exist it does not necessarily mean that the client cannot do business with the financial professional, but it is required to make clients aware of COI so they can make informed decisions. COI can include anything from owning shares of the same stock to having overlapping business interests. COI disclosure agreements usually need to be signed by the client before the business relationship can start. This, honestly, is a difficult thing to regulate and for even the best intending of advisors to keep up to date. As a note, many of the disclosure requirements for retail investors are not required when dealing with institutions. It is assumed these clients have done their due diligence. (STC, 2022)

Professionals in other sectors often have differing or no disclosure requirements. This means that the investor needs to be proactive in identifying where COI exist, and deciding how to avoid, eliminate, mitigate, or if of a low-risk nature live with them.

The Precious Metal Dealer

Precious metals dealers make money by selling bullion and coins. As discussed in previous chapters, they need to constantly sell products to keep the lights on. They are perpetual gold bugs. In addition to marketing materials, they often publish articles or books about investing in physical metal. Any idea what the recommendation is? Buy, buy, buy. The reasons are constantly recycled, be it inflation, the end of the dollar, end of the world. Every market goes up and down. Precious metals may very well be appropriate for your portfolio, and you should do your own research. Part of that research is identifying any COI or bias of the sources providing the research material.

The Brokerage

Brokerage houses generally make money in two ways, trading fees/commissions and interest paid on cash securities. Traditionally, the push has always been increasing the frequency of trades, thus increasing the frequency of receiving commissions. Did you notice any changes once commission free trades began?

1- Brokerage houses began offering higher interest paying money market funds than banks to attract capital and increase their market share at the expense of the banks. They still keep a portion of the interest usually in the form of a management fee.
2- Suddenly, options and futures trading was being pushed to retail investors. These trades still carry fees and commissions, and they were back to the same business of making high frequency traders out of everyone.

The Investment Bank

Another interesting COI that exists with investment banks is trading against their clients. The investment bank has all the investment data on their clients and will regularly place trades opposite their clients. A pretty good strategy considering a 2017 study by UC Berkley estimates that 80% of day trades are unprofitable (Barber et al., 2017). Many investment banks also engage in prop trading, meaning these investment banks will put out ratings, recommendations, or upgrades/downgrades on different securities based on their research divisions findings and will trade ahead of announcements. (Charitou & Karamanou, 2020)

High Frequency Trading

One of the most lucrative applications of the supercomputer is the ability to execute algorithmic trades, known as High-Frequency Trading (HFT). It has come to dominate daily trading volume. HFT technology allows institutional traders to execute their orders of multimillion-share blocks ahead of other investors, capitalizing on fractional upticks or downticks in share prices. When subsequent orders are executed, profits are instantly obtained by HFT traders who then close out their positions. This can occur dozens of times a day, reaping huge gains for HFT traders. Though different in application and execution, it functions the same as frontrunning, which is a prohibited practice in the U.S. Sadly frontrunning even in the traditional sense, where brokers receiving large orders will place trades ahead of those orders in order to capitalize on the movement is still a problem. The SEC as recently as 2022 filed a frontrunning case worth $47 million. (Chen, 2022; SEC, 2022)

Dark Pools

Dark pools are private exchanges that allow large block orders of securities to be traded anonymously between buyers and sellers. Executed trades are not reported until after the transaction is completed. These started in the 1980s to add efficiency and save costs between large brokerage houses without having to go through public exchanges. The incentive for large institutional investors to use dark pools has increased as market participants try to mimic or take trade cues from the actions on large players. Additionally, the now pervasive HFT makes it extremely difficult for these traders to place large block orders on public exchanges. Even when spread over several exchanges, the large block size and HFT activity around it not only alerts everyone to the trade but often can disadvantageously move the price. The dark pool allows institutional investors to avoid this. Today, no less than 64 highly regulated dark pools are operating in the United States. The anonymity and overall lack of transparency around dark pools, however, make frontrunning much easier to pull off unnoticed, and with the sheer volume of trades taking place in dark pools, it makes average investors question the accuracy of market depth and even price data. (Chen, 2022)

Investment Advisors and their Representatives

Investment advisors (IA) are usually large companies that sell investment advice and management services. Many are also broker/ dealers and have insurance products, as well. They attract business through a network of investment advisor representatives (IAR), which are contracted individuals who solicit mutual funds and insurance products for the IA. The IARs are what most people would call their financial advisor. The contracts between the IA (company) and their representatives limit the IAR (person) to the defined lines of business and specific investments or products offered by the IA (company). This in effect makes the IAR a captive agent. Even when the contract does not limit the agent to solicitation of outside products, compensation plans, sales bonuses, and other competitive metrics used by the IA discourage the solicitation of outside products in all but the rarest of cases. Depending on the representative's licensing, they will be able to offer either commission-based products or charge a service or management fee. Understanding your financial representative's licensing and how their firm's agreement with them works will help you understand how you will pay for their services, what services and investments they can offer, and what kinds of COI may exist. The licensing part is usually advertised on their card or can be quickly looked up. Agreements with the firm, however, are closely safe-guarded. It is generally accurate to view all investment adviser representative as "captive agents", meaning they will only present you with the firm's insurance products and mutual funds offered directly through them or close affiliates. While some IARs may argue this, the reality is the bonus structures these firms have negate any incentive to solicit outside business even if contractually they are able to. This affects the client in several ways that are usually never fully disclosed, or if disclosed, rarely understood:

1- The client is usually under the impression that their financial advisor (the IAR) is the actual person choosing and managing the investments. This is true in part. The IAR is choosing from a list of company approved mutual funds for which the IAR will receive a commission (if it's a load fund) or a management fee if they are serries 65 licensed. Your IAR usually receives about half of the management fee; the IA (company) receives the balance. Neither the IA nor the IAR play any role in management of the fund. Unless the IAR has proper licensing (series 65 or series 7 with a series 66), they will not be able to invest in individual stocks or ETFs for clients. In essence, they exist to market mutual funds. One of the biggest surprises for me when I was one of these people was that we spent 40% of our training on product knowledge and 60% on marketing language and psychology.

2- The vehicle your IAR will often choose for retirement accounts is a deferred annuity, which has some advantages when buying the load funds they are likely selling you. Basically, changing investments in a load fund when held in an IRA would require repaying the load fee or commission each time there is a fund change if held in an IRA, but in the differed annuity, due to their structure, load fees are not recharged money is simply reallocated. That part is all good and fine. However, most clients would be interested to know that the deferred annuity counts as an insurance sale for your IAR's sales and bonus metrics. This is a common COI rarely disclosed.

3- The IAR is prohibited from discussing investment options outside of what is offered by the broker/dealer. Physical investments in precious metals, real estate, and crypto are relevant examples. This is usually under the pretense of the "selling away" rule which is a prohibited practice for buying products from a broker/dealer other than your own. The big firms, out of caution, interpret this (at least when it concerns their IARs) to include investments in non-securities as well. While there are legitimate regulatory concerns the IA (company) is trying to avoid, this in turn can create another COI. When clients express interest in investing in physical precious metals, real estate, or crypto, the IAR is to direct the client instead to commodity mutual funds, securitized real-estate funds (like REITS or mortgage-backed securities), or something else. The choices must come from the IA approved list. Thus, the IA (company) can maximize their funds under management, which may or may not be in the client's best interest.

Commodity mutual funds offered through the large broker/dealers usually drastically underperform the asset they are meant to track. (Financial Times, 2025) This was discussed previously but is because such funds typically purchase long-dated futures contracts, which have storage costs and possibly some time-decay factored in. As these near expiration they are rolled into more long-dated contracts so that in a flat market you are constantly buying high and selling low. Additionally, these funds are subject to the manager's timing ability and fees. Being leveraged, poor timing can exacerbate poor performance. Finally, management fees are high. This has caused many IARs to have a negative bias toward commodities in general, because the only funds they see are the struggling ones. Many will not even touch commodity funds and given the performance of the ones they are allowed to solicit I don't blame them.

As we observed in chapter 3 many commodities in inflation adjusted dollars are going down in price through time due to improved production technology and efficiency. A commodity fund needs an experienced trader, not an investor-minded manager of the fund if it is to be successful. That is an almost non-existent find with the commodity mutual funds these firms throw together just so they have something to offer in the asset class.

In short, do not plan on having meaningful discussions around precious metals with an IAR who is part of a big firm. Firstly, because it is out of their line of business and they will be ignorant of many important aspects. Secondly, they will try and direct you into another investment vehicle that they can sell, which may not even be related to precious metals.

The Independent Registered Investment Advisor (IRIA)

For those who want to have meaningful discussions around outside investments like precious metals, real estate, and crypto as part of their portfolio, the best option is probably the independent registered investment adviser (IRIA). In this scenario there is still an IA (company) and an IAR (person), the difference is that the IAR is one of the principles or owners of the IA (company), often the sole owner. These professionals are all series 65 licensed and the independent structure and licensing allows fee based instead of commission-based compensation, which removes many of the COI we encounter with the IA/broker-dealer/IAR relationship. Many of these professionals are also insurance licensed and offer comprehensive financial planning, which can also be a COI, but maybe one you are OK with.

These professionals still make money by managing money, so they will probably push you in the direction of market-based instruments. That said, you can probably find someone that is willing to discuss metal ETFs, mutual funds, futures, and maybe even physical products. Market-based instruments will be subject to their established management fees. For physical products, they will probably charge you a service fee for purchases/sales, due diligence, and arranging shipping or storage. It is a fee sized to their time requirement and work involved, legally it cannot be structured as a commission. This is the fairest, least COI way. In this situation, be aware of frequent recommendations to completely cycle into and out of physical metals investments. This activity would be considered a form of churning, another prohibited practice, that involves frequent trading in order to collect additional fees.

An IRIA will usually cost about the same as the IA/IAR arrangement, they will have nearly unlimited investment options and are brokers regarding insurance. They also keep all the service fees. While a lot of that extra money is allocated to their overhead and compliance expenses, they generally keep more than the IAR, which translates to needing to maintain fewer clients, meaning more time is spent on account management and less in soliciting new business. Many who understand the financial industry choose to use an IRIA even if their person does cost more, because for them it is a small price to pay for conflict free and unbiased advice.

Research Firms

In the U.S. research firms that deal in securities are considered investment advisors and are required to register with either the state or the SEC. Those who do not deal in securities are not required to register and by their nature usually have less COI. This can be complicated, however, when registered investment firms have contracts with the research firms that allow special or advanced access or when publicly listed companies pay a research firm to publish reports or give interviews to executives.

Research firms tend to focus on a particular market, political environment, or region of the world. Seeking out firms providing conflict free, unbiased, accurate, and timely advice is the quest of any active market participant.

An important part of doing your own research is both learning how to recognize the bias of those giving advice but also identifying your inherent biases. Looking at any market objectively is critical, and understanding your biases will help you avoid many costly mistakes.

Training Providers

Training providers are usually a business that trains or educates retail investors about investing and trading. They often have contracts with large brokerage houses that compensate them for bringing in new clients and accounts. The brokerage then pushes the training provider to train clients in higher frequency/higher commission strategies, which as discussed before, statistically are less successful for the retail investor.

Other training providers hold themselves up as successful retail traders who, through showy ads with themselves enjoying expensive things, entice investors into expensive subscription services that may offer trade ideas or training materials. However, the training providers are not necessarily good traders themselves, but rather, are good marketers, and their success is derived from their subscription business. There are plenty of ways to cheat in this business, historically a common one was to tell half the clients to buy and the other half to sell, ensuring that half got profitable advice and would keep subscribing. Initially, it can be difficult to distinguish good players from the bad. If you use such a service, go in with both eyes open, and frequently access the value of the advice or services received.

The Certified Public Accountant (CPA)

The CPA, along with a few other specialized legal professionals, is unique in that they do not require securities licensing, or additional training beyond that required by their profession to offer investment advice. So long as they are not charging a fee specifically for that advice, they do not require state registration. Many choose to register and will charge fees for both tax and investment advice. It is important to understand which licenses and registrations your CPA in order to put both their advice and fees in context. They can be very good resources for both market based and outside market investments, and they understand the tax ramifications of all related decisions. They are also a natural choice as trustees of estates or advisory boards. This broad scope, however, creates many potential COI when interacting with clients. For example, they could simultaneously be the advisor of both a buyer and a seller of a property or other investment and often advise clients (for a fee) on multiple investment decisions, while also filing taxes (also for fees) that those investment decisions have made more complicated. While I am a proponent for every individual using a qualified tax professional, they need to be aware where COI could arise. Many individuals intentionally have both an investment and a tax professional for this reason and may even add legal, real estate, and insurance professionals, if their case merits to avoid COI. In best case scenarios, these individuals will collaborate on the case, each bringing their experience and expertise in the client's best interest.

CPAs tend to fall into the trap of giving tax advice, looking backward, as they prepare the previous year's taxes. This may or may not be the best investment or financial planning advice looking forward.

The western world has built a massive infrastructure around the financial sector. Retail investors/traders need to remember that, while this infrastructure can create many opportunities, it was not necessarily built for their benefit. Training themselves to identify, avoid, eliminate, and mitigate conflicts of interest is a key element of navigating the risks within this infrastructure. While this chapter only highlighted a few examples, hopefully it will help readers think and act more proactively.

Summary

1- Conflicts of interest (COI) exist all around in the financial industry. Some professionals must disclose COI while others don't. You must be proactive in identifying COI.
2- You should not base a decision to buy or sell precious metals off of what the dealer recommends; they have an inherent COI.
3- Be aware of the COIs that exist with brokerage houses and investment banks. If there is a lot of advertising or push around a particular financial product, it is reason for deeper investigation.
4- Investment adviser representatives for large firms are ill suited to speak about or recommend products around precious metals due to their contracts with the investment advisor which create a serious COI between them and the client.

Independent registered investment advisors are usually a better choice, if one with expertise in precious metals can be found.

5- Using research firms that do not deal in securities is usually best, because it eliminates COI.
6- Seek educators and trainers who do not receive compensation from brokerage firms or investment banks to remove COI around taught trading strategies.
7- CPA's have unique rules that allow them to give financial advice without additional licensing. While it is highly recommended to use such a professional, be aware of how the one stop shop service could create COI with your situation.
8- Consider building a team of professionals to handle your estate. Ideally, this would consist of a tax, investment, and legal professional but could also include a real estate and insurance consultant. Make sure they collaborate to maximize the benefit from each.

Notes

Chapter 11: Precious Metals in a Financial Plan

Thus far, we have discussed how precious metals were formed, where they are located, and in simple terms how they are extracted. We have also discussed their physical properties, some of their historical uses, and the roles they play in industry and our modern economy. We reviewed the historical relationships between gold and currency and discussed how this has led to several misconceptions that are today often presented as common knowledge.

We have looked at mining companies and the differences between majors and juniors, their differing objectives and codependences. Most importantly for understanding mining companies, we explored the various risks that could be applicable. We discussed streaming and royalty companies that are the financiers of mines and how their business models operate. We investigated the various financial instruments investors and traders can use to invest in precious metals and the taxation laws regarding each and have highlighted some of the major pros and cons, while looking at examples and strategies.

In this final chapter, we bring it all together and discuss how precious metals can be used as part of one's financial plan. This information is specific to U.S. residents. While some aspects are true for those in other jurisdictions, tax laws vary significantly from country to country. In addition to the investment vehicle, one must consider the classification or account type that is to be used.

See figure 11-1, The Value of Creating Options. Though a simple diagram, this illustration, like the periodic table, provides an invaluable reference with a depth of information for those who know how to read it. Each box represents a different financial instrument in the United States. In truth, each box also has several un-displayed categories within it. Each box has its own advantages and disadvantages, tax implications, timelines, and rules. It is far from a perfect system, it is complex and often cumbersome, however, the reality is that this system has evolved in the U.S. because, for those who know how to navigate it, it creates (for all income levels) maximum flexibility, financial freedom, security, tax mitigation, growth, asset protection, and the ability to own and transfer property between individuals, organizations, and generations.

You may have heard the maxim "If you want to be rich, you have to do rich people stuff." This is a diagram of what that stuff looks like. While none of these boxes is terribly complicated to understand by itself, the true strength is in how they can interact with each other. A good financial coach can teach you to use them synergistically to maximize their value and minimize your risks. While most people will not use every box, everyone will want to have significant assets in at least 6 boxes by the time they retire. This ensures that no matter what market cycles, physical ailments, or perils take place, they will be able to make a wise financial decision. (Batholith, 2024)

As we have just demonstrated, a book literally can be written on each of these topics. Let us discuss how to best use what we have learned regarding precious metal investments and apply it to a personalized financial plan.

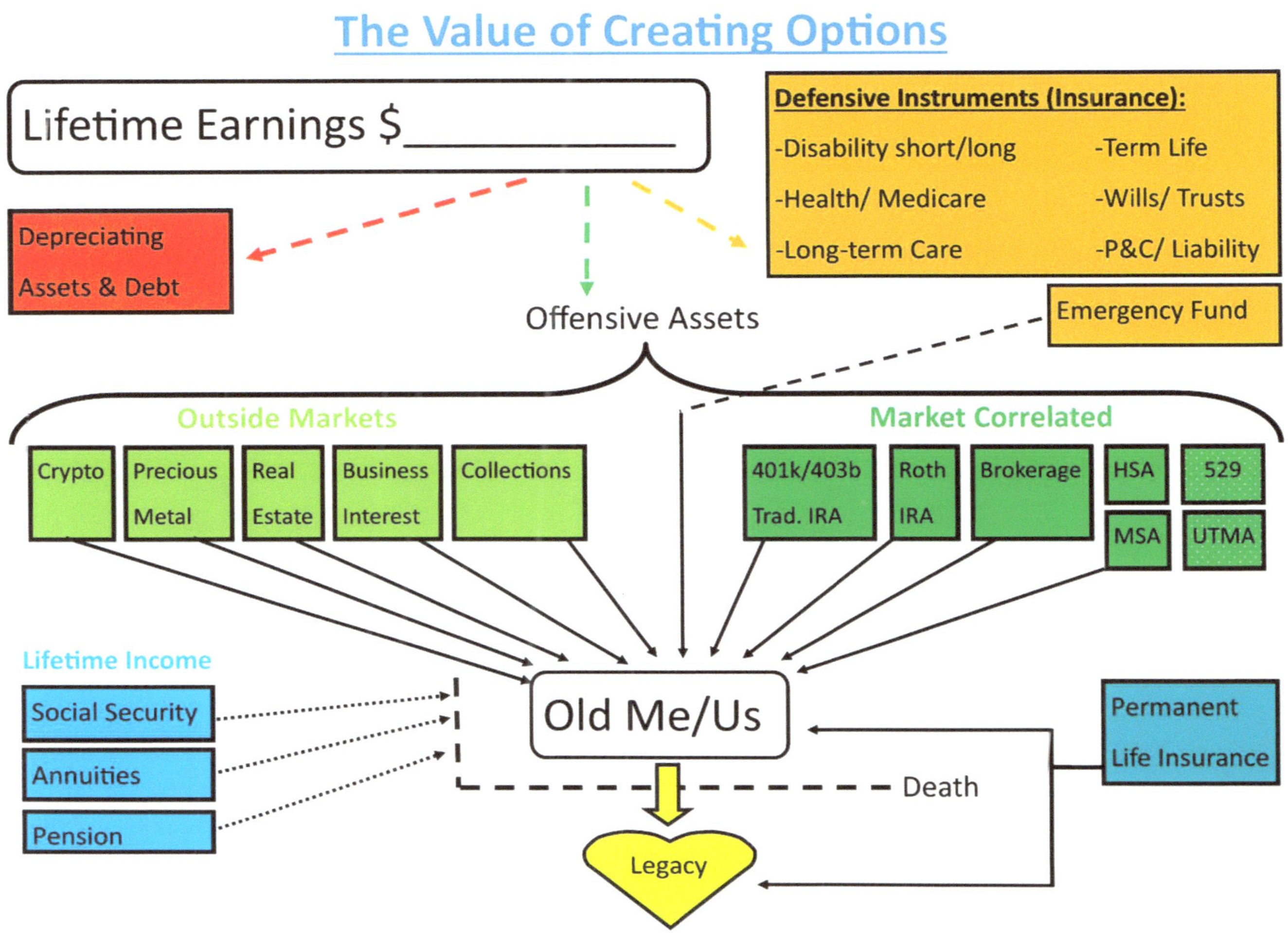

Figure 11-1: The Value of Creating Options*, considered by some to be the periodic table of money organization, this diagram helps individuals quickly categorize asset classes based on purpose, general function, taxation, and legacy potential. It also helps individuals realize that some of the best financial benefits come from synergies between the different boxes. In general, everybody will want to have significant assets in at least 6 of the boxes by the time they reach retirement. (Batholith, 2024)*

Chapter 11: Precious Metals in a Financial Plan

Physical precious metals usually occupy two boxes. The precious metals box, typically constrained to non-collectable bullion products, and the collectable box. Both these are usually long-term assets, and capital gains are taxed similarly at the collections rate, as discussed in the taxation chapter. An advantage of these assets over retirement accounts is that you have no restrictions on how much you can put in or when you can take them out. They can be kept short-term or long, it is up to you; however, the nature of both is that they will be intermediate to long-term assets because transaction costs will be high. Some less frugal people like this, because it makes it more difficult for them to access when impulse spending but is still available to supplement their emergency fund in a crisis. Privacy is a key reason why both have a place in the financial plan. The right collectables will generally keep up with or outpace inflation; whereas, bullion is not a perfect inflation hedge but sees its best appreciation when confidence in government deteriorates. Between the two, bullion will be much more liquid. (Armstrong, 2017; Armstrong, 2019)

Unlike retirement accounts, where you will be forced at age 72 to begin making distributions, you can leave your metal invested, and only cash it in when needed. I know a couple old folks who bought an ounce of gold a month while they were working and now cash in an ounce of gold a month in retirement.

Precious metals IRAs do exist. A reminder to what was discussed earlier, I do not recommend using an IRA for physical precious metals. Other than cash, physical precious metal is the most liquid asset you can own that has complete privacy. Once put into an IRA that privacy goes away. Also remember what Martin Armstrong said: *"Gold is the hedge against government."* Putting physical precious metal in an IRA negates the two primary reasons it should be part of your financial plan.

Finally, because of their privacy, physical metals are difficult assets to track when it comes to taxation. Dealers are not required to report purchases or sales under $10,000.00. The onus is on you to report capital gains on your metal sales. Keep good records of purchases and sales so as to not overpay.

Chapter 11: Precious Metals in a Financial Plan

Often people buy and hold physical precious metals as a hedge against government instability or some kind of apocalypse. Indeed, if there is a war, revolution, or authoritarian market cycle, it is the physical assets that survive, and precious metals and certain collectibles are both popular choices due to their high store of value and portability. However, nearing the end of life without a crisis materializing, the assets are passed to heirs. In this case, they receive a stepped-up basis for tax calculations, and again there is no required distribution schedule as with an inherited IRA.

If you have the right collectables, they tend to appreciate faster than bullion. The tradeoff is, in a crises it can be difficult to know what value to expect. Crises tend to increase the value of certain collectables, as collectors try to acquire them while they are still available. After a crisis or war prices may be higher, as some number of the collectables were lost or destroyed; or, inflation, which is most extreme in times of war, has eroded the purchasing power of the currency. But, if everyone is struggling to survive, all that may be received is whatever utility value the collectable may have, such as its metal content, but no collectable value. In these scenarios it will be more difficult to find a buyer, and it may be better to solicit potential buyers outside of the area of crisis. (Armstrong, 2017)

Investors in collectables need to have sufficient assets to weather crises, otherwise they may be forced to sell collectables at inopportune times. This is one reason that individuals should have a mix of asset types. Collectables and bullion generally do not generate income; it is an appreciation only type investment. These and liquidity are some reasons why collectable assets typically comprise a significantly smaller proportion of total assets than other asset classes.

Still many collectors enjoy their collections, and having a hobby that builds value is a strong argument. Investors that do not have a genuine interest in collectables in general or in a particular type of collectables should generally not invest in them.

Assets Best Suited for the Brokerage Account

Futures and option-spread-trades usually will only be available in a brokerage account. This is because of their highly speculative nature. The government is giving a tax break with retirement accounts, because they realize social security alone will not be sufficient to support you in retirement. They want you to be able to support yourself instead of going on welfare, as an estimated 47.9 million U.S. retires have, as of 2022. (Sekulic & Djordjeric, 2023) They want you to save money, not speculate with it.

Mining stocks and leveraged metal ETFs also fit well in the brokerage account. My rule of thumb is that anything risky goes in the brokerage. The reason for this is that in this account losses can be used to offset gains, minimizing tax liability. Losses can also be rolled over from year to year as discussed in the tax chapter. Yes, it still hurts to lose money, but the silver lining is you now have some tax hedging ability in your financial plan. This can be used to offset income (within limits) or capital gains from the sale of a property or other asset. The strategy is to apply losses to the highest taxed gains and work your way down.

Assets Best Suited for Retirement Accounts

In retirement accounts, we usually invest more than trade. In my experience, most metal/mining securities fluctuate more than they appreciate, meaning trading strategies are more effective than investment strategies. Therefore, most are not appropriate for retirement accounts. That said, some of the majors (large mining companies) have relatively stable dividend paying stocks. Coupled with a covered call strategy, this can work well as part of a retirement account portfolio. This can also be said for some of the metal/mining ETFs. Even so, you will probably want to cycle into and out of positions trying to catch major cycle highs and lows. Preferred stocks that are usually relatively stable and have healthy dividends are also a good option, when they can be found. Many of the broad market mutual funds and ETFs will have some exposure to the metals and mining sector. These are highly recommended, as all sectors help to balance each other through various market cycles. A retirement account can also negate many of the capital gains distribution challenges faced by mutual funds. (Maverick, 2025)

If you are a good trader, paying down dept and funding retirement accounts from some of the gains in your brokerage account is a smart idea. This strategy helps take some of your winnings and allocate them to a lower risk profile. It will also limit interest and tax exposer, either now or in the future.

It is important to have money in both a traditional and a Roth IRA. The traditional IRA will save on taxes now, but the Roth protects all gains from taxes. If you are a household with variable income you will want to contribute to the traditional IRA in good years, reducing tax exposure, and in lean years, when tax burdens are less significant, contribute to the Roth. In extremely lean years, you may even consider doing a traditional to Roth conversion of some funds in the traditional IRA. When doing this, taxes are owed on the money being converted, because it wasn't taxed when it went into the account. If the conversion is made during a low-income year the applicable tax bracket is lower. The strategy is to convert as much as you can, stopping before it puts you back into a higher tax bracket. Once in the Roth, this money can grow tax free for the rest of your life.

The Roth IRA also allows you to withdraw contributions (not earnings) before age 59 ½ without penalty. While this generally should be avoided, because you can't put the money back in, it does give a little more flexibility in an emergency situation. It will be interesting to see how the new proposed tax laws of the second Trump administration evolve. If enacted, they may change some of these recommendations.

Assets Best suited for a Health Savings Account (HSA)

If you have a health savings account, you may consider moving funds to a self-directed HSA to avoid custodial fees and gain access to investment options. In my opinion, Fidelity currently offers the best self-directed HSA account, and you can still have it and keep your work-related HSA qualified health insurance plan and associated HSA account. Fund the self-directed HSA with earnings and potential gains from the brokerage account, like as discussed with IRAs. Be sure to pay attention to applicable contribution limits and make sure employer plus personal contributions do not exceed these limits.

HSAs can be powerful tools in a financial plan because contributions reduce your taxable income, and they also grow tax free. Literally the best of both worlds, but you can only use these funds to pay for approved medical expenses, which do include Medicare and long-term care insurance premiums for retirees. These funds should be used before death, if possible, because they are fully taxable at death for non-spouse beneficiaries. Meaning the entire account balance is taxable as income for the non-spouse beneficiary. This is significantly more expensive and less flexible than how inherited retirement accounts are treated. (Murray, 2024)

Growing an HSA will take several years of disciplined saving. Once $10-20k has accumulated, they are especially well suited for income producing portfolios, as owners will have a need for several small distributions throughout the year. A good dividend-paying mining stock, or ETF, coupled with a covered call strategy is appropriate as part of an income producing portfolio in an HSA. Preferred stocks are also ideal in income producing portfolios; be aware not all preferred stocks are able to be bought in a Fidelity HSA.

Also, be aware that a common trait among dividend stocks, especially higher paying ones, is that their share performance will typically not be very good, as they are shelling out a bunch of money for dividends each quarter. Often, the share price may even go down. The goal is to have it stay at least flat while collecting the dividend. Timing is important. The advantage of buying a dividend stock low is that as it appreciates, you are still getting a rate based on your purchase price, with the share appreciation to boot. Beware of dividend traps, however. If it looks too good to be true, it probably is, and these stocks tend to fall hard if there is a dividend cut.

The preferred stocks will be more stable and have less risk this way. Generally, their share prices tend to fall with rising interest rates, and rise with falling rates, as capital seeks higher returns, but of course, a company's financial strength plays into this. One risk specific to preferred stocks, being debt instruments, is the company can call (buy) them back, essentially paying off their loan. This may force you out of a well-working position. The risk of this is greater during times of falling interest rates, as the company may refinance, or when company performance is strong and it has abundant free cashflow. This risk tends to be low in rising interest rate environments, as new financing options tend to be worse for the company than sticking with their preferred stock plan.

Finally, when building a dividend portfolio, plan on taking at least a year to reach your full allocation. This will allow a few market cycles to play out. Selling good dividend payers can be a difficult decision when they reach cycle highs. In such cases, you will want to evaluate the company and dividend strength, chance of increased payouts, value of continued payouts, appreciation of the share price, likely timeframe and depth of a potential pullback, and potential investment options to take its place in the portfolio.

Considerations for Trusts & Estate Planning

Some may have developed the thought of using precious metals to hide assets from the government, thus helping qualify for Medicaid and paid for long-term care. While this is in theory doable, it is probably not a wise thing to do for a few reasons.

1- Medicaid has set limits on what they will pay providers, which is significantly below what they usually charge. Because of this, many facilities will not accept Medicaid patients. Those that do, subsidize their Medicaid beds from profits off of privately funded clients. The care received by Medicaid paying patients usually involves a shared room with only the legally required minimum level of care. After visiting several facilities, I can say that this option is not for me.

2- Old people are really easy to steal from, and due to their off-the-grid nature, precious metals, like cash, can be easily stolen. Maybe, most concerning is that 25% of elder fraud cases involve a family member, 7% a fiduciary, and 4% a non-family in-home care giver. (CFPB, 2019)

Individuals can and should structure their assets now in ways to protect themselves for when they are their most vulnerable. Proper use of retirement planning techniques involving trusts and various insurance products can remove many of the conflicts of interest that may arise, especially if an inheritance is involved, in caregiver/family/fiduciary relationships. A well thought out and executed trust/insurance plan can also significantly reduce tax exposure and facilitate the protection of assets and their transfer after the owner's death. One of the reasons people buy long-term care (LTC) insurance or permanent life insurance with an LTC rider is to remove the risk of a family member spending funds intended for their care on something else.

It is usually more difficult to defraud someone of assets that can be tracked vs those that cannot. Where privacy is ideal when we are in a good state of mind, it becomes a risk when we enter mental decline. Putting precious metals into a trust removes the privacy around them but also puts them under the management of a trustee. Though statistics show family members are three times more likely to defraud their elder relatives than fiduciaries, the fiduciaries are not infallible. (CFPB, 2019)

Structuring a trust so that it has both a trustee and a fiduciary can mitigate this risk, as the separate parties keep each other in line. Trusts can be very flexible in design. Naming at least two individuals and regular auditing requirements written in the formation documents provides an extra layer of protection.

Trusts can take many forms. Most often they are described as either **revocable trusts**- the owner controls and makes changes without the beneficiary's consent or **irrevocable trusts**- designed to take assets out of the owner's name. While the owner still has a say, the consent of beneficiaries is required to make changes. Another option is to form a company, usually structured as an LLC taxed as a corporation, assets in this case are the corporations and are taxed accordingly, yet the individual retains an interest in, or ownership of, the company and thus can still receive benefits from their assets.

Specifically in regard to precious metals:

Revocable Trust-

Assets go into the trust. You can name yourself or another trusted individual as the trustee. It offers a layer of protection by making it difficult for non-trustees to mismanage assets. Typical bullion tax rates apply if metal in the trust is sold for a capital gain. Depending on how it is structured, the beneficiary may or may not receive a stepped-up tax on assets (including bullion/collections) upon the owner's death. This option provides the highest level of control for the owner, but typically fewer benefits. (Rodriquez, 2021)

Irrevocable Trust-

Irrevocable trusts are commonly used by individuals trying to qualify for Medicaid. Assets go into the trust; documents include terms and a named beneficiary(s). While the original owner has a say if changes are made, the beneficiary(s) must consent to the changes. The owner cannot be the trustee and, ideally, neither should the beneficiary. Bullion/collections still receive the collections rate for capital gains. Beneficiaries receive a stepped-up tax basis on property within the trust; however, this has been made more complicated by IRS REV. RUL. 2023-2. The new ruling states that "complete gifts" are excluded from the step-up basis. Wording and structure of the trust protecting "incomplete gifts" keeps the step-up basis intact. (Carrabus, 2023; IRS, 2023f; Rodriques, 2021)

Irrevocable trusts, typically, offer a higher level of protection, because more people are involved approving the management of assets but relinquishes the most control. This arrangement will probably require bullion assets to be held at a repository.

Assets held in a Company-

Companies set up for this purpose are usually limited liability companies (LLC), as they offer more flexibility and tax benefits than a sole proprietorship, but less reporting requirements than a corporation. Assets held in the company are considered company property. Capital gains rates still apply. How taxes are actually paid and how specific estate planning goals are met will depend on whether it is set up as an LLC partnership or an LLC taxed as a corporation. The former is a pass-through entity, the LLC files form 1065 and reported profits and losses are passed onto the partners' returns using the schedule K-1 form. An LLC that wishes to be taxed as a corporation must file form 8832 which, for tax purposes, makes the LLC its own entity. The LLC taxed as a corporation will file its taxes using form 1120 (the standard C corporation form). (IRS, 2024a)

The LLC taxed as a corporation is usually better when the goal is to separate names from ownership of property and retain significant control, as the LLC becomes its own entity. One of the household members is usually listed as a company officer. It is often chosen as a vehicle when someone in the household needs to qualify for Medicaid, or when the beneficiary is a special needs minor, a minor with assets the parent wants to keep private, or a disabled adult beneficiary. The corporate tax rate applies, and then any income received from the company is taxed at the marginal tax rate of the recipient. This results in double taxation if not managed properly. The primary advantages are privacy and control. (Allied, 2024)

The LLC partnership will not separate names from the property but does create several tax advantaged opportunities for parents to transfer assets to children. In this strategy both parents and children are partners. It is typically used to minimize estate and gift taxes. A key detail with these is that in some states the LLC must dissolve upon the death of one of the partners. Dissolution can be avoided by putting transfer of ownership provisions in the LLC's operating agreement. You could also put the LLC into a revocable trust. (Ulman, 2024)

Both options streamline the ability to count expenses (legal, storage, management fees, insurance premiums) against profits or gains. Also, beneficiaries can receive benefits (income, access to property, paid for expenses) from the LLC. If the LLC taxed as a corporation is chosen, the double taxation can be mitigated by offsetting gains with expenses, which could include management expenses for rental property or investment accounts, insurances, or even vehicle related expenses on any vehicles transferred into the corporation. (Allied, 2024; Ulman, 2024)

In both types of organization, intended beneficiaries have part-ownership. It can be flexible in how the timing of voting rights or level of involvement of part owners is awarded. This usually gives all control initially to the funding member, and they distribute voting rights, shares, and access to management of assets according to how they see fit. Protection is as good as the people managing the business accounts. As an added layer of protection, operating agreements may dictate how certain assets are managed, for example the management of rental properties may be delegated to a property manager and in the case of precious metals, it is commonly dictated that a repository be used for physical products. (Allied, 2024; Ulman 2024)

Using a company for estate planning is typically a good option for families who want to retain control, though it does require more effort than either trust option typically will. Owners can hand over more control to the beneficiaries (part owners) as their capability increases and trust is earned.

Both the LLC partnership and an LLC taxed as a corporation may receive a step-up or potentially a "step-down" basis for assets depending on several factors, and it works differently for each. The LLC partnership is the more complicated in this regard. Some key points for the partnership:

1- Assets sold before the death of a partner do not receive a step-up basis.
2- Property can receive a step-up basis after the death of a partner, but it is not automatic. In order to get a stepped-up basis, a 754 election must be made, which realigns property with fair market values. You will likely need the help of a tax professional to make this election and understand all the tax implications. (HMB Law, 2023; IRS, 2024b)

Assets in the LLC taxed as a corporation do not receive a stepped-up basis. Rather, the shares of the corporation itself receive the stepped-up basis. This works because the value of the company is dependent on the value of all its assets, which could include real property, precious metals, cash/brokerage accounts, but also things like brands and royalties. This can greatly simplify things, especially with estates that have several diverse assets. To avoid probate, operating agreements should be drafted or amended to outline the distribution of shares upon death to intended heirs of the primary share holder. This may also include making them officers in the company if they are not already. (HMB Law, 2023; IRS, 2022) Life insurance is used to provide capital for taxes and buying out heirs not intended to manage the company instead of being forced to sell assets upon death, which may happen at an inopportune time in the market cycle.

While the above is the "letter of the law" interpretation, the practicality is that companies in estates with a total value under the federal gift tax limits ($13,990,000.00 for 2025) are usually not scrutinized at the federal level and receive a stepped-up basis. However, below is a list of states that have their own estate tax limits. Most state limits are significantly lower than the federal amount. If estate valuations are above the applicable limit, these states will likely scrutinize, to make sure they receive their due. (Allied, 2024, IRS, 2024c)

List 11-1: States with an Estate Tax and its Corresponding Limit for the 2024 Tax Year. (Pendell, 2024)

Connecticut - $13,610,000
District of Columbia - $4,710,000
Hawaii - $5,490,000
Illinois - $4,000,000
Maine - $6,410,000
Maryland - $5,000,000
Massachusetts - $2,000,000
Minnesota - $3,000,000
New York - $6,940,000
Oregon - $1,000,000
Rhode Island - $1,774,583
Vermont - $5,000,000
Washington - $2,193,000

Applicable for all Estate Planning Entity's

In each structure, precious metal assets will go from being private, which is one of the main reasons to own them, to non-private. In my opinion, the only reason one would want to give up the privacy aspect of their precious metals is when the risk of having them lost or stolen begins to outweigh the privacy benefits. Many may choose to divest their precious metal assets before reaching a state of mental decline simply to avoid having them lost or stolen all together. Otherwise, they should plan on using one of the above structures (trust or LLC), along with a depository acting as the custodian to gain protection. This, of course, adds expense, but it is better than losing the asset.

If drafted appropriately, each structure will allow the assets to avoid probate, saving legal fees and streamlining taxation. Before setting up a trust an individual should consider all the assets that will be held in it and the implications. For example, a primary residence put into an irrevocable trust would lose its primary residence tax exemption. The same may or may not apply to a company depending on how it is structured, and ownership allocated. (Allied, 2024; HMB Law, 2023)

Remember, assets do not need to be put into the trust immediately. While some types of property may be put into the trust upon formation, an individual could opt to wait to transfer precious metals until they no longer trust themselves or want the responsibility.

While maybe obvious to those of us in the financial services industry, it may not be to others that there is a lot of specialty within the estate planning space. Most professionals will only be well versed in a few trust and company options. While I feel this section is a good guide to get people started, you will want to speak to at least a few specialists in different areas to decide what is the best structure for your needs. It would improve the process significantly if, before meeting with these people, you had a list of goals or estate planning objectives you want the entity to achieve and be prepared to talk in detail about your asset mix. Otherwise, you are at risk of just getting what they give everyone else, which may or may not work out well for you.

Lastly, determining who will be your trustee, fiduciary, and authorized representative, for health-related decisions, is not something you decide overnight. Make sure to devote serious thought and observation to this years before you think it will need to apply. Just like how pad locks keep honest people honest, having a few trusted individuals as part of your plan, who are required to check or audit each other, does the same thing.

Liquidating a Collection

Many readers at some point will be in the position where they need to liquidate a collection, either their own or a loved one's. This can be one of the most difficult parts of distributing an estate, especially if the collection is large and diverse. I am going to address this from the perspective of a coin collection, but several of the principles apply regardless of what the collection is.

Step 1- Cataloging

The first step is always to know what you have. Hopefully, the collector has kept a catalog. If you are the collector, the best insurance you can provide for your collection is to keep a detailed and up to date catalog. The catalog enables an accurate and timely appraisal. If you have an elderly parent who has already expressed that they want you to handle their collection when they pass, begin working with them now, while they are alive, to get the catalog assembled. If they have already passed, this will be a more difficult process, especially if you are a non-collector. In this case, do your best. Do not divest anything until it is properly cataloged and you have at least a vague idea of its value. Anticipate the need to seek outside information. Internet forums, books, and local collecting clubs are all good resources. Likely, there are reference materials with the collection that offer a good place to start. Once you have a catalog, you can move on to the appraisal. USA Coin Book offers a free online catalog. The advantage in this situation is that once entered, you can look up coin valuations easily and even list them for auction. Which will help with the next two steps.

Step 2- Appraising

You can choose to do this yourself or have it done by a professional. Most coins are relatively easy to do yourself, if you know what they are. Simply looking at several listings on eBay will give one a good feel for retail value. Do this with a copy of your catalog handy and start affixing valuations.

If you choose to go with an appraiser, they will probably go about it in a similar way. The only difference is they will be quicker and may even know the rough valuations of several specimens without having to look them up. An appraiser may choose to appraise the collection based on groups of similar coins. This is appropriate if wanting to sell the collection in one lot. Collections sold this way usually bring less than full retail value, but it ensures that the entire collection is sold and is faster. If you want to capture the full retail value, you will want a more specimen-specific appraisal. Now, with a catalog and appraisal you can move on to selling.

Step 3- Selling

When it comes to selling, there is the fast and easy way, which results in less money, or the more involved way which usually results in more money.

Coin dealers are often the best buyer for fast and easy. They have the capital and are constantly in need of more inventory to replace sales. Often, individuals will have a coin dealer do the appraisal and then sell the collection to that dealer. While this can work, realize there is an inherent conflict of interest. It is usually better to get an independent appraisal and then approach several different dealers with the complete catalog and appraisal to see which will give the best price. These need not all be local. Internet coin dealers often make very competitive offers, as their overhead costs are usually lower and they churn through inventory faster. Many dealers will want to visually inspect the collection, which is a reasonable request. Expect to receive bids 25-50% below retail. It is to your benefit to solicit several bids.

The next option is selling to local individual collectors or collectors you meet at coin shows. This will bring the closest to full retail. They may haggle with you, but you will not need to worry about auction house premiums and shipping fees. The challenge here is many will try to cherry pick the collection, as most will not be interested in the entire lot or if it is a large collection, they may not have the capital to afford it. Dealers may also try to cherry pick, and this can make your collection more difficult to sell, if the "trophies" have already been taken.

Lastly, you can use online auctions like eBay and GreatCollections.com. Be aware that Great Collections only deals with graded coins. USA Coin Book is a good option, especially for non-graded coins and items in the <$300 market. You can build a catalog on the site, then list auctions directly from the catalog. There are no listing fees, and a 2% commission is due only upon sale. Selling the collection yourself usually involves the most work, as you need to take time to list lots, manage sales, and ship specimens. You will receive full retail, but you will also have listing and shipping expenses. One advantage of eBay is that for smaller items that are difficult to appraise, you can list the specimen with no minimum bid for a long duration, and the market will essentially price it for you. Make sure you have excellent photos and lots of information about the piece in the listing if you do this, so buyers have confidence that it is a genuine item. Several AI apps are in development that can identify and appraise coins for you from a photo, while the tech is not quite where I would like it to be, on the identification end it is an extremely helpful and time saving tool for those new to collecting when dealing with modern coin issues. On the appraisal end, it is only going to be as good as the photo, and at this time, would only be appropriate for low value common issues.

Additional Considerations

Remember, appraisal and selling expenses, which could include coin show fees and travel expenses, need to be subtracted from money received for accurate capital gains calculations. Also, dealing with graded coins makes the appraising process significantly easier. Having all the high value items graded before selling is usually worth the trouble. Typically, at the very least, the coin should be worth the cost of grading before slabbing the coin. If pieces are made of precious metals, pay attention to current commodity prices to make sure it is an opportune time to sell. Finally, sell the coins during "Coin Season" or basically the late fall and winter months. This is when collectors generally are the most active, and you will have the most bidding activity on your listings.

How Big a Part of My Financial Plan Should Precious Metals Be?

Determining allocation levels in a financial plan depends on objectives, timelines, and risk tolerance. I like to look at all the boxes in my financial plan and put numbers on them. After several years, I started to feel I had too much or too little in a particular box and began developing ratios for myself. Allocation ratios, though not discussed frequently, is a key concept of financial planning.

Many find they are comfortable with placing 2-10% of their total net worth in physical metal, but this is by no means a rule. Physical precious metals are not something to go overboard on, but also not something to ignore. On the con side, they do not pay dividends or interest, have storage expenses, are cumbersome to trade, and at best are an imperfect hedge against inflation. On the pro side, they have the most privacy, are <u>the</u> hedge against government and major calamities, can be an unrestricted and mobile store of wealth, and are often used as a "deep" emergency fund. Overallocation with a buy and hold strategy will slow portfolio growth over long periods. Under allocation may leave one with limited options in a time of crisis. Well-timed purchases and sales, usually on a 7 to 10-year cycle, can greatly enhance a portfolio's performance. As discussed in chapter 3 the correlation of precious metal price movements is lower than other market related assets, this is usually more so for collectables. Good collectables also hold up better against inflation, their "collector's value" tends to insulate them when commodity prices fall. The tradeoff is their liquidity is lower, and selling expenses are usually higher.

Regarding metal-related instruments trading on the exchanges, I calculate these as a percentage of my total portfolio, and they usually fluctuate between 5 to 20%. Trading metal-related financial instruments offers great opportunity because when their volatile cycles arrive, they tend to be pronounced.

Anton Kreil, a well-known trader, stressed the importance of trading a mix of markets and said his ideal portfolio mix was 65% equities, 20% commodities, 10% forex, and the remaining 5% as cash. His reasoning is that successful trading is dependent on volatility, which historically is greatest in equities, followed by commodities, with forex being the least. His ideal time frame for most trades is about a month. The cash allocation is used to take advantage of short-term opportunities (1 to 5 days). (Kreil, 2013)

While every trader's portfolio is different, many successful traders find their mix ends up being similar to Kreil's. It does not need to be a hard-set rule, but it is something that naturally works. In today's world, many traders set an allocation for crypto, which as a group is currently the most volatile asset class. As a trader, do not try to subdivide the allocations into smaller sectors, as one might with an investment portfolio. Precious metals make up just a few of the commodities, and a trader is going to go where the volatility is. One quarter, for example, they may be trading gold because that is where all the activity is, but the next could be oil or grains.

Conversely, if taking an investment approach to building a portfolio, a 5-10% allocation in metal-related equities or ETF's is often used to balance other sectors. They have a cyclical nature both in terms of the businesses themselves and how they are traded, and you should plan on entering and closing positions in line with the cycles. Use the chapters on mining stocks and exchange traded products to identify traditional risk areas, and then do research on the specific securities being considered, seeing which risks apply before taking positions. Various technical analysis studies can be used to help time entries/exits and select price targets. Be prepared to dig when doing research, as many of the relevant risk factors will not be noticeable with a few quick internet and AI searches.

Chapter 11: Precious Metals in a Financial Plan

Summary:

1- Physical precious metals make a good addition to a financial plan by adding privacy and a hedge against government.

2- Precious metal collectables can be a hedge against inflation. The "right" collectibles with the best chance of appreciation will be those that are:

   a. Well known, possibly with historical significance
   b. High grade or exceptional quality
   c. Rare
   d. Easily identified as genuine with established provenance

3- Care and research should be used when cataloging and divesting of a collection.

4- Putting precious metals into an IRA negates the privacy of the investment and is therefore not recommended.

5- Understanding the different types of assets and the rules around the account in which they are held empowers individuals to minimize taxes and create maximum gains and flexibility in financial plans.

6- For traders, volatility = opportunity, and they benefit having an allocation to commodities due to the volatility they bring.

7- The cyclical and lower correlation nature of precious metal securities compared to the general market can be used in investment portfolios to balance other sector holdings.

8- Trusts and limited liability companies are both vehicles used for estate planning. Determining which structure is best will depend on the amount of control desired, how removed from property the owner wants their name, and the tolerated tax burden.

9- Life insurance is used to cover taxes and give heirs timing flexibility for divesting assets.

10- Putting precious metal assets into a trust removes their privacy but may be appropriate later in life to protect the assets from fraud, theft, or loss.

11- Investors and traders should determine what allocation ratios they are comfortable with, 2 to 10% is common for physical metal, and 5 to 20% for market-based assets in investment or trading portfolios.

Conclusion

Congratulations, you have just completed reading the most comprehensive work published to date on the precious metals markets. I can confidently say you are now among the most informed retail investors and traders in the sector, and I expect the enclosed information to improve your risk assessments and hopefully help with idea generation.

My first goal with this project was to open readers to the integral part these metals play in our everyday lives and economy. Beyond that, it was to help investors and traders understand these investments at a deeper level, teaching them to identify risks, and help them see opportunities.

I believe I have accomplished both. I went into this work, arrogantly perhaps, viewing myself as an expert. The research conducted has tried, refined, and redefined in some cases my ideas and understanding. Formats such as this will never provide timely enough information to be taken as trade advice. Yet, this work, which addresses the macroeconomics of precious metals and key considerations with these companies and financial instruments, will accelerate and enhance the reader's research and risk identifying efforts. Similarly, understanding how they can be used in both a financial and estate planning informs individuals on how they can grow and transfer wealth while mitigating taxes. Even if not one copy of this book sells, the research efforts expended have already allowed me to generate new trade ideas, execution strategies, and modify my financial structure.

I didn't want to write "just another book on gold," spewing opinions and a few ideas like so many in the marketplace but, rather, present a thoroughly researched resource for those ready to advance from the beginner level of understanding. To that end, I have provided all of my references. You don't have to take my word for it, go see for yourselves, please.

You also need to know that the majority of the investment and trade strategies discussed are ones I have used or seriously considered for myself with my own money. Like they say, "you know nothing about a stock until you own it." Understand that my research is coupled with real trading and investing experience. And, yes, researching and writing this book has caused me to adapt and improve many of my strategies and try out new ones. I will be honest; some experimenting was required with the new-to-me instruments and trading strategies before I learned how to make them work and ultimately felt comfortable enough with them to write about. Doing is learning, as with trying any new market, start small and do your research, if you fail to do so, all I have done is make you dangerous. As you get a feel for what works, you can scale up to full-sized positions.

Another rut we sometimes fall into is wanting a list of what to do and not to do. We want to just read a book on something and then be successful. Unfortunately, there is no easy way. In addition to knowledge, trading specifically requires maintaining an optimal metal state, controlling emotions, having humility and confidence, and depending on the circumstance, the ability to be patient or take immediate and decisive action. Trading is just as much self-mastery as technical acumen, and self-mastery is a life-long process.

You can read lots of books and learn lots of good principles, but in the end, you still need to write your own book. This work presents several principles and lots of knowledge, and I feel it is a good contribution. Use it, but you need to write your own story. Happy hunting to all!

The End

I would like to personally thank you for taking the time and energy to read my book. If you have enjoyed this work, or found the information useful, please consider leaving a positive review. With enough, I may consider writing similar works in the future.

-T. Forbush

For those who would like to leave a review, wanting to order additional copies with wholesale pricing, or who may be interested in learning more about Forbush's financial advising services, they may do so by emailing him at: batholith@batholith.net

Impressions & Goals

References:

Allied Financial Services (2024), Tax Implications for Various Trusts & Entities in Estate Planning, *Batholith Wealth Management & Insurance*, Interview, December 12.

Anderson, J. (2018), Does USPS Ship Gold?, SD Bullion, WEB access: Dec 2023, Does USPS ship Gold? (sdbullion.com)

Angelo, S. (2017), Total World Gold & Silver Production: Fact vs Conspiracy, *SRSrocco*, August 21st, WEB access: May 2025, Total World Gold And Silver Production: Fact vs Conspiracy | Gold Eagle

APMEX (2022), Mormon Gold - Salt Lake City - 1849-1860, *APMEX.com*, May 22nd, WEB access: Apr. 2025, Mormon Gold – Salt Lake City – 1849 – 1860 - APMEX

Armstrong, M. (2024), Why Are Central Banks Buying Gold?, *Armstrong Economics*, April 3, WEB access: Dec 2024, Why Are Central Banks Buying Gold? | Armstrong Economics

Armstrong, M. (2023a), Hoards Are Vital to our Understanding of History, *Armstrong Economics*, January 26th, WEB access: Dec 2024, Hoards Are Vital To Our Understanding Of History | Armstrong Economics

Armstrong, M. (2023b), Should Argentina Peg its Currency to the Dollar?, *Armstrong Economics, December 6*, WEB access: Dec 2025, Should Argentina Peg Its Currency To The Dollar? | Armstrong Economics

Armstrong, M. (2022), Federal Reserve & Misconceptions, *Armstrong Economics*, Dec 20, WEB access: Jan 2024, Federal Reserve & Misconceptions | Armstrong Economics

Armstrong, M. (2021), Private Money, *Armstrong Economics*, February 24, WEB access: Dec 2024, Private Money | Armstrong Economics

Armstrong, M. (2020), Gold in Currencies & Cryptocurrencies, *Armstrong Economics*, Feb 20, WEB access: Aug 2025, Gold In Currencies & Cryptocurrencies | Armstrong Economics

Armstrong, M. (2019), Gold & The Hedge Against Government, *Armstrong Economics,* June 12, WEB access: Mar 2024, Gold & The Hedge Against Government | Armstrong Economics

Armstrong, M. (2018), The Hunt for Taxes Brings Down Governments Every Time, *Armstrong Economics*, January 19th, WEB access: Dec 2024, The Hunt For Taxes Brings Down Governments Every Time | Armstrong Economics

Armstrong, M (2017), What About Collectibles?, *Armstrong Economics,* January 15th, WEB access: Dec 2024, What About Collectibles? | Armstrong Economics

Armstrong, M. (2015a), Did Gold Survive the Depression, *Armstrong Economics: Americas Economic History*, Sept. 25, WEB access: Jan 2024, Did Gold Survive The Depression? | Armstrong Economics

Armstrong, M. (2015b), Currency Pegs & Their Risks, *Armstrong Economics*, Aug 15, WEB access: Jan 2024, Currency Pegs & Their Risks | Armstrong Economics

Armstrong, M. (2015c), Indian Ancient Imitations of Roman Coins, *Armstong Economics*, Oct 3, WEB access: Sept 2025, Indian Ancient Imitations Of Roman Coins | Armstrong Economics

Atasu, A., Duran, S., & Van Wassenhove, L. (2021), The Dark Side of Solar Power, *Harvard Business Review: Sustainable Business Practices,* June 18, WEB access: Aug 2025, The Dark Side of Solar Power

Baldridge, R. (2022), What Are Stock Warrants?, *Forbes Advisor: Investing*, March 2nd, WEB access: Dec 2024, What Are Stock Warrants? – Forbes Advisor

Banton, C. (2022), Currency Peg: What It Is, How It Works, and Fixed Exchange Rates, *Investopedia*, July 11, WEB access: Jan 2024, Currency Peg: What It Is, How It Works, and Fixed Exchange Rates (investopedia.com)

Barber, B., Lee, Y., Liu, Y., Odean, T., & Zhang, K. (2017), Do Day Traders Rationally Learn About Their Ability?, *Haas School of Business, University of California, Berkley*, October, 34p.

Batholith, (2024), The Value of Creating Options, *Batholith Wealth Management & Insurance*, Educational Materials, November, 2p

Bauder, S. (2020), 10.8% of Americans Own Gold, While 11.6% Own Silver, According to New Survey, *Gold IRA Guide,* Sept. 1, WEB access: 10.8% Of Americans Own Gold, While 11.6% Own Silver, According To A New Survey (goldiraguide.org)

BeMetals (2020, BeMetals Commences Phase 2 Underground Drill Program At High-Grade South Mountain Zinc-Silver-Gold-Copper Project, press release, *BeMetals Corp*, September 16, 8p.

Bennet, M. (2023), Sukuk are just another capital market (and that is a good thing), *All About Finance*, Apr 18, WEB Access: Sept 2025, Sukuk are just another capital markets instrument (and that is a good thing)

Besta, S. (2020), Profiling the world's top five platinum mining companies, *NS Energy*, Oct 26, WEB access: Jan 2024, The top five platinum-mining companies in the world (nsenergybusiness.com)

BigstackMcgee (2022), Full 1200oc Silver Bar Stack, *youtube.com*, December, WEB access: Jun 2024, https://www.youtube.com/watch?v=6CJbKH8XqxM

Bird, B. (2022), What is an Unrecaptured Section 1250 Gain?, the balance, WEB access: Dec 2023, What Is an Unrecaptured Section 1250 Gain? (thebalancemoney.com)

Blackstone (2021), Blackstone Tactical Opportunities to Acquire the Certified Collectibles Group, a Leading Provider of Tech-Enabled Authentication, Grading and Conservation Services for the Global Collectibles Industry, *Blackstone Inc.*, press release, July 2021, WEB access: Dec 2024, Blackstone Tactical Opportunities to Acquire the Certified Collectibles Group, a Leading Provider of Tech-Enabled Authentication, Grading and Conservation Services for the Global Collectibles Industry - Blackstone

Blakely, S. (2021), What Miners Need to Know About Smelter Charges, *Canadian Mining Journal,* November 5th, WEB access: Dec 2024, What miners need to know about smelter charges - Canadian Mining Journal

Blanchard™ (2024), Top-5 Discoveries from the SS Gairsoppa: Silver Bars, Coins and More, *Blanchard* ™, Blog, March 7, WEB access: Dec 2024, SS Gairsoppa Silver Coins & Bars: TOP-5 Gairsoppa Silver Findings

BLM.gov (2022), Mining Claim Fees, US Department of the Interior: Bureau of Land Management, WEB access: Apr 2022, Mining Claim Fees | Bureau of Land Management

Bovolo, C. (2005), The physical and chemical composition of the lower mantle, *Philosophy Transactions of the Royal Society*, vol 363, issue 1837, 2811–2836p.

Brewster, N. (2017), How mining companies should hedge (or not hedge) commodity prices, LinkedIn, WEB access: Dec 2023, (20) How mining companies should hedge (or not hedge) commodity prices | LinkedIn

Brittanica (2024a), Silver, *Encyclopedia Brittanica*, Jan 5, WEB Access: Jan 2024, Silver | Facts, Properties, & Uses | Britannica

Brittanica (2024b), Gold, *Encyclopedia Britannica*, Jan 5, WEB Access: Jan 2024, Gold | Facts, Properties, & Uses | Britannica

Brownlow, A. (1996), Geochemistry (2nd ed.), *Prentice-Hall inc.*, New Jersey, 580p.

Bryant, J. (2021), How a Catalytic Converter Works, *NAPA Auto*, Apr 29th, WEB access: Jan 2024, How A Catalytic Converter Works » NAPA Blog (napaonline.com)

Carcody (2020), 7 Symptoms of Bad or Failing Spark Plugs, Feb 16, WEB access: Jan 2024, 7 Symptoms of Bad or Failing Spark Plugs (carcody.com)

Carpathian, J. (2024), Gold and Silver Legal Tender States: Mapping the Expansion, *Carpathian Gold,* Blog, WEB access: Dec 2024, Gold and Silver Legal Tender States: Mapping the Expansion | Carpathiangold.Com

Carrabus, W. (2023), Can an irrevocable trust beneficiary claim a step-up in basis: understanding IRS Rev. Rul. 2023-2, *Futterman Lanza LLP*, July, WEB access: Dec 2024, Can an irrevocable trust beneficiary claim a step-up in basis: understanding IRS Rev. Rul. 2023-2

CFPB (2019), Suspicious Activity Reports on Elder Financial Exploitation: Issues and Trends, *Consumer Financial Protection Bureau*, February, 36p.

Charles Schwab (2023), Mark-to-Market & Trader Taxes, WEB access: Dec 2023, Mark-to-Market & Trader Taxes | Charles Schwab

Chase, R. (2025) Assets and Liabilities Mining Companies Acquire Through Mergers and Acquisitions, *Batholith LLC,* Interview with Chase Specialty Services LLC, an environmental engineering firm servicing the mining industry, Sept. 2.

Chang, Z. & Meinert, L.D. (2008), Empire Mine Idaho: Exploration Implications of Unusual Skarn Features Related to High Fluorine Activity, *Economic Geology vol 103 #5,* 909-938p.

Charitou, A. & Karamanou, I. (2020), Sleeping with the Enemy: Should Investment Banks be Allowed to Engage in Prop Trading, *Review of Accounting Studies,* vol. 25, 513-557p.

Chen, H. (2024), Explore Pure Silver and Silver Alloy Materials Used for Jewelry, *Sobling Jewelry,* Sept 14, WEB access: Aug 2025, Explore pure Silver and Silver Alloy Materials used for Jewelry - A Comprehensive Guide To Silver and silver Alloy Materials' Properties And Features

Chen, J. (2024a), Troy Ounce: Definition, History, and Conversion Table, *Investopedia,* May 23, WEB access, Jun 2024, Troy Ounce: Definition, History, and Conversion Table (investopedia.com)

Chen, J. (2024b), What is a Straddle Options Strategy and how is it Created, *Investopedia: Options Trading Guide Ch 5,* August, WEB access: December 2024, What Is a Straddle Options Strategy and How Is It Created?

Chen, J. (2022), What Are Dark Pools? How They Work, Critiques, and Examples, *Investopedia: Investing, Alternative Investments*, March, WEB access: Dec 2024, What Are Dark Pools? How They Work, Critiques, and Examples

Chernicoff, S. & Whitney, D. (2002), Geology (third ed.), *Houghton Mifflin Company,* Boston-New York, 648p.

Cleary, L. (2023), How Much Are Auction Prices? A Detailed Guide, lauracleary Solo Travel, WEB access: April 2022, How Much Are Auction Fees? A Detailed Guide - Laura Clery

Coghlan, G. (2021), Platinum's drive to replace Palladium in catalytic converters, FXSTREET, WEB access: Apr 2022, Platinum's drive to replace Palladium in catalytic converters

Collectors Corner (2023), 1673-S M8 Esc Calico-1012 Spain AU50, PCGS Coin# 721390, *collectorscorner.com*, Oct 29, WEB access: Jan 2024, Collectors Corner - 1673-S M 8 Esc Calico-1012 Spain AU50 PCGS - #63711634

Common, D. and Malik, G. (2018), How crematoriums are recovering precious metals from inside the dead, *CBC News*, May 14, WEB access: Jan 2024, How crematoriums are recovering precious metals from inside the dead | CBC News

Cooksongold (2025), Bullion: Product Specifications, *Cookson Precious Metals Ltd,* Birmingham, England, WEB access: Mar 2025, Gold and Silver Bullion

Coplan, C. (2013), Newmont Begins Commercial Production of Copper in Nevada, *High Desert News*, October 31.

Cowely, A. (2022), PGM Market Report, *Johnson Matthey*, May, 60p.

Crooks, E. (2015), The US Shale Revolution: How it changed the world, and why nothing will ever be the same again, *Financial Times*, April 24.

Curry, S. (1957), Platinum Catalysts in Petroleum Refining, *Platinum Metal Review,* vol 1, issue 2, 38-43p.

Dabilis, A. (2013) Bailout Cuts Cyprus Bank Accounts-Withdrawals Barred, Greek Reporter, March 16-2013. WEB access: Apr 2022, Bailout Cuts Cyprus Bank Accounts, Withdrawals Barred - GreekReporter.com

Dalrymple, G.B. (1991), The Age of the Earth, *Stanford University Press*, 492p.

Desjardins, J. (2016), Currency and the Collapse of the Roman Empire, *The Money Project*, WEB access: Apr 2022, Infographic: Currency and the Collapse of the Roman Empire

Desjardins, J. (2015), A Miner Problem, $2 Billion in Negative Working Capital, *Visual Capitalist*, March 27, WEB access: January 2024, Chart: A Miner Problem, $2 Billion in Negative Working Capital (visualcapitalist.com)

Deseta, N. (2020), Geology of the PGE Deposits in the Bushveld Complex, South Africa, *Geology for Investors*, Sept 18, WEB access: Jan 2024, Geology of the PGE Deposits in the Bushveld Complex, South Africa | Geology for Investors

DiStefano, J., (2023), Federal investigation is looking for at least $75 million in missing silver and gold from a Delaware warehouse, *The Inquirer,* December 28th.

Doak, E. (2023), Exchange-Traded Notes: The Facts and the Risks, *Charles Schwab: Investments*, May 18th, WEB access: Dec 2024, Exchange-Traded Notes: The Facts and the Risks | Charles Schwab

Doak, E. (2023b), ETFs and Taxes: What You Need to Know, *Charles Schwab: ETFs*, July 17th, WEB access: Mar 2025, ETFs and Taxes: What You Need to Know | Charles Schwab

Donnelly, J., Lapeyrouse, N., and Rex, M. (2023), Chemistry Fundamentals: CH 19, Nuclear Chemistry, *University of Central Florida*, WEB access: Jan 2024, Why It Matters: Nuclear Chemistry – Chemistry Fundamentals (ucf.edu)

Downey, L. (2024), 10 Options Strategies Every Investor Should Know, *Investopedia: Options Trading Guide Ch 1,* October, WEB access: Dec 2024, 10 Options Strategies Every Investor Should Know

Downey, L. (2022), 10 Options Strategies to Know, *Investopedia*, WEB access: Apr 2022, https://www.investopedia.com/trading/options-strategies/

Duncan, K. (2012), The History of the Trade Dollar, *Coinweek*, May 31, WEB access: Aug 2025, The History of the Trade Dollar

Edelen, A. (2020), With a narrow vote Lucky Friday miners union accepts contract after more than two years on strike, The Spokesman-Review, WEB access: Apr 2022, With a narrow vote, Lucky Friday miners union accepts contract after more than two years on strike

Egan, C. (2024), Precious Metals Comparison for Fine Jewelry, *CoreyEgan.com*, Jewelry Knowledge, WEB access: Mar 2025, Precious Metals Comparison for Fine Jewelry – Corey Egan

Elamroussi, A, Yan, H., & Vera, A. (2022), Canadian Authorities Freeze Financial Assets for those Involved in Ongoing Protests in Ottawa, *CNN*, February 20th, WEB access: Dec 2024, Freedom Convoy in Canada: Authorities freeze financial assets for those involved in ongoing protests in Ottawa | CNN

Els, F. (2016), Idaho Silver Mine Shaft Sunk to Final Depth of 9,587 ft., *mining.com*, May 24, WEB access: Aug 2025, Idaho silver mine shaft sunk to final depth of 9,587 feet - MINING.COM

Elwell, C. (2011), Brief History of the Gold Standard in the United States, *Congressional Research Service*, 7-3700, #R41887, 18p.

EPA (2024), Solar Panel Recycling, *U.S. Environmental Protection Agency,* Nov 13, WEB access: Aug 2025, Solar Panel Recycling | US EPA

Erkoyun, E. (2019), Turkey to issue gold-backed bond and sukuk to corporate investors, *Reuters*, Sept 17, WEB access: Sept 2025, Turkey to issue gold-backed bond and sukuk to corporate investors | Reuters

ESA (2025), Classification of Mineral Deposits, *Earth Science Australia,* WEB access: Oct 2025, https://earthsci.org/mineral/mindep/class_dep/class_dep.html

Eveland, T. (2023), List of Medieval Coins, *The Medieverse*, Oct 6, WEB access: Dec 2024, List of Medieval Coins (150+ Terms with Photos!)

Fahey, M. (2014), Fake Proof Silver American Eagles from China, *Coin World*, Jun 26, WEB access: Jun 2024, Fake Proof silver American Eagles from China (coinworld.com)

Farooki, M. (2018) China's Mineral Sector and the Belt & Road Initiative, *STRADE: European Policy Brief No. 2/2018,* 11 p. China's Mineral Sector and the Belt & Road Initiative

FasterCapital (2025), Basket Peg: Diversifying Stability: The Strategy Behind Basket Peg Currencies, *FasterCapital: Content,* Apr 9, WEB access: Dec 2025, Basket Peg: Diversifying Stability: The Strategy Behind Basket Peg Currencies - FasterCapital

Faure, G. (1998), Geochemistry (2nd ed.), Table A-4: Average Chemical Composition of Selected Lunar Rocks, *Prentice-Hall inc.*, 600p.

Federal Reserve Bank of Atlanta (2024), The Story of Money: Section 13- The Civil War Era, Tour, WEB: access: Jun 2024, https://www.atlantafed.org/about/tours/story-of-money/13-civil-war-era/

Feliu, G. & Gorné, R. (translator)(2018), Money and Coinage in the Middle Ages: Money & Currency, *Brill,* Boston, 21-40p.

Financial Crimes Enforcement Network (FinCEN), (2023), History of Anti-Money Laundering Laws, U.S. Dept. of Treasury, WEB access: Dec 2023, History of Anti-Money Laundering Laws | FinCEN.gov

Financial Crimes Enforcement Network (FinCEN), (2017), Report of International Transport of Currency or Monetary Instruments, Form 105, U.S. Dept. of Treasury, WEB access: Dec 2023, FinCEN Form 105 (Rev. 7-2003)

Finance Monthly (2015), Swiss Franc Breaks from Euro Peg, January 16, WEB access: Apr 2022: Swiss Franc breaks from euro peg - Finance Monthly | Personal Finance. Money. Investing

Financial Times (2025), Fund Comparison Tool, *The Financial Times Ltd.*, WEB access: Mar 2025, Fund Comparison Tool - compare performance, risk and ratings - FT.com

Forbush, T. (2025), Four Gold vs Silver Ratios to Understand, *GeoTech LLC,* internal report, May 9th.

Forbush, T. (2024), Fluorite, Implications for H_2SO_4 Leaching of Copper Ores: Empire Mine, Idaho, *GeoTech LLC*, 11p. Fluorite: Implications for H2SO4 Leaching of Copper Ores, Empire Mine, Idaho, Forbush, T. , Little, W.W., eBook - Amazon.com

Forbush, T. (2016), Mobile Metal Ionization: Effectiveness in Gold Exploration, *University of Alaska Fairbanks,* August, 187p., WEB access: Dec 2024, Mobile metal ionization: effectiveness in gold exploration

Ford, E. (2024), The Olympic Medals in Paris Will Literally Contain a Piece of the Eiffel Tower, *NBC Insider,* February 9th, WEB access: Dec 2024, 2024 Paris Olympic Medals Will Contain Piece of Eiffel Tower | NBC Insider

Fowler, E. (2023), Why investors are sick of gold miner's hedging, *Financial Review*, April 23, WEB access: Aug 2024: ASX RRL: Investors are sick of gold miners squandering the rally on hedging (afr.com)

Ganti, A, (2024), Preferred Stock: What it Is, How it Works, *Investopedia: Stock Trading Strategy & Education*, June, WEB access: Dec 2024, Preferred Stock

Ganti, A. (2022), Condor Spread: Definition, Types, and Strategy Examples, *Investopedia: Options and Derivatives, Advanced Concepts*, January, WEB access: Dec 2024, Condor Spread: Definition, Types, and Strategy Examples

GCSE (2025), Alloys, *Science-revision.co.uk*, WEB access: Mar 2025, Alloys

Goldback (2025), What are goldBacks?, *Goldback.com,* WEB access: Mar 2025, About Goldbacks: 24K Gold-Backed Currency

Goldcoinbalance.com (2024), The easy way to detect fake gold coins, *Gold Coin Balance*™, copyright 2011-2019, WEB access: July 2024, The Best Fake Gold Coin Detection Tool | Gold Coin Balance

Gold Daughters (2024), Gold Panning Tours, *golddaughters.com*, WEB Access: Jan 2024, Alaska Gold Panning Tour - Fairbanks, Alaska | Gold Daughters

GoldSilver (2024), What is a Troy Ounce?, *GoldSilver.com: Investing Guide*, Feb 2, WEB access: Jun 2024, What is a Troy Ounce? (goldsilver.com)

Grice, S. (2008), Look On The White Side, *Hoover & Strong: technical articles*, Jan 1, WEB access: Aug 2025, Look on the White Side – Technical Articles

Grok 3 (2025a), How Many People in the U.S. are Capable of being a Mineral Exploration Geologist Considering the Education, Training, Physical Requirements, and Lifestyle?, *xAI*, Personal Interview, April 13th.

Grok 3(2025b), Is AI Best Used to Replace or Augment Mining and Minerals Exploration Professionals?, *xAI,* Personal Interview, April 13th.

Haughton, B. (2016), The Roman Hoxne Hoard, *World History Encyclopedia*, August 23rd, WEB access: Dec 2024, The Roman Hoxne Hoard - World History Encyclopedia

Hayes, A. (2024), How This Options Strategy Works, With Example, *Investopedia: Options Trading Guide Ch 6,* June, WEB access: Dec 2024, Strangle: How This Options Strategy Works, with Example

Hayes, A. (2022), Christmas Tree Options Strategy: Meaning, Overview, Examples, *Investopedia: Options and Derivatives, Advanced Concepts*, May, WEB access: Dec 2024, Christmas Tree Options Strategy: Meaning, Overview, Examples

Habbache, N., Alane, N., Djerad, S., & Tifouti, L. (2009), Leaching of copper oxide with different acid solutions, *Chemical Engineering Journal*, vol. 152, issues 2-3, October, 503-508p.

Harvey, C. (2023), Red Giant Star: Definition, Temperature & End, *General Studies Earth and Space Science: Ch. 8 Star Formation & Evolution*, Study.com, WEB access: Jan 2024, red_supergiant.png (350×196) (study.com)

Hemestine, T. (2021), Abundance of Elements in Earth's Crust- Periodic Table and List, *sciencenotes.org*, WEB access: Jan 2024, Abundance of Elements in Earth's Crust - Periodic Table and List (sciencenotes.org)

Hirose, K., Wood, B. & Vočadlo, L. (2021), Light elements in the Earth's core, *Nature Reviews Earth & Environment*, vol 2, August, 645-658p.

History.com Editors (2020), FDR takes United States off gold standard, *A & E Television Networks*, WEB access: Apr 2022, https://www.history.com/this-day-in-history/fdr-takes-united-states-off-gold-standard

HMB Law (2023), Step-Up in Basis for Assets Held in an Entity, *Hancock, McGill & Bleau*, January, WEB access: Dec 2024, Step-Up in Basis for Assets Held in an Entity

Hoff, D. (2016), Non-Traditional Assets, *Mountain West IRA*, WEB access: Dec 2023, Non-Traditional Assets - Mountain West IRA Blog

Holland, E. (2023), Russia's Challenges in Mineral Extraction, *Colorado School of Mines: Critical Minerals & Clean Energy Transition Workshop,* Sept 21, 7p. Holland-Russias-Challenges-in-Mineral-Extraction.pdf

House, A. (2018) Phoenix Mine Metallurgy, Mill, and SX/EW plant tour, *Newmont Corporation,* October 23, Battle Mountain, Nevada

Howe, A. (2024), Supreme Court strikes down Chevron, curtailing power of federal agencies, *SCOTUSblog,* June 28, WEB access, July 2024, Supreme Court strikes down Chevron, curtailing power of federal agencies - SCOTUSblog

Hyde, T. (2008), Exchange Traded Funds Invested in Metal, memo: CC:ITA:B01:LAAyres, Chief of Office Counsel, *Internal Revenue Service*, 2p.

Idaho Legal Aid Services, (2020), Questions and Answers about Medicaid for Those Needing Long-Term Care in Idaho, *Idaho Legal Aid Services*, July, WEB access: Dec 2024, Questions and Answers about Medicaid and Long-Term Care updated July 2020.pdf

IDHW, (2022), Application for Medicaid, *Idaho Dept. of Health & Welfare: Forms & Applications,* HW 2014 | REV 02/04/2022, WEB access: Dec 2024, Application for Medicaid

IMS, (2024), First US Bitcoin ETF Launches using Cayman Structure, *IMS,* Apr 9th, WEB access: Mar 2025, First US Bitcoin ETF launches using Cayman structure

INN (2021), An Investor's Guide to Royalties and Streams, *Investing News Network: Gold Investing*, March 9th, WEB access, Dec 2024, An Investor's Guide to Royalties and Streams | INN

Internal Revenue Service (IRS) (2024a), LLC filing as a corporation or partnership, *Internal Revenue Service: Small Business & Self Employed*, August 22nd, WEB access: Dec 2024, LLC filing as a corporation or partnership | Internal Revenue Service

Internal Revenue Service (IRS) (2024b), FAQs for Internal Revenue Code (IRC) Sec. 754 election and revocation, *Internal Revenue Service*, June 24th, WEB access: FAQs for Internal Revenue Code (IRC) Sec. 754 election and revocation | Internal Revenue Service

Internal Revenue Service (IRS) (2024c), Estate Tax, *Internal Revenue Service,* October 29th, WEB access: Dec 2024, Estate tax | Internal Revenue Service

Internal Revenue Service (IRS) (2023a), Capital Gains and Losses, Topic No. 409, WEB access: Dec 2023, Topic No. 409, Capital Gains and Losses | Internal Revenue Service (irs.gov)

Internal Revenue Service (IRS) (2023b), Wash Sales, Publication 505, WEB access: Dec 2023, Publication 505 (2023), Tax Withholding and Estimated Tax | Internal Revenue Service (irs.gov)

Internal Revenue Service (IRS) (2023c), Gains and Losses From Section 1256 Contracts & Staddles, form 6781, WEB access: Dec 2023, 2023 Form 6781 (irs.gov)

Internal Revenue Service (IRS) (2023d), About Publication 590-A, Contributions to Individual Retirement Arrangements (IRA's), WEB access: Dec 2023, About Publication 590-A, Contributions to Individual Retirement Arrangements (IRAs) | Internal Revenue Service (irs.gov)

Internal Revenue Service (IRS) (2023e), Form 8300 and Reporting Cash Payments of Over $10,000, WEB access: Dec 2023, Form 8300 and Reporting Cash Payments of Over $10,000 | Internal Revenue Service (irs.gov)

Internal Revenue Service (IRS) (2023f), 26 CFR 1.1014-1: Basis of Property Acquired from a Decedent, *Internal Revenue Service*, Rev. Rul. 2023-2, 9p., WEB access: Dec 2024, RR-2023-02

Internal Revenue Service (IRS) (2022), Publication 551: Basis of Assets, *Internal Revenue Service,* December, WEB access: Dec 2024, Publication 551 (12/2022), Basis of Assets | Internal Revenue Service

Jakaitė, L. (2019), Feldspars, *Strike-Dip.com*, WEB access: Aug 2025, Feldspar Poster (Digital)

Japan Currency Museum (2008), Chinese Shell Money 16th to 8th Century BC, *photograph*, WEB access: Jan 2024, File:Chinese shell money 16th 8th century BCE.jpg - Wikimedia Commons

Jewelry Informer (2024), The Top 11 Different Types of Silver, *Jewelryinformer.com*, Jan 8, WEB access: Jan 2024, The Top 11 Different Types of Silver - Jewelry Informer

John, J. (2008), Sulfidic serpentinite (platinum-palladium ore) (Johns-Manville Reef, Stillwater Complex, Neoarchean, 2.71 Ga; Stillwater Mine, Beartooth Mountains, Montana, USA, *flicker.com*, photograph, Aug 4, WEB access: Jan 2024, Sulfidic serpentintite (platinum-palladium ore) (Johns-Man… | Flickr

Johnson, B. (2019), How Much More Tax Efficient are ETFs than Open-end Funds? A Look in 9 Charts, *Morningstar*, Jul 31st, WEB access: Apr 2025: How Much More Tax Efficient Are ETFs Than Open-End Funds? A Look in 9 Charts | Morningstar

Jones, E. (2025), Lunch Interview with Thunder Mountain Gold Inc CEO Eric Jones & Consulting Geologist Dr. Steven Reynolds about the South Mountain Mine project, *GeoTech LLC*, September 29, Boise, Idaho.

Jones, E. (2024), Thunder Mountain Gold Announces Private Placement Financing, *Thunder Mountain Gold*, press release, November 28th, WEB access: Dec 2024, Thunder Mountain Gold Announces Private Placement Financing

Jones, E. (2023), Thunder Mountain Gold, Inc. Updated 43-101 Mineral Resource Estimate at South Mountain Shows Significant Increase, *Thunder Mountain Gold Inc.*, Press Release, December 21, WEB access: Dec 2024, Thunder Mountain Gold, Inc. Updated 43-101 Mineral Resource Estimate at South Mountain Shows Significant Increase.

Jung, S., Kröner, A, Hauff, F., and Masberg, P. (2015), Petrogenesis of synorogenic diorite-granodiorite-granite complexes in the Damara Belt, Namibia: Constraints from U-Pb zircon ages and Sr-Nd-Pb isotopes, *Journal of African Earth Sciences*, vol. 101, 253-265p.

Keane, J.M. (2015), Forensics of a Failed Operation: Equatorial Tonopah, *Society of Mining, Metallurgy, & Exploration*, 21p.

Kobayashi, C., Karakas, A., and Lugaro, M. (2020), The Origin of Elements from Carbon to Uranium, *The Astrophysical Journal*, 900:179, September, 33p.

Kowalski, C. (2023), Filing Taxes on Commodities, *the balance*, WEB access: Dec 2023, Filing Taxes on Commodities (thebalancemoney.com)

Kreil, A. (2013), Interview with the Institute of Trading and Portfolio Management's Managing Partner, *Cass Business School, City University of London*, February 7th, WEB access: Dec 2024, Anton Kreil | Ex Goldman Sachs Trader Tells Truth about Trading

Kusimba, C. (2017), When-and why- did people first start using money?, *The Conversation: Science + Tech*, June 19, WEB access: When – and why – did people first start using money? (theconversation.com)

Lamkin, A. (2021), What Are the Countable and Non-Countable Assets for Medicaid?, *Andrew M. Lamkin P.C.*, legal blog, December 20th, WEB access: Dec 2024: Medicaid Countable and Non Countable Assets

Langmuir, C. & Broecker, W. (2012), How to Build a Habitable Planet: The Story of Earth from the Big Bang to Humankind, *Princeton University Press*, 179–183p.

Lewis, T.K., Spilker, B.C., & Call, K.S. (2019), The taxation of collectibles, *The Tax Advisor*, WEB access: Dec 2023, The taxation of collectibles (thetaxadviser.com)

Macro Trends (2025a), Gold Prices-100 Year Historical Chart, *Macro Trends LLC,* Nov 1, WEB access: Dec 2025, Gold Prices - 100 Year Historical Chart

Macro Trends (2025b), Crude Oil Prices (1946-2025), *Macro Trends LLC,* Nov 1, WEB access: Dec 2025, Crude Oil Prices (1946-2025)

Maverick, J., (2025), Tax Efficiency Differences: ETFs vs. Mutual Funds, *Investopedia,* June 1, WEB access: Aug 2024, Tax Efficiency Differences: ETFs vs. Mutual Funds

Maus, V., Giljum, S., Gutschlhofer, J., Luckeneder, S., and Leiber, M. (2020), Global mining uses more than 57,000 km^2 of land, *Vienna University of Economics and Business,* FINEPRINT, Brief No. 12, 4p.

McClay, R. (2023), Exchange Traded Notes: An Alternative to ETFs, *Investopedia*, December 17th, WEB access: Dec. 2024, Exchange Traded Notes: An Alternative to ETFs

McGinley, S. (2022), Inflation raises old debate on currencies being pegged to dollar, *Arabian Gulf business Insight: Economy*, July 28, WEB access: Jan 2024, Inflation raises old debate on currencies being pegged to dollar | AGBI

McGuinn, D. (1991), What Happens to My Safe Deposit Box if My Financial Institution Closes?, *Bankers Online*, May 1, WEB access: Jun 2024, What Happens To My Safe Deposit Box If My Financial Institution Closes? | Bankers Online

MedBroadcast (2025), Metal Hypersensitivity, *medbroadcast.com,* WEB access: Mar 2025, Metal Hypersensitivity - Causes, Symptoms, Treatment, Diagnosis - MedBroadcast.com

Medeiros, E. (2017), Trading Leveraged ETFs for Max Profits, *Trade Risk*, WEB access: Apr 2022, https://www.thetraderisk.com/trading-leveraged-etfs-for-max-profits/

Mercier, J. (2022), 2022 Supplemental Budget Brings Increase in Inflation Adjusted Per-capita Spending, *Washington Policy Center,* April 20, WEB access: Mar 2024, 2022 supplemental budget brings huge increase in inflation-adjusted per-capita spending

Milligan, M. (2011), Odyssey Confirms Discovery of SS Gairsoppa Shipwreck, *Heritage Daily*, September 27, WEB access: Dec 2024, Odyssey Confirms Discovery of SS Gairsoppa Shipwreck

Mitra, A. and Rimstidt, J. D. (2009), Solubility and dissolution rate of silica in acid fluoride solutions, *Geochimica et Cosmochimica Acta*, vol 73, issue 23, December, 7045-7059p.

Mitchell, C. (2024a), Butterfly Spread: What it is, with Types Explained and Example, *Investopedia: Options Trading Guide Ch 8,* April, WEB access: Dec 2024, Butterfly Spread: What It Is, With Types Explained & Example

Mitchell, C. (2024b), Iron Condor: How this Strategy Works, with Examples, *Investopedia: Options Trading Guide Ch 7,* April, WEB access: Dec 2024, Iron Condor: How This Options Strategy Works, With Examples

Moen, J. & Tallman, E. (2015), The Panic of 1907, *Federal Reserve History*, Dec 4, WEB access: Jan 2024, The Panic of 1907 | Federal Reserve History

Monetary Metals (2025), Corporate Website, *monetarymetals.com,* WEB access: Sept 2025, Monetary Metals & Co. Earn interest on your gold & silver.

Money Metals (2025), Wyoming Goldback State Bundle, *Money Metals,* Listing Image, March, WEB access: Mar 2025, Wyoming Goldback State Bundle - One .9999 Gold-Backed Bill of Each Denomination (1, 5, 10, 25 and 50)

MUAMALAT Gold (2025), Gold Backed Sukūk and Modern Islamic Finance: Embracing Physical Gold in Shariah Compliant Investments, *MUAMALATgold.com.,* Jun 11, WEB access: Sept 2025, Gold-Backed Sukūk and Modern Islamic Finance: Embracing Physical Gold in Shariah-Compliant Investments - Muamalat Gold

Murray, K. (2024), The Best (and Worst) Types of Accounts to Inherit, *Serving those who Serve,* Mar. 20th, WEB access: Apr 2025, The Best (and Worst) Types of Accounts to Inherit

NASA (2017), NASA Missions Catch First Light from a Gravitational-Wave Event, *press release,* Oct 16, #17-083.

NCS-Import (2003), Judgement entered in suit over Tonopah copper mine, *Northern Nevada Business Weekly,* Aug 19, WEB access: Aug 2024, Judgment entered in suit over Tonopah copper mine | Serving Carson City for over 150 years (nevadaappeal.com)

Noble Gold Investments (2022), Sales Tax on Gold and Silver: Where You Stand, State by State, WEB access Dec 2023, Sales Tax on Gold and Silver - Rules For Every State (noblegoldinvestments.com)

Norton-Rose-Fulbright (2017), Royalty Finance- The New Normal, *Mining World,* August, WEB access: Apr. 2025, Royalty finance - the new normal? | Global law firm | Norton Rose Fulbright

Numista (2024), 6 Pence- George VI, *Numista.com>catalog>Fiji,* WEB access: Dec 2024, 6 Pence - George VI - Fiji – Numista

Olympics.com (2024), Olympic Medals, *Olympics.com>Olympic Games>Olympic Medals,* WEB access: Dec 2024, Olympic Medals - History, Design, Photos

Oommen, M. (2020), Compliance Considerations for S-K 1300: Preparing for the New SEC Regulations, *WSP,* November 30, WEB access: Dec 2025, Compliance Considerations for S-K 1300: Preparing for the New SEC Regulations

Osterberg, S. (2025), South Mountain Project Idaho Site Tour & Discussions with Steve Osterberg, Vice President of Exploration for Timberline Resources, *GeoTech LLC,* November 3-5, Jordan Valley, Oregon.

Parshley, L. (2023), "An Alaskan Native tribal council greenlit a gold mine. Some tribal members aren't happy.", *Alaska Public Media*, WEB access: Dec 2023, An Alaska Native tribal council greenlit a gold mine. Some tribal members aren't happy. - Alaska Public Media

Pappas, S. (2021), Deepest earthquake ever detected should have been impossible, *Live Science*, Nov 8, WEB access: Jan 2024, Deepest earthquake ever detected should have been impossible | Live Science

PCGS (2024a), CERT VERIFICATION #19951877, *Collectors Universe Inc.*, WEB access: Dec 2024, PCGS Certificate Verification Coin Details for Cert #19951877

PCGS (2024b), 20th Century Coin Index, *Professional Coin Grading Services: Price Guide*, December 13th, WEB access: Dec 2024, PCGS Price Guide - 20th Century Coin Index

PCGS (2024c), Morgan Dollar, 1893-S MS, *Collectors Universe Inc.,* Historical Auction Prices, WEB access: Dec 2024, Morgan Dollar, 1893-S MS - PCGS Auction Prices

PCGS (2024d), Key Dates & Rarities Index, *Professional Coin Grading Services: Price Guide*, December 17, WEB access: Dec 2024, PCGS Price Guide - Key Dates and Rarities Index

Pearson, O. (2018), Can Creditors Seize a Safe Deposit Box?, *Pocket Sense: Managing Your Money*, Oct 25, WEB access: June 2024, Can Creditors Seize a Safe Deposit Box? | Pocketsense

Peeler, T. (2021), Law Pertaining to Safety Deposit Boxes, *Legal Match,* May 21, WEB access: Jun 2024, Safe Deposit Box Rules & Regulations | LegalMatch

Pendell, C. (2024), The Complete List of States with Estate Taxes (Updated for 2024), *JRC Insurance Group*, January, WEB access: Dec 2024, The Complete List of States with Estate Taxes (Updated for 2024) | JRC Insurance Group™

Pendleton D. & Javier, L. (2020), Steve Cohen and D1 Capital Team Up For Collectors Universe, *Bloomberg: Deals*, November 30th, WEB access: Dec 2024, Steve Cohen and D1 Capital Team Up For Collectors Universe

Perez, L. (2023), What You Need to Know About the Capital Loss Tax Deduction, *smartasset*™, WEB access: Dec 2023, All About the Capital Loss Tax Deduction - SmartAsset | SmartAsset

Prata, D. (2025), Sovereign Gold Bonds Discontinued In FY25 On Price Volatility, Global Economic Headwinds: Finance Minister, *NDTV/Profit*, April 1st, WEB access: Apr 2025, Sovereign Gold Bonds Discontinued In FY25 On Price Volatility, Global Economic Headwinds: Finance Minister

PUBLIC LAW 99-185 (1985), Gold Bullion Coin Act of 1985, *99th U.S. Congress*, December 17th, 3p.

Pylas, P. (2015), Switzerland Stuns Markets By Giving Up On Currency Peg, *Associated Press*, January 15, WEB access: Aug 2025, Switzerland stuns markets by giving up on currency peg | AP News

QuandaryFX (2020), PSLV: The Physical Silver Play, *Seeking Alpha*, WEB access: Apr 2022, https://seekingalpha.com/article/4393895-pslv-physical-silver-play

Ramesh, A. (2024), 42 Chart Patterns for Effective Intraday, Swing, and F&O Trading, *Strike Blogs: Technical Analysis*, Oct. 18th, WEB access: Apr 2025, 42 Chart Patterns for Effective Intraday, Swing & F&O Trading

Rawluk, C. (2023), National Instrument 43-101: An Overview for Investors, *Geology for Investor*, June 21, WEB access: July 2024, National Instrument 43-101: An Overview for Investors | Geology for Investors

Reams, Lee Sr. (2017), Recaptured and Unrecaptured Real Estate Rental Section 1250 Gain, *Counting Works Learning Center*, WEB access: Dec 2023, Recaptured and Unrecaptured Real Estate Rental Section 1250 Gain – CountingWorks Learning Center (taxcpe.com)

Reinicke, C. (2020), Warren Buffett's right-hand man said that he'd never buy or short Tesla stock, *Markets Insider: News: Stocks*, February 19th, WEB access: Dec 2024, Charlie Munger Would Never Buy or Short Tesla Stock - Markets Insider

Reuters (2013), As Cyprus sells gold to help bailout, other troubled eurozone countries could be next, *Financial Post: Economy*, April 11, WEB access: Jan 2024, Cyprus gold sale may be prescription for Italy, Portugal | Financial Post

Robb, L. (2020), Introduction to Ore-Forming process, 2nd ed., *Wiley-Blackwell*, 496p.

Rodney, R., Simmons, G., and Smith, M., (2023), Technical Report on the Updated Mineral Resource Estimate at the Black Pine Gold Project, Cassia & Oneida Counties, Idaho, USA, *Liberty Gold Corp.*

Rodriquez, J. (2021), Types of Trusts for Elderly Parents, *Griswold: Estate Planning*, April, WEB access: Dec, 2024, Types of Trusts for Elderly Parents

Rogers, J. (2014), California Couple Uncover Rare Gold Coins Worth $10 Million While Walking Their Dog, *The Prince George Citizen, February 25th*, WEB access: Dec 2024, California couple uncover rare gold coins worth $10 million while walking their dog - Prince George Citizen

Ross, M. (2025), Working With Islamic Finance, *Investopedia*, Jan 10, WEB access: Sept 2025, Working With Islamic Finance

Roy, D. (2025), The U.S. Critical Minerals Delema: What to Know, *Council on Foreign Relations*, July 30, WEB access: Aug 2025, The U.S. Critical Minerals Dilemma: What to Know | Council on Foreign Relations

Royal, J. (2025), What is the Long-erm Capital Gains Tax?, *Bankrate*, Feb 2025, WEB access: Aug 2025, 2024-2025 Long-Term Capital Gains Tax Rates | Bankrate

RSC (2024), Periodic Table, *The Royal Society of Chemistry*, WEB access: Jan 2024, https://www.rsc.org/periodic-table

Saville, S. (2015) Why Gold Mining Companies Should Never Hedge, *Seeking Alpha*, Apr 24, WEB access: Aug 2024, Why Gold Mining Companies Should Never Hedge | Seeking Alpha

Science 2.0 (2007), Calvera Is Earth's Closest Neutron Star, *Scientific Blogging*, Aug 21, WEB access: Jan 2024, Calvera Is Earth's Closest Neutron Star | Science 2.0 (science20.com)

SEC (2022), SEC Charges Financial Services Professional and Associate in $47 Million Front-Running Scheme, *Securities and Exchange Commission*, Press Release, December, 2022-228.

SEC (2024), U.S. GoldMIning Inc., *United States Securities & Exchange Commission,* Form 8-K, November 21, WEB access: Dec 2024, sec.gov/Archives/edgar/data/1947244/000149315224010489/form8-k.htm

Sekulic, R. & Djordjevic, N. (2023), How Many People Are on Welfare in 2024?, *Moneyzine,* February, WEB access: Dec 2024, How Many People Are on Welfare in 2023?

Sensible Collector (2025), Golden Legacy: The Remarkable Story of Mormon Gold Coins, *Sensible Collector,* articles, WEB access: Apr 2025, Golden Legacy: The Remarkable Story of Mormon Gold Coins | Articles | Sensible Collector

Shadel, D. and Eaton, J. (2016), Older Americans Lose Millions Through Coin Scams, *AARP*, WEB access: Apr 2022, https://www.aarp.org/money/scams-fraud/info-2016/gold-coin-investment-scams.html2016

Shivaprasad, A. and Hobson, P. (2022), Analysts slash platinum and palladium forecasts amid global slowdown, *Reuters*, Aug 3, WEB access: Jan 2024, Analysts slash platinum and palladium forecasts amid global slowdown | Reuters

Sieroń, A. (2016), How Do The Gold ETFs Really Work?, *Gold-Eagle.com*, WEB access: Apr 2022, https://www.gold-eagle.com/article/how-do-gold-etfs-really-work

Shaikh, K. (2025), 30-million-ton discovery makes China world's second-largest EV battery power, *Interesting Engineering,* Jan 9, WEB access: Dec 2025, China hits lithium jackpot with estimated 30 million ton reserve

Simanjuntak, W., Harahap, D., Hasibuan, A. (2024) Analysis of the Effectiveness of Gold and Sukuk as a Hedge, *Morfai Journal,* Dec, 1614-1619p.

Sillitoe, R. (2010), Porphyry Copper Systems, Society of Economic Geologists Inc., *Economic Geology*, v. 105, 3-41p.

Singer, C. (2016), Will the Government Find Out I'm Buying Precious Metals, *Money Metals Exchange*, WEB access: Dec 2023, Can the Government Track Your Gold & Silver Purchases? (moneymetals.com)

Silver Gold Pill (2020), Top Collectible and Rare Silver Bars to Watch For, *silvergoldpill.com,* Blog Post, May 11, WEB access: Jun 2024, https://www.silvergoldpill.com/blog/which-silver-bars-are-collectible

Silver Institute (2022), World Silver Supply & Demand, *The Silver Institute: press releases,* Apr 20, WEB access: Aug 2025, Global Silver Demand Surged in 2021

SMI (2024), Technologies: Mint Mark SI, *Sunshine Minting Inc*, WEB access: July 2024, TECHNOLOGIES | Sunshine Minting

Smerten, R. (2001), White Gold Alloys, *Orchid.Ganoksin.com*, Jewelry Discussion, WEB access: Mar 2025, White gold alloys - Jewelry Discussion - Ganoksin Orchid Jewelry Forum Community for Jewelers and Metalsmiths

Sociable (2023), Governments Can Program CBDC to Restrict Undesirable Purchases, Set Expiry Dates: WEF 'Summer Davos' in China, *The Sociable*, June 28th, WEB access: Dec 2024, Governments Can Program CBDC to Restrict Undesirable Purchases: WEF 'Summer Davos' in China

Solå, A. (2024), Investing in hobbies can be money well spent — just don't take on debt, *CNBC: Finance*, January 13th, WEB access: Dec 2024, Investing in hobbies can be money well spent — just don't take on debt

Soltani, E. (2024), U.S. Nominal vs. Real House Price Index Trends (1970–2024), *Visual Capitalist: Voronoi*, November 13th, WEB access: Dec 2024, 📈 U.S. Nominal vs. Real House Price Index Trends (1970–2024) - Voronoi

SSR Mining (2018), Updated Marigold Life of Mine Plan Confirms Near-Term Production Growth and Robust Economics, *SSR Mining Inc.,* News Release 18-09, June 18, 11p.

Stack's Bowers (2016), Significant 1854-S Double Eagle PCGS# 70030, *Stack's Bowers Galleries,* March 2016, Baltimore - Session 4 - Lots 13001-13251, WEB access: Dec 2024, 1854-S Liberty Double Eagle. Variety-11A. Broken A. AU-55 (PCGS). CAC. | Stacks Bowers

STC (2022), Serries 65-NASAA Uniform Investment Advisor Law Examination Study Manual, 44th ed., *Securities Training Corporation*, 313p.

TABARAK Investment Capital Ltd. (2025), The Safest Way To Own And Hold Physical Gold, *Gold Reserve Sukuk*, Fact Sheet, 2p. WEB access: Sept 2016, FACT SHEET ENG.pdf

Taylor, C., Schulz, K., Doebrich, J., Orris, G., Denning, P., and Kirschbaum, M. (2009), Geology and nonfuel mineral deposits of Africa and the Middle East: Bushveld Igneous Complex, *USGS,* Open-File Report 2005-1294-E, 247p.

Taylor, S. (2012), Solar System Evolution-A New Perspective: Ch 5- Composition and chemical evolution of the solar nebula, *Cambridge University Press*, Cambridge, U.K., 73-104p.

Thomas, A. (1989), 90 Golden Years: The Story of the Perth Mint, *Gold Corporation*, 59p.

Thompson, C. (2024), Using the 'Greeks' to Understand Options, How to Deploy Options Sensitivity Analysis To Improve Your Trading, *Investopedia: Options and Derivatives Strategy & Education,* September, WEB access: Dec 2024, Using the 'Greeks' to Understand Options

Torres, I. (2003), World Copper Smelters, *U.S. Geological Survey*, WEB access: Dec. 2024, World copper smelters | Data Basin

Total Materia (2024), Key to Metals AG, WEB access: Jan 2024, Total Materia: Subscribers Home

TPB (2020), Securities Industry Exam Test Prep & Practice Test, *Test Prep Books,* 2nd ed., 33-35p.

Tseytlin, B. (2017), The Benefits of Acquiring Junk Silver, *Coin Exchange*, March, WEB access: July 2024, https://www.coinexchangeny.com/blog/benefits-acquiring-junk-silver/

Tukos Minerals (2024), Argentite with Quartz, Uchucchacua Mine, Peru, *Tukosminerals.com*, WEB access: Jan 2024, Argentite with quartz | Takos Minerals

TurboTax (2025), Tax Efficiency: ETF vs Mutual Fund, *turbotax.intuit.com*, Aug 2, WEB access: Aug 2025, Tax Efficiency: ETF vs Mutual Fund - TurboTax Tax Tips & Videos

Ulman, M. (2024), How to Use an LLC for Estate Planning, *Investopedia: Wealth> Trust & Estate Planning*, May 8th, WEB access: Dec 2024, How to Use an LLC for Estate Planning

U.S. Gold Bureau (2012), Four Ways to Avoid Buying Fake Gold Bullion Coins, Feb 12, WEB access: Jun 2024, Avoiding Fool's Gold: 4 Tips to Help Recognize Fake Gold (usgoldbureau.com)

U.S. Mint (2017), US Mint History: The Crime of 1873, *Office of Corporate Communication*, Mar 22, WEB access: Jan 2024, The "Crime of 1873" | U.S. Mint (usmint.gov)

USDA (2024) Inflation Adjusted Corn, Wheat, Soybean Prices, 1912-2018, *U.S. Department of Agriculture,* WEB access: Mar 2024, https://www.ers.usda.gov/webdocs/charts/58365/commodity_fig15.png?v=42594

U.S. Forrest Service (2022), Mining In National Forests, U.S. Department of Agriculture: Forest Service, WEB access: Apr 2022, https://www.fs.fed.us/geology/includes/minerals/1975MiningInNationalForests.pdf

U.S. Supreme Court (2018), S. Dakota vs. Wayfair Inc., et al., No 17-494, *Heritage Reporting Corporation*, Washington, D.C., 62p.

Vagi, D. (2013), Ancients Today: Roman coinage often imitated around world, *Coin World*, world coins, July (special issue), WEB access: Apr 2022, Ancients Today: Roman coinage often imitated around world

Valcambi (2025), Products: CombiBar™, The best ever produced multi-functional bar, designed to serve as an investment bar, *Valcambi SA,* WEB access: Mar 2025, CombiBar™ - Valcambi

Venditti, B. and Ma, J. (2023), All the Metals We Mined in One Visualization, *Visual Capitalist,* WEB access: Jan 2024, All the Metals We Mined in One Visualization

Villar, V., Cowperthwaite, P., Berger, E., Blanchard, P., Gomez, S., Alexander, K., Margutti, R., Chornock, R., Eftekhari, T., and Fazio, G. (2018), Spitzer Space Telescope Infrared Observations of the Binary Neutron Star Merger GW170817, *The American Astronomical Society*, The Astronomical Journal Letters, Vol 862, num 1, 5p.

Wall, M. (2023), James Webb Space Telescope spots huge star about to go supernova, *space.com*, March 14, WEBB access: Jan 2024, James Webb Space Telescope spots star about to go supernova | Space

Wehner, M. (2020), Scientists Spotted an Explosion so Intense it Defies explanation, *BGR*, Nov 12, WEB access: Jan 2024, Scientists spotted an explosion so intense it defies explanation (bgr.com)

Wile, R. (2012), How A Manhattan Jeweler Wound Up with Gold Bars Filled with Tungsten, *Business Insider,* Sept 19, WEB access: Jun 2024, Tungsten Filled Gold Bars Found in New York - Business Insider

Wilson, L. (2023), Gold & Silver Warrants: What Are They? Why Own Them? How Are They Bought & Sold?, *munKnee.com*, June 6th, WEB access: Dec 2024, Gold & Silver Warrants: What are They? Why Own Them? How are They Bought & Sold? (+27K Views) - munKNEE.com

Wilton, J. (2020), BeMetals Confirms Significant Gold and Silver Component from its Phase 2 Underground Drill Program at the High-Grade South Mountain Zinc-Silver-Gold-Copper Project, *BeMetals Inc.*, press release, December 9th, WEB access: Dec 2024, 20201209.pdf

WPIC (2025), Platinum Market China Update, *World Platinum Investment Council,* Jul 2, WEB access: Dec 2025, Platinum Market China Update - CME Group

Winter, J. (2001), An introduction to Igneous and Metamorphic Petrology, *Prentice-Hall inc.*, New Jersey, 697p.

World Gold Council (2024), Gold Facts, WEB access: Jan 2024, 24 Facts About Gold | World Gold Council

World Gold Council (2023a), Above-ground stocks, WEB access: Jan 2024, How Much Gold Has Been Mined? | World Gold Council

World Gold Council (2023b), Gold Demand Trends Q1 2023, WEB access: Jan 2024, Supply | World Gold Council

World Gold Council (2023c), Historical demand and supply, Oct 31, WEB access: Jan 2024, Gold Demand & Supply by Country | World Gold Council

World Gold Council (2022), Gold Demand Trends Full Year 2021, WEB: access Apr 2022, https://www.gold.org/goldhub/research/gold-demand-trends/gold-demand-trends-full-year-2021/

Yeend, W., Shawe, D., & Wier, K. (1989), Gold in Placer Deposits, *U.S. Geological Survey*, Bulletin 1857-G, 27p.

Young, E., Kohl, I., Warren, P., Rubie, D., Jacobson, S. and Morbidelli, A. (2016), Oxygen isotopic evidence for vigorous mixing during the Moon-forming giant impact, *Science*, vol 351, no 6272, 493-496p.

Zimmerman, R., Ibrado, A., Dunn, G., Kirkham, G., Martin, C., Kowalewski, P., Roos, C., & Rosenthal, S., (2021), Stibnite Gold Project Feasibility Study Technical Report, Valley County, Idaho, *M3 for: Midas Gold.*

Zucchi, K. (2023), Top Exchanges Pegged to the U.S. Dollar, *Investopedia*, Sept 7, WEB access: Jan 2024, Top Exchange Rates Pegged to the U.S. Dollar (investopedia.com)

About the Author

Tyson John Forbush was raised near Rexburg, Idaho, on an 80-acre farm which was an auxiliary business to his father's accounting and tax preparation practice. He is the oldest of seven children. As a youth he enjoyed outdoor adventures, camping, and alpine skiing. He spent summers working the family farm, other agricultural jobs, and at a local welding shop. In school he excelled at science but struggled with English and writing. He made his first precious metal investment at age 17 when his dad convinced him to buy silver instead of spending his potato harvest money on a new pair of skis. Like many in his community, at age 19 Forbush served an LDS mission. After two years in eastern Ukraine, he returned home and gained a B.S. in Geology with a Russian minor from BYU-Idaho. He still reads, writes, and speaks fluent Russian to this day.

Exploring for gold, Central Alaska 2012

After graduation and two failed marriage proposals to his college girlfriend, Forbush worked as a drill site geologist on a remote project. He was surprised late one night when the same girlfriend arrived at his hotel and proposed to him in the courtyard. He said yes, and after the marriage they both worked geothermal exploration for a year before moving to Alaska where Forbush entered a graduate program at the University of Alaska Fairbanks. He went on to complete a Master of Science in Economic Geology & Geochemistry, his research focused on improving geochemical soil surveying methods, and his thesis remains the most definitive study of Mobile Metal Ionization's™ effectiveness in gold exploration.

Forbush has received many accolades over the years. He is an Eagle Scout. In high school he was recognized as the most outstanding science student in his class. While at college he was recognized as the top performing geologist in his class's capstone mapping course. Months later his undergraduate research project was awarded 1st place in a university wide exposition. In graduate school his team finished top five globally in the 2013

Imperial Barrel Awards, an oil and gas industry funded competition, that included 316 international graduate teams. Later, in 2016, he was honored with the District Award of Merit from the Boy Scouts of America, for his volunteer work with local scouting units.

Professionally he has been a productive explorationist. Forbush made his first gold discovery as a senior in college and has made significant contributions to total ore tonnage of every project he has worked in a position of decision. From 2013-14 he provided the initial data capture and assessment on over 100 mineral sites involved as part of a major land exchange between the U.S. Forest Service and State of Alaska. The exchange was finalized as part of the *Consolidated Appropriations Act of 2017, Public Law 115-31*. Forbush is a Certified Professional Geologist through the AIPG, the highest professional and ethical standard in the field, and "Qualified Person" by SEC regulation SK-1300 mineral property reporting and disclosure standards.

Never afraid of a full day's labor Forbush worked as many things paying his way through school including time at a grain elevator, as a ramp agent for Alaska Airlines, as a motor coach driver/guide for summer cruise guests, and a handyman. He endearingly refers to their fixer upper starter home in Alaska as his *"third degree"* and considers his advanced auto maintenance class possibly the most practical course of his college experience.

Forbush has known his share of difficulties as well. While in Ukraine he received word that his mother and grandmother had been killed in a car accident when a dump truck rolled through a stop sign into their lane. His mother's siblings sued Forbush's father because in their view their sister (the driver) killed grandma. The next several years were tumultuous and challenging for the family, as many relationships were lost and the family adapted to being a one-parent household. Upon returning from Ukraine, he helped maintain the farm while attending university.

Later after graduate school, Forbush and his wife relocated back to Idaho, in Boise near his in-laws. Initially the move was meant to be temporary until permanent work could be secured. His immediate family now consisted of his wife and two young sons with another on the way. Soon after the birth of Forbush's third son, the oldest was diagnosed with Autism, and within the next three years similar diagnoses were given to the other two boys. As most exploration projects and mines are far away from metropolitan areas, which have the services his children needed, this significantly limited Forbush's ability to secure consistent work and he found several traveling jobs that still afforded him a degree of flexibility. During this period, he developed his geologic consulting business, exposure to the diversity and rapidity of the different projects allowed him to quickly gain experience beyond his years. Still the weeks at a time away from home and employment volatility were taxing on the family and Forbush sought additional lines of business that offered decent compensation and high flexibility.

In 2020 during the Covid-19 crisis he went to work for one of the major financial institutions as an investment advisor representative. Such positions are 100% commission, so he worked 40hrs/ week for the firm and still consulted another 20hrs nights and weekends for a junior exploration company as he was building his practice.

Despite meeting his obligations to the firm, 18 months later new management threatened to end his contract unless he gave up the geological consulting completely. The reality, as Forbush learned, is that when an advisor builds their business with a large firm it really is not their business but the firms, who can take it away at a whim. Sadly, these scare tactics are often used even against senior advisors, threatening their business to keep them in line. Not wanting to throw away his education and experience to help the new managing partner's metrics and knowing he could better serve clients without the limitations and conflicts of interest being inherent of association with a firm/broker/dealer Forbush left. This was a costly decision, however, as the firm retained his book of business as well as all residual commissions on insurance he had placed, effectively taking his business and resetting him back to square one.

He went back to exploration as a consulting project manager, in 1 year building a client's project from a 150,000 oz gold resource to an 875,000 oz gold resource. The evenings at the cheap motel or in field RV were spent studying for and securing the appropriate licenses to restructure his financial advising firm to be completely independent. After building the exploration project from literally a three walled shed into the most promising exploration property in the company's portfolio, his contract was terminated. This is not terribly uncommon in the exploration space as companies will often hire consultants to do what they do not have the capability of doing themselves, taking over once a project is established. By this time Forbush had reestablished his financial planning practice enough to pivot himself back to that business, regaining most of his former clients.

Today Forbush still lives in Boise and maintains a small but loyal clientele in both his geological consulting firm and his financial advising practice. He doesn't solicit much, preferring to focus on service and receiving referrals. Professionally he splits his time between the two businesses and trading his personal account. He enjoys helping his clients navigate the complex financial/insurance landscape and seeing them achieve their goals of financial security and independence. He enjoys the variety, flexibility, and complementary nature of the three lines of business. In his personal life, he enjoys looking after the needs of his family, DIY projects, coin collecting, writing, and whatever hobby the family may currently be experimenting with.

www.ingramcontent.com/pod-product-compliance
Lightning Source LLC
LaVergne TN
LVHW071243210926
848486LV00007B/329